LAW & ORDER

LAW & ORDER

The Unofficial Companion

Kevin Courrier *and* Susan Green

RENAISSANCE BOOKS
Los Angeles

Library of Congress Cataloging-in-Publication Data

Green, Susan
    Law & order : the unofficial companion / Susan Green & Kevin Courrier.
        p. cm.
    Includes bibiographical references and index.
    ISBN 1-58063-022-7 (alk. paper)
    1. Law & order (Television program)   I. Courrier, Kevin.   II. Title.
    PN1992.77.L395G74 1998
    791.45'72—dc21   98–7012
                                                                           CIP

10 9 8 7 6 5 4 3 2 1

Design by Tanya Maiboroda

Distributed by St. Martin's Press
Manufactured in the United States of America
First Edition

For Grandmother Courrier,

who made it possible for me to fulfill the dream

of writing this book.

—*Kevin Courrier*

For my father,

who imagined a masterpiece and left this world

with sweetness in his soul.

—*Susan Green*

CONTENTS

Above all, we have to thank the person who said yes to the mere kernel of an idea for this book in 1994 and kept saying yes to everything we ever asked of him: Dick Wolf. ("Awoo!" to you too.) We also will forever appreciate: our agent with the charming British accent, Peter Rubie; Rene Balcer; our champion, Gene Ritchings; Joe Stern; Leon Ortiz; Gus Makris and all his great Gus-isms; the entire hospitable, hardworking *Law & Order* crew; Robert Nathan; Chris Noth; Audrey Davis of the Lippin Group; Marilee Mahoney of NBC; Lydia Friedman; Dena Morean; Lorna Nowve; Jessica Burstein; James Jackson; David Kalat (our *Homicide: Life on the Street* counterpart); Jim Parish; and Norby of the eternal poker game.

And we're more than grateful to the many friends, colleagues, and family members who helped us in so many material and spiritual ways: Shlomo Schwartzberg; Steve Vineberg; Ron Levine; Jeff Chown; Steven Lungley; Avril Orloff; Deborah Straw and Bruce Conklin; Suze Rotolo and Enzo Bartoccioli; Sheila Courrier and Albert Vezeau; Shawn Courrier; Bob Green and Bill Coil; Jennifer Green; Esther, Ryki, Steve, and Sylvia Zuckerman; Joel and Phyllis Greenberg; Donald Brackett and Mimi Gelman; David Churchill; Bob, Helen, and Andrew Plumley; Annie Bryant; Ellie Skrow; Chris Trebilcock; Bob Douglas and Gayle Burns; Betsy Liley; Maggie Maurice and Michelle Demers; Tom Fulton; Anton Leo, Dave Downey, Geoff Pevere, Greig Dymond, Diane Collins, Kate Pemberton, Kevin O'Leary, Neil Sandell, and Nancy Kelly; Donna R. Lemaster and other knowledgeable fans on the Internet; Anne and Al; Bob Kopf; Jean Jinnah; Stan Chan; Igor Svoboda and Thomas Graydon; Mark Bradley; the late William Kunstler; Bob Rae; and our furry muses,

COPPING A PLEA

*Television has brought back murder
into the home... where it belongs.*

—ALFRED HITCHCOCK, *Observer* (1965)

MANY PEOPLE have discovered that *Law & Order*, the television drama seen Wednesday nights on NBC and in daily cable TV reruns on the Arts & Entertainment Network, tends to get under the skin. Viewers find themselves addicted, despite, or perhaps because of, the fact that the show boasts few big stars, few personal details about the characters, much legal mumbo-jumbo, and stories that examine thought-provoking contemporary issues.

And so it was for us, long before the show won its well-deserved 1997 Emmy Award for Outstanding Drama Series. However, the decision to turn a favorite pastime into a career path by creating a companion book arrived through both choice and destiny. The choice in that process—some of which took place during the first O. J. Simpson trial, which augmented our *Law & Order* crash course in the criminal justice system—involved certain perceptions about the series. This show has some of the best acting on television, and the writing is clever, but never underestimates the audience's intelligence. No other episodic drama is better at scrutinizing the moral complexities of every social issue it tackles on camera. As seasoned film critics, we rarely witness this caliber on the big screen today.

We are not alone. Other *Law & Order* aficionados keep crossing our path with an eerie regularity.

We open a book at random—in this instance, *New York* magazine critic David Denby's *Great Books*, a 1996 non-fiction tome—and find the following quote: "A movie made without courage, without faith in the audience left me in a state of dull-eyed disgust, and most of them were made that way. Increasingly, they were made without storytelling craft as well. (For that, one turned to Dick Wolf's *Law & Order* on TV.)"

Begin chatting with someone in a chiropractor's waiting room and what does he say? A spiritually-inclined friend of his was so devoted to this show that, after checking into an ashram (a Hindu religious retreat) for a one-year vow of silence, he continued watching episodes on a VCR, and would hum the *Law & Order* theme as part of his meditations.

Sit down in a restaurant and what does the waitress bring to the table? She's been a *Law & Order* fan ever since performing with the Stratford Shakespeare Festival, where Douglas Rain (the voice of "HAL" in Stanley Kubrick's 1968 film *2001: A Space Odyssey*) advised all his colleagues to catch the show as an example of fine acting.

Perhaps the most astonishing *Law & Order* conceptual continuity came as we were leaving Quebec in the fall of 1997. Susan had driven to Montreal to meet Kevin, in hopes that crossing the border to America by car rather than bus would give him more credibility. Over the years, he had frequently encountered problems at U.S. Customs, enduring questions about why a Canadian citizen might want to visit Vermont. Freelance journalism apparently is a rather abstract profession in the eyes of officials charged with regulating the nation's borders.

In this case, Kevin was coming south to work on this book, carrying the contract from our publisher to prove it. "Why can't he just write it up there?" we overheard one Customs official ask another. Things were not going well for us until the supervisor took a closer look at the contract. "Your book is about *Law & Order*?" he asked and, seeing us nod, added, "That's my favorite program. I love that Jerry Orbach!"

Voila! We were ushered through Customs with speed. Such serendipity also tells us something about this TV show's remarkable reach, intriguing both a sophisticated New York film critic and an officer of the law in a remote northern Vermont town.

During two weeks on the set in Manhattan, however, we discovered that *Law & Order*'s magic is tempered by some *Rashomon*-like divisions. Filmmaker Akira Kurosawa himself might find it daunting to chronicle the variety of perspectives on the truth of this long-running series. That revelation shaped our book in a manner we had not anticipated: This could not be a tidy little overview. We had a responsibility to include conflicting voices, to consider the pain of creation.

Despite the legacy of rough times at *Law & Order,* virtually everyone we interviewed, no matter how alienated or for whatever reason disenchanted, believes that nothing can compare with this TV series. Aesthetic common ground can sometimes eclipse emotional divides. *Law & Order* always manages to attract people who are nothing less than passionate about their own work. Although gathered separately, the various commentaries fall quite naturally into something resembling the company's "roundtable" script meetings. To us, it is as if these people from different eras throughout the show's long production history are sitting in the same room—not necessarily peacefully, but together.

Nevertheless, most of what we encountered was joyous during our sometimes arduous, often amazing, *Law & Order* book-writing experience. Phone interviews frequently went on for hours because the subjects were so enthusiastic about sharing recollections and expressing opinions. On the set, everyone was gracious. Many were hilarious.

During rehearsal of a scene from Episode 167: "Ritual," Jerry Orbach (who plays Det. Lennie Briscoe) asked us: "You two still working on that book? It must be an epic."

S. Epatha Merkerson (who plays Lt. Anita Van Buren) chimed in: "It's going to be two volumes, *Law & Order* and *S. Epatha Merkerson....*"

Orbach, that favorite of border guards the world over, cut her off with the perfect quip: "*...the Early Years.*"

Maybe that'll be our next project, Epatha. Stay tuned.

THE FOUNDING FATHER

Nothing ever becomes real till it is experienced—Even a proverb is no proverb to you till your Life has illustrated it.

—JOHN KEATS, 1819

HIS PROFOUND influence on television has been slow to build but impossible to deny. As the man who created *Law & Order* in 1988, executive producer Dick Wolf has blazed impressive new trails in a terrain that many thought already fully conquered.

To begin with, this was a man who could not be satisfied with slogans. "My father had been in advertising," explains Wolf, a Manhattan native with a Jewish-Catholic heritage. "I started working in a couple of agencies during one summer [1969] in college and just sort of naturally segued into it. I was basically the way most twenty-two-year-olds are: I really didn't know what I wanted to do, but I'd never earned a dime that wasn't somehow connected to writing."

By the time he fled the Madison Avenue world of advertising in the mid-1970s, the University of Pennsylvania graduate had dreamed up more than one hundred commercials and national campaigns, including such memorable slogans as "You can't beat Crest for fighting cavities," and the more controversial "I'm Cheryl; Fly Me" for National Airlines.

Why did Wolf forego such dizzying career heights? "I turned thirty and realized I didn't want to sell toothpaste for the rest of my life," he says.

"I optioned a book called *Trucker* and wrote a screenplay, made a bunch of contacts. Then, I wrote *Skateboard* [1977]. *Trucker* never got made."

After ten years and five films, including the poignant *School Ties* of 1992 (with Brendan Frasier), Wolf reassessed his situation and decided that television would become his new medium.

"It was a very easy change for me to make. *School Ties*, for example, took eleven years to get made," he recalls. "Development hell is truly development hell in features. I wrote a *Hill Street Blues* [1981–87] script because my agent called and asked if I wanted to do television and I said no. Then he told me it was *Hill Street*, which was my favorite show, so I wrote a script."

His freelance days took a tumble when "I was sitting in my office at home with my wife and our, at the time, one-year-old daughter. My agent called to say they liked the script at *Hill Street* and wanted me to go on staff. I said, 'No, I don't want to go into an office....' She said, 'Dick, don't you understand the way the television business works? They pay you all this money every week to be on staff and then they pay you to write the scripts on top of that....' My wife leaned over, because it was on the speaker phone, and said: 'He'll be there Monday morning.' And I obeyed."

Wolf worked on *Hill Street* in 1985, ran *Miami Vice* (1984–89) for two years beginning in 1986, then formed his own company in 1988, and began dreaming up shows (eleven, to be exact). Although a fair number of these TV series crashed and burned, many of the people who worked on them with Wolf also gained *Law & Order* credentials.

Two of Wolf's newer programs, *New York Undercover* (1994–) and *Players* (1997–), are still on the scene midway through *Law & Order*'s eighth season. For reasons that Wolf probably would love to pin down, this minimalist cops-and-courts show that tackles the issues became his long-distance runner, finally earning an Emmy Award for best drama in 1997.

"You don't have to worry about who's sleeping with who," says Wolf, who grew up in the late 1950s and early 1960s with lean, televised yarns of urban crime like *Dragnet* and *Naked City*. "If you don't see the show for three weeks or three months or three years, you come back and it's the same show. It may be different people playing different characters but the structural integrity has basically remained unsullied. We haven't fixed what isn't broken."

CHAPTER 1

THE
MOMENTUM

*Take nothing on its looks; take every-
thing on evidence. There's no better
rule.*

—CHARLES DICKENS, *Great Expectations* (1860)

IT SEEMS doubly ironic that Ronald Reagan was still president in 1988 when Dick Wolf dreamed up a series for Universal Television with a relatively positive outlook on American justice.

Only thirty-five years before, in 1953, the ultimate law-and-order politician was a B-movie actor starring in an eminently forgettable Universal-International cowboy saga called—you guessed it—*Law & Order*. However, Wolf initially had in mind a title with less oomph. "I played around with *Night and Day*, and all sorts of other things," he explains. "Then I came up with *Law & Order* and was very proud of myself: 'Oh, my God! I had an original idea.'"

Wolf decided that the first half of this show would chronicle two particular New York City detectives and their commander solving a violent crime. After that, he wanted each episode to visit the district attorney's office and the courts, where three prosecutors attempt to convict the perpetrator. In this *Law & Order*, some of the larger issues of the day could come into focus through stories based on real cases that were making headlines.

When Wolf revealed his brainstorm to the man who was then president of Universal Television, Kerry McCluggage, that executive knew it was

Law & Order *creator and executive producer Dick Wolf, a former ad man and screenwriter who turned to episodic television.* [Copyright ©1997 by Universal City Studios, Inc. Courtesy of Universal Publishing Rights, a Division of Universal Studios Licensing, Inc. All rights reserved.]

not such an original idea. "He said, 'Oh, yeah. *Arrest and Trial* in 1963,'" Wolf recalls. "And I said, 'What?' Kerry said, 'Ben Gazzara. Chuck Connors.' I told him I never saw it."

Together, they looked at the pilot for *Arrest and Trial,* a crime drama with two forty-five minute segments that ran on ABC for one year. "Ben Gazzara plays a detective," Wolf says. "He arrests a guy for armed robbery; then Chuck Connors comes on as the defense attorney and he gets the guy off. It was the wrong guy."

When the lights came back on, Wolf turned to McCluggage. "I asked him if Ben Gazzara arrested the wrong guy every week, and he said, 'It was a problem.'"

Although Wolf envisioned *Law & Order*'s detectives as occasionally fallible, he planned a fresh approach to the genre that would move from police procedural to prosecution with a slice of hard-bitten realism. Moreover, he intended to explore a new angle. "It turned out to be a really original idea because, up until that point, there had never been a legal show featuring prosecutors," he says. "I believed the heroes weren't the defense attorneys who were getting these scumbags off. The heroes were the prosecutors, working for a tenth of the money and putting them away. It seemed like a very natural meld."

Natural, yes. Doable? Not right away. "We sold the show to FOX [Broadcasting] initially," Wolf explains. "Not a pilot. They wanted thirteen [episodes]. Then, [network head] Barry Diller called and said, 'I love this idea but it's not a FOX show. We shouldn't do this.' We then went to CBS, which ordered a pilot. They liked the pilot but didn't put it on because there were no breakout stars. So, it was a dead pilot."

"Everybody's Favorite Bagman," the pilot written by Wolf, tackled a story of corrupt city officials and the mob. In the summer of 1989, he screened it for NBC's top executives, Brandon Tartikoff and Warren Littlefield. "Brandon really liked it and asked, 'But can you do this every week?' Because it was quite intense."

The names are the same, but it's cowboys instead of cops...

Law & Order, the 1942 movie starring Buster Crabbe as Billy the Kid. *[courtesy of Archive Photos]*

Law & Order, *the 1932 movie about Wyatt Earp directed by John Huston.* *[courtesy of Archive Photos]*

Law & Order, *the 1953 movie about Wyatt Earp starring Ronald Reagan* (left). *[courtesy of Archive Photos]*

Long before NBC's Law & Order, other television dramas offered the hard-boiled approach to crime...

Dragnet *(NBC, 1952–63), with Ben Alexander (left) and Jack Webb as Officer Frank Smith and Sgt. Joe Friday, respectively, always searching for the facts.* [courtesy of Archive Photos]

Naked City *(ABC, 1958–63), each week featured James Franciscus (left) as Det. Jim Halloran and John McIntire as Det. Lieutenant Dan Muldoon investigating one of eight million stories.*
[courtesy of Archive Photos]

Arrest and Trial *(ABC, 1963–64), with John Kerr as Assistant Deputy District Attorney Barry Pine in court.*
[courtesy of Archive Photos]

Littlefield, president of NBC Entertainment, agrees. "I looked at the pilot and believed there was a pretty intriguing series there. I'm kind of a crime junkie . . . so it was instantly attractive to me. I loved the concept of a split focus, with the first half being police investigators and then going into the legal proceedings. It was remarkably simple for such complex storytelling. I felt instinctively that it had the potential for a pretty broad-based audience."

Joe Stern is a producer who had worked with Wolf on *No Man's Land*, a 1986 feature. Stern left Los Angeles to help launch the new show that ended its hour segment with a mournful cry of "Awoo!" over a lupine logo. "Stylistically, it was innovative," Stern says of the early *Law & Order*. "It was basically hand-held. We shot the pilot in 16 mm. It was totally unsentimental. First, I showed *The Battle of Algiers* [1966] to the director of the pilot, John Patterson, so there was a real vision there. It ended up resonating."

The Battle of Algiers was director Gillo Pontecorvo's depiction in newsreel style of the bloody 1950s uprising that eventually ended French colonial rule in that corner of North Africa. Stark and dry-eyed, the film presents virtually no personal information about its ambiguous characters, who symbolize the inexorable forces of history.

"The pilot is the most frenetic, the grittiest of all the shows," Stern continues. "We knew we were on to something; when we started making them, we knew even more so."

Actor Dann Florek, who appeared in the pilot and, later, returned to play Capt. Donald Cragen for four seasons, also was intrigued with the show's concept. "The style—I had never seen anything quite like this— the sense of, almost, News at Eleven. The hand-held camera. The immediacy of it. The visceral quality. It was muscular. There were no establishing shots. . . . I was really taken with it. I felt more like I was reading a movie."

Richard Brooks, whose assistant district attorney character appeared on the *Law & Order* pilot of 1988 and then, later, for three seasons, has similar sentiments. "I knew it was going to be a great show because the writing was so intense. I hadn't really wanted to do episodic TV before that. . . . But this one struck me right off. The concept was great, with the hand-held and shot in 16mm. It was from the point of view of the characters, rather than [being] about the characters."

A Manhattan-based writer, David Black, also joined the production team. "Dick had this new cop show he wanted to do in New York and make New York a main character," he says. "We had a screening before it was picked up by NBC. [Fellow scribe] Robert Nathan was there and said, 'Boy, I never wanted to do TV but I want to do this. This is the smartest, classiest

Joe Stern, who served as the New York-based executive producer of Law & Order on the 1988 pilot and from 1990 through 1993.

[courtesy of Joe Stern]

show I've ever seen.'" Recently, Nathan elaborated on his initial impression: "I thought the language and the storytelling was dazzling, and very new for television."

Wolf recruited Montreal-born writer Rene Balcer in 1990. "When I first saw the pilot, what came to mind was *The French Connection* [1971]," he remembers. "That graininess, that [William] Friedkin documentary feel. It seemed to hark back to those cop movies of the early '70s—*Across 110th Street* [1972], *Dog Day Afternoon* [1975]—a genre that I really like. Also the format seemed to be a great vehicle for every week just addressing any kind of topic you can imagine and not having to service all these personal stories that end up overtaking most series."

It was time to grapple with the logistics of actually having an hour-long television show to put on the air. Wolf says, "I told [Kerry McCluggage], 'Let me get six scripts written and we'll prove it to you.' And we turned in the six scripts in December and he ordered the show and we started shooting, I think, the first week of March 1990."

"In the first year, Nathan and I together wrote or rewrote nine of the first thirteen episodes, seven of the second nine," Black says. "He lived down the block. We'd start at breakfast, have lunch together, walk through the park, have dinner and be up till three in the morning. We were cranking these out, like, one a week. We were exhausted all the time."

Producer Jeff Hayes, who joined *Law & Order* in the first season, has similar memories: "I didn't think I would like it at all. Who the hell wants to work at this crazy pace? Then, halfway into it, it was almost, like: 'How could I ever go back?' I was working so fast. But it's fun to work this fast. You have to think on your feet, moving real quick. It does not get boring and you can't make mistakes."

But how do you avoid mistakes when you're essentially inventing the process as you go along? "We had to find out how to do the show, especially learning how to do the courtroom scenes," Hayes says. "We were working around the clock. This is shot like a movie....It's stuff that seems so easy to us now, but it took a long time to learn how to do it."

The scripts had to be crafted to make *Law & Order*'s frenetic pace possible. "The scenes are very, very short," David Black explains. "You start very deep in and get to the emotional heart of the scene and you get out. It's fast. I think we changed the speed at which shows move on TV. We were the first show to do that. It's very efficient."

Arthur Forney is a supervising producer and, periodically, a director. "We were shooting a lot more in the first four, five, six years. We had more exterior scenes. We were out in the streets more and that gave the show more of an edge than it has now."

Robert Palm, who worked on *Law & Order* from the beginning through the end of Season Two, was also smitten: "It was snappy and hard-boiled, and it appealed to the journalist in me. I liked the immediacy of it. *Law & Order* was a very black-and-white show in its initial state, and the writers played with the gray areas and filled it with ambiguity."

Robert Nathan, head writer and story editor on Law & Order *from 1990 through 1994.* [courtesy of Robert Nathan]

Wolf was unyielding. "Dick remained absolutely steady in his vision of what the show should be. I remember the tremendous pressure he was under to warm it up and make it a soap like *L.A. Law*," says Black, who rounded up writers for the project. "I went to novelists, playwrights and journalists—none had ever written for TV. I had barely written for TV."

Michael Chernuchin was a practicing attorney for seven years before he signed on with *Law & Order* as a writer during the first season. "Back then, there really weren't any reality-based shows on television, shows that gave you the feel of New York....And I loved the idea of telling a story from beginning to end. We travel a huge distance in just under forty-five minutes. We show a criminal investigation from soup to nuts. It's essentially a study of the criminal justice system presented in an entertaining fashion."

William Fordes, a former real-life prosecutor, has been a legal consultant with the show since 1990. "*Law & Order* is as authentic as you can get within the confines of drama. I spent six years at the DA's office in Manhattan and, short of Court TV, it doesn't get any more realistic than this.... It means compressing twenty-minute legal arguments into a page and a half or two pages, so that we're true to the law, the audience understands what's going on, and lawyers wonder if it's a real case."

Two genuine New York City cops, Mike Struk and Jerry Giorgio, helped the writers devise accurate police procedures for their scripts and showed the ropes to actor Chris Noth, who would portray *Law & Order*'s charismatic Detective Logan for five seasons. "You see how a New York cop responds and it's usually less baroque than anything in TV movies or fiction," Noth says. "Once a scene was written that I thought was a cliché, I knew how to go in the other direction. If they wrote the cop tough, it was wrong. They always try to do that with cops, write them tough—like, get in your face. And what New York cops taught me was a certain seduction in interrogation."

Stern had immigrated to New York to do only the first thirteen episodes of the show but wound up staying with the crew for three years. "I had no intention of remaining but it was a good project. I felt that we were onto something." With Wolf in L.A., he was responsible for maintaining the heartbeat of the New York production. "Each show was, to me, life or death. We weren't just making television—we were making great television."

THE CAST

Never mind the character, stick to the aleybi.

—CHARLES DICKENS, *Pickwick Papers* (1836)

FROM the very first, Dick Wolf's design for *Law & Order* was a hyperkinetic yet remarkably spare TV production, with the acting talent to match.

The pilot, "Everybody's Favorite Bagman," starred Chris Noth and George Dzundza as Mike Logan and Max Greevey respectively, detectives in the 27th Precinct headed by Capt. Donald Cragen (Dann Florek). These characters all had Irish working-class backgrounds. The prosecutors were more of a mixed bag. Executive Assistant District Attorney (EADA) Ben Stone (Michael Moriarty) had an Emerald Isle heritage, but Assistant District Attorney (ADA) Paul Robinette (Richard Brooks) was African-American. They worked for a WASP-like DA played by Roy Thinnes, the veteran TV actor who has starred in such series as *The Invaders* (1967–68).

Producer Joe Stern recalls, "Dick had his eye on Moriarty and he was an old friend of mine as well. Moriarty and James Naughton [were the two choices]. The network liked Naughton and we all liked Moriarty, because he was such a strange actor."

Noth was up against Michael Madsen, later featured in Quentin Tarantino's film *Reservoir Dogs* (1992). "Madsen sort of had the part until the last reading at the network," Stern says. "The [acting] mannerisms kept repeating themselves and we got a bit disenchanted."

For the ADA, it was between Brooks and Eriq LaSalle, now an ever-somber surgeon on the famed TV hospital drama *ER* (1994–). "The network wanted LaSalle and Dick wanted Richard Brooks," Stern continues.

Almost two years passed before the series went into production. "After making the pilot, we had an option on the four main characters and they were paid holding money for the additional year," Wolf says. "But we didn't have options on Roy Thinnes or Dann Florek. Luckily, Dann didn't have anything else going on. I called up Roy, who told me he was the star of a new show, *Dark Shadows* [1991]. *Law & Order* was definitely a supporting role for him."

So Steven Hill was hired to replace Thinnes as the DA and almost missed being dubbed Adam Schiff. "I remember Dick was going to call him Schlesinger," Stern says. "I said, 'It's too long a name.'"

The pilot was aired on the NBC network, but not until the middle of the first season's fall schedule. "After all thirteen episodes were cut, we

Four members from Law & Order's first set of police and prosecutors: From left, Richard Brooks as ADA Paul Robinette, George Dzundza as Sgt. Max Greevey, Chris Noth as Det. Mike Logan, and Michael Moriarty as EADA Ben Stone. *[courtesy of Photofest / Copyright ©1990 by Universal City Studios, Inc. Courtesy of Universal Publishing Rights, a Division of Universal Studios Licensing, Inc. All rights reserved.]*

Michael Moriarty and Richard Brooks (EADA Ben Stone and ADA Paul Robinette), Law & Order's initial prosecutors starting with the 1988 pilot. *[courtesy of Photofest / Copyright ©1990 by Universal City Studios, Inc. Courtesy of Universal Publishing Rights, a Division of Universal Studios Licensing, Inc. All rights reserved.]*

Steven Hill, the show's crusty District Attorney Adam Schiff since Season **One.** *[Copyright ©1997 by Universal City Studios, Inc. Courtesy of Universal Publishing Rights, a Division of Universal Studios Licensing, Inc. All rights reserved.]*

Dann Florek (left), playing Capt. Don Cragen from the 1988 pilot through 1994, and George Dzundza as Sgt. **Max Greevey.** *[courtesy of Photofest / Copyright ©1990 by Universal City Studios, Inc. Courtesy of Universal Publishing Rights, a Division of Universal Studios Licensing, Inc. All rights reserved.]*

decided on the air order. I think the pilot ran seventh [actually sixth]," says Wolf, who does not think this mix-and-match caused confusion. "That's the beauty of the show and why, I think, it's still on. The audience knows that you tune in and every week you get a totally contained, complete story."

Costar Chris Noth remembers that "most of us knew that this thing was head and shoulders above anything else on TV at the time. With *Law & Order*, I saw the potential for a cinematic experience on television, for stuff that was uncomfortable for people to watch in terms of issues, language, situations, depth of character. We were shooting in New York when no one else was. This was on a level TV had never reached."

Despite irreconcilable tensions on the set, the experience was thrilling. "I used to run to work. It was very exciting to be on the show those first two years. It was the only game in town," Noth says.

"It was real guerrilla filmmaking," Stern suggests. "That's what made it so exciting."

CHAPTER 3

THE METAMORPHOSES

The universe is change; our life is what our thoughts make it.

—MARCUS AURELIUS, Second Century A.D.

ELECTRIC as the show was to shoot and to watch, internal problems began surfacing even in *Law & Order's* earliest, headiest production days. The creative teams on both sides of the camera were forced to negotiate the minefield that underlies television talent and ego. For more than half a decade, not a year would go by without significant, often startling, defections and dismissals.

George Dzundza quit the detective duo after the first season, replaced by Paul Sorvino (as Det. Phil Cerreta) from September 1991 through November 1992, and then Jerry Orbach (as Det. Lennie Briscoe) ever since. When Michael Moriarty departed at the end of Season Four (1993–94), Sam Waterston came on board in September 1994 as the new EADA, Jack McCoy.

As Season Three drew to a close, Dann Florek and Richard Brooks were replaced by the first women ever to break into *Law & Order's* male sanctuary, S. Epatha Merkerson and Jill Hennessy (Lt. Anita Van Buren and ADA Claire Kincaid). Then, in 1995, it was goodbye Chris Noth, hello Benjamin Bratt (as Det. Reynaldo Curtis). Hennessy flew the coop at the end of Season Six (1995–96), with Carey Lowell arriving soon afterwards to play ADA Jamie Ross.

For a while, it seemed as if every time viewers tuned in characters were tuning out. Wolf jokes about the anticipation this might have generated: "I think the audience is waiting, 'Who's next?'"

Although no major *Law & Order* alterations took place between late spring and early fall of 1997, one important recurring figure did disappear without explanation. Dr. Elizabeth Olivet was no longer the prosecution's psychiatric expert because actress Carolyn McCormick accepted a lead role in the American version of the British-spawned *Cracker* on ABC. J. K. Simmons suddenly showed up in Episode 159: "Denial," the second episode of Season Eight (1997–98), as Dr. Emil Skoda.

Then, another surprise near the end of Season Eight: Carey Lowell announced she was quitting the show to spend more time with her seven-year-old daughter, Hannah. No replacement was immediately named, but sources in Dick Wolf's office suggested that "he has all summer to find someone."

At the same juncture, late April 1998, *Law & Order* had not yet been automatically renewed for a ninth season. Cast members were reportedly asking for higher wages, not long after Universal Television became the USA Networks—renamed when Barry Diller took over the TV arm of the studio a few months earlier.

OUT WITH THE OLD

Series creator Dick Wolf never worried about *Law & Order* surviving its many cast fluctuations. "Going from George Dzundza to Paul Sorvino to Jerry Orbach, or from Michael Moriarty to Sam Waterston, or Richard Brooks to Jill Hennessy to Carey Lowell: It's a plethora of riches."

Be that as it may, depending on the source of recollections, tales vary about who did what and why and how. "George left because his family is in California," Wolf says. "He said to me, 'Moriarty gets to kill the bull every week.'"

Producer Joe Stern recalls that, "Dzundza was jealous of Moriarty, felt Moriarty had the better part....Dzundza was a very unhappy guy, unhappy through the whole second half of the first season."

Contrast that with how much joy Dzundza expresses six years later, in 1997: "I was happy to be a part of it; I was happy to leave it. I'm happy with what I left behind. I'm happy that Dick Wolf is making a fortune and has the opportunity to do other shows. I'm happy for the actors. I'm happy for the writers who have a chance to address material that you don't always get to do.... I'm happy for all the good things that came out of it."

In 1991, however, happiness was on hold. "It was a very tough time and Dzundza was very hard on [co-lead Chris] Noth. George wouldn't come out of the trailer on the abortion show [Episode 12: 'Life Choice'] because he thought he'd been slighted by Noth; it took me forty-five minutes to get him out. There was personal tension in that episode. He wanted Noth fired. It was never gonna happen," Stern says.

Some crew members perceived a benefit in the charged emotional atmosphere on the set. "That first year, everything seemed a little more raw," sound mixer David Platt says. "Dzundza and Noth really didn't get along. They'd fight. Oh, did they fight. . . . In the grand scheme of things maybe they liked each other but, as partners, there was friction—and that friction worked on the show."

George Dzundza (Det. Max Greevey) and Chris Noth (Det. Mike Logan), who played devoted police partners for one year but feuded when the cameras weren't rolling.
[courtesy of Photofest / Copyright ©1990 by Universal City Studios, Inc. Courtesy of Universal Publishing Rights, a Division of Universal Studios Licensing, Inc. All rights reserved.]

Spike Finnerty, both a stand-in and precinct detective with rare oncamera lines since the pilot, observed the ongoing Dzundza-Noth discord: "There was always an undercurrent of angst, the little sarcasms, the biting back and forth. The outcome of that was some really dynamic acting. That made the stuff [on screen] very, very strong."

Noth says he and Dzundza had "a love-hate relationship. I found out later that, behind my back, he was trying to take credit for my acting and, at the same time, trying to get rid of me. . . . As soon as he saw it was an ensemble show and it wasn't going to be *The George Dzundza Hour*, he was out of there."

Dzundza remembers that he was already miserable just two weeks into the first season (1990–91). "There were personality issues. When I came on, I had a certain amount of experience in films and there were some people there that didn't. . . . Chris and I were at loggerheads about things because we have different lifestyles, different ways of working, different points of view."

On the tender side of life, Dzundza brooded about playing the role of a cop on the show versus the role of being a dad on the home front, where his wife was pregnant with their third child. "When you're doing a television series, you're working twenty-two, twenty-three hours a day and then you fly home to see your family for a day or two. The rest of the time you're not there to kiss a boo-boo or put them in bed or to listen to their problems....You become a phantom."

Noth sums up the situation with typical brio. "There's a lot of *Law & Orders* created out of conflict: conflict between the actors, conflict between the producers and the actors, conflict between the writers and the producers. We were all conflicted. We all basically f***ing hated each other."

(In July 1992, the *New York Post* reported that Noth and Michael Moriarty roughed each other up at a Manhattan club where the company was celebrating six Emmy nominations. Paul Sorvino, who by then had replaced Dzundza on the series, reportedly stepped in to break up the fight.)

As it turned out, Sorvino didn't fare much better than Dzundza. "Paul left because he'd gotten bronchitis from shooting [episodes] outside and was worried he wouldn't be able to sing. So he literally left to pursue his opera career," Wolf says.

Paul Sorvino (left), playing Det. Phil Cerreta and seen here with Chris Noth (Det. Mike Logan), replaced George Dzundza (Det. Max Greevey) as Logan's partner in 1991 but lasted less than two seasons. *[courtesy of Photofest / Copyright ©1991 by Universal City Studios, Inc. Courtesy of Universal Publishing Rights, a Division of Universal Studios Licensing, Inc. All rights reserved.]*

Paul Sorvino says, "Frankly, one of the reasons I left is there wasn't enough of an opportunity [to highlight Cerreta's personality]. I had been told that a number of episodes would [take me] into the law segment. I said to them, 'There's not enough for me to do. I don't get to kill the bull,' " the actor adds, echoing Dzundza's matador metaphor. "That was Michael Moriarty's job. But I needed more of a fight and I needed more closure."

A third of the way into his second *Law & Order* season, Sorvino was written out of the show. "One of the frustrating things about that role— one of the reasons George [Dzundza] left, I assume, and certainly why I left—is there wasn't enough range.... It wasn't a large enough vehicle for me to express what it was I want to express as an artist."

Producer Joe Stern remembers that "Sorvino started rumbling early in his first season. He wanted his hours shortened. He wanted this; he wanted that. Then he started wearing that Russian hat because he was cold. Dick was not going to split up the two cops; they were always in scenes together. And that's what we would have had to do to shorten Sorvino's workload."

According to series regular Dann Florek, "Dzundza was difficult and mean. Sorvino was difficult but never mean. Sorvino was just kind of a blowhard. On the set one day he said, 'I am one of the five greatest living actors.' We all just looked at each other and no one knew what to say. It was his shot and he had a line like, 'Are you sure the car was brown?' He screwed it up about four times. I just turned to him and said, 'Paul, maybe you should make that one of the *seven* greatest living actors.' Everyone laughed. He laughed."

The most painful replacements were gender-related, according to Wolf. "I can honestly say I had nothing to do with it when [NBC president] Warren Littlefield called up and said, 'The show's too testosterone-driven. There aren't any women watching it. I love *Law & Order*, but it's over next year without women.' I said, 'What are you telling me?' and Warren's answer was, 'I'm telling you to put women in the show.'"

Wolf suddenly realized, "There are only six characters, so that meant I had to fire somebody. Warren said, 'Hey, your choice. I think it will really make a difference.' And he was right. The ratings have gone up every year since the women came on the show.... They are a comfort zone."

Delivering the news to Florek and Brooks in 1993 certainly was not so comfortable. "It was awful; literally, the two worst phone calls I ever had to make in a business context. I said, 'Dann, there's nothing I can tell you. You've been a mainstay on the show. Everybody loves you. You were always there whenever you were needed. You came prepared; you knew your lines. You're fired. What can I say? It has nothing to do with you.'"

Florek doesn't care for the way it was handled. "Everything was kind of hushed and hidden. Then people say, 'Oh, that's the hardest thing I ever did!' Dick, don't even pretend here, pal."

Chris Noth still bristles about the situation. "In the first two years, our time slot was changed, like, four different times. When we first went on Tuesday nights, we got really high numbers; we were winning our time slot. When [Warren] Littlefield switched us to nine o'clock, against

Roseanne, we got killed. Then he moved us to Friday. Nowhereland. So he starts to say, 'It's because you don't have women.' But people who loved the show couldn't find it."

Dann Florek recalls how Richard Brooks learned he was to leave the series. "He came home from vacation, ready to go to work, found a message on his machine, and that's how he knew. I think it was flat out just like a kick in the privates."

Brooks admits it caught him by surprise: "I thought I had a lot of support from the production people, the critics, the audience.... I felt really strongly loved. I'd passed on some films because I thought I'd be coming back. I didn't hear about it till a week before we were supposed to start shooting again."

In 1995, executive producer Ed Sherin told Entertainment Weekly that Brooks "didn't get along with [Michael] Moriarty and he was grousing all the time. We needed a new mix....It was nothing but testosterone here."

Sound mixer David Platt mourns the bygone days. "With the combination of Florek and Noth, we lost a lot of time laughing," he says. "That's what I think is missing now, that kind of familiarity, that dynamic. I loved the good-old-boy thing they had—no knock on Epatha or Jill or Carey. For the crew, it was a stunner. We loved those guys."

Newcomer Jill Hennessy was well aware of *Law & Order* on-the-set love. "It's like coming into a wound that hasn't healed yet," she says. "When Epatha and I arrived on set, I think we both got completely the opposite [of what we expected].... I know everybody was upset about the way Dann and Richard had been taken off the show. If anything, [they were] so welcoming and really made a point of including us."

The Brooks-Florek exodus may have been disturbing, but viewers and critics became downright apoplectic when Dick Wolf fired Chris Noth in 1995. Three years later, the complaints still haven't abated. *Entertainment Weekly* critic Ken Tucker recently wrote that although most of the cast changes work pretty well, "I invariably miss the presence of beefy, blunt Chris Noth."

Beefy? The actor's many smitten fans are more likely to think hunky than chunky. Noth has had to hire assistants to handle the volume of mail still coming in for him. On the Internet, an active *All Things Noth* Web page (http://members.aol.com/dwalheim/noth.html) is one of several by and for devotees of his tough, sexy, sensitive cop. One such cyber zealot, with the moniker Capella, proposed in late 1997 that "no one out-Noths the Noth."

The Noth speaks: "Once they got rid of Danny and Brooks, and Ed Sherin got on board [as executive producer], I was, like, saying goodbye.

I had two more years on my contract but, for me, the show ended right then and there."

In retrospect, Dick Wolf believes he made a rational, albeit difficult, production choice. "The writers were going crazy," he says. "They had nothing to write to because Briscoe and Logan agreed with each other about everything. They could finish each other's sentences and that gave them no dynamic to play with."

Noth acknowledges that the two detectives were cut from the same cloth, but it was not a fabric of his own making. "When they hired Jerry [Orbach] I thought it was a mistake because there wasn't enough differentiation between our characters. It was playing the same notes. You put a Sorvino or a Dzundza in there, we can't help but bounce off each other."

He asserts that Wolf is no friend to actors and therefore "shouldn't be in show business. If you fundamentally don't trust them and don't respect them, then why are you in this at all?...Go make ads for Seagram's Scotch."

As a man who left advertising for entertainment, Wolf protests his ogre image: "We try to maintain good relations, as much as it looks like I'm a serial killer. We're doing a movie with Chris that's being written right now: *Logan in Exile*. He's a detective on Staten Island. It's a two-hour movie for NBC. . . . If it works, we can do a couple a year. He's enormously popular."

That praise pales in comparison with Wolf's admiration for Benjamin Bratt, who was hired in an attempt to sort of out-Noth the Noth. "He brings sex appeal. Ben's one of the ten sexiest men on television according to *TV Guide*. The guy is built like a Peruvian god."

With the addition of a Peruvian god and a glamorous ex-Bond girl like Carey Lowell (from the 1989 James Bond spy thriller *License to Kill*), the show can no longer boast, as a 1991 article in the (Toronto) *Globe and Mail* mentions, that "[t]here are no stars or pretty faces on *Law & Order*."

Good looks aside, Bratt has yet to earn the critical acclaim or Internet activity that Noth enjoys. No matter how often his musculature is displayed—and the detective's revealing undershirt has became something of another character on the show—viewers seem to have a tough time warming to the frosty Curtis, portrayed by an actor who is exceedingly warm and witty off screen. The show's producers, however, appear confident that he's a crowd pleaser. Executive producer Ed Sherin told *TV Guide* in 1996 that "[e]very time we've shown Ben Bratt in an undershirt, we get a lot of female mail."

As wrenching as the Florek/Brooks/Noth employment pink slips were, nothing quite matched the horrific time Wolf went through when the mercurial Michael Moriarty (who declined to be interviewed for this book) bid the show farewell. This action followed his very public attacks against Attorney General Janet Reno, who had warned that the government might step in to curtail the current state of television violence. Moriarty seemed to take the threats personally.

Apparently, the furor started at a November 1993 dinner with Moriarty, Wolf, and other television executives in Washington, D.C. "It was kind of surreal," Wolf recalls. "I asked Reno, 'Well, don't you think the parents of America should decide what their children watch and not the federal government?' She said, 'You can't trust parents anymore.' I said, 'Excuse me?' And she said, 'No, it's not like when I was growing up and my father would tear out the offending pages of *Superman* and *Batman* comics before we could read them.' And I just went, 'Yow!'"

Wolf believes that "it pushed every one of Michael's buttons about censorship and everything else. I didn't disagree with him. But I told him, 'Michael, it does not lead to meaningful dialogue when you go around calling the attorney general of the United States a psychotic Nazi bitch.' He said, 'I'm suing her.' I said, 'You can't sue her, Michael. She's immune from prosecution in performance of her official duties.'"

At that point, according to Wolf, Moriarty made a declaration: "'If that's your advice, I'm getting myself another attorney.' I said, 'Michael, I am not an attorney. You are not an attorney. You play an attorney on television.' About a week later, he resigned."

His resignation letter, submitted in January 1994, describes a nightmarish scenario of government censorship. Although Wolf and others at *Law & Order* were equally repulsed by the attorney general's remarks, they felt alarm about the extreme nature of Moriarty's reaction.

On the cover of *The Gift of Stern Angels*, Michael Moriarty's rambling 1997 memoir, Reno's face is superimposed on a dragon being pierced with a lance held by a knight bearing Moriarty's countenance. In the text, he proclaims his Lone Ranger stance: "Knowing I'm the only one that has taken an unequivocal stand against this censoring from Washington . . . knowing it's David and Goliath for real, I press on, pushing and pushing my words out through interviews, lectures and faxes."

As he publicly trumpeted his anti-Reno rhetoric, the actor reportedly became increasingly unpredictable on the set, but on camera continued to perform with astonishing, even unparalleled, grace. "For my money, you can't replace Moriarty," producer Joe Stern says. "I think Sam [Waterston] is good, but the complexity of Moriarty you can never replace. He brought this incredible self-righteousness to it. He was, as critic John Leonard called him [on *CBS News Sunday Morning*], 'a samurai warrior.'"

Former *Law & Order* writer Robert Nathan feels that, "separate from all the external issues of Michael leaving the show, he is a consummate pro. The line between character and actor is pretty blurry because the actor brings so much of himself. The writing is so minimal that the actor has to make those moments come alive. John Leonard saw the blending of Ben Stone and Michael Moriarty. Michael knew that, by [his last] episode, the warrior he created was out of control."

To this day, Dick Wolf continues to be upbeat about replacing Moriarty with Sam Waterston. "[Jack] McCoy is a hundred and eighty degrees away from Ben Stone. When Michael resigned, I got this panic call from Warren [Littlefield]: 'This is insane....What are we going to do? The guy is the heart of the back half of the show.' I said, 'I have two words: Sam Waterston.' He said, 'Fine.'"

Even greater ire resulted when Wolf told *TV Guide* in November 1994 that "Michael did a fantastic job for years, but Sam projects more sex appeal." In an *Entertainment Weekly* story on the show, Moriarty shot back: "I hope that's on Sam's grave—'Here lies a man who's sexier than Mike Moriarty.'"

For co-producer Arthur Forney, the Moriarty-Waterston comparison is a matter of degrees. "When we made the transition from Michael to Sam, the show evolved too. There were different rhythms in the way the actors responded to things, in the way they delivered their lines, that also changed the style of the editing. Michael could do a lot of things with a type of look, whereas Sam might do it with an additional line—and that tells a story sometimes."

One TV critic, from Toronto's *Globe and Mail*, observed in early 1995 that McCoy was "steadier, a little more emotionally anchored than Moriarty's Ben Stone, who always...seemed in danger of becoming unhinged at any moment."

However, there was a sweet side to this quixotic actor, according to actress Jill Hennessy. "Michael was very helpful and fatherly. I learned a lot from him." When he left the show, Hennessy was sad to see him go.

Former camera operator Christopher Misiano, who now directs episodes on *Law & Order* or substitutes as cinematographer, believes that "each generation has had a different flavor. One of the unique things about the show is that it survived all those things. There aren't that many TV shows in history that have done this, changed that many people."

Now, toss into this volatile then-versus-now debate the great leap forward in public awareness of *Law & Order* when the Arts & Entertainment Network (A&E) began broadcasting reruns in September 1994, just as Sam Waterston was making his debut on the NBC version. "So many people say, 'I started watching your show on A&E,'" says producer Jeff Hayes.

For viewers whose maiden *Law & Order* experience comes via cable television reruns, there is often confusion. "I still get stopped by people, probably more than when I was actually on the show," Dann Florek says. "They yell out, 'Hey, Captain! How ya doin'?' Some only watch the show on A&E. One person told me, 'What a wonderful idea. You don't [usually] see revolving casts, different combinations of people.' I said, 'Well, it's not exactly that way.'"

Noth is bemused by this phenomenon. "Do you really believe the show's new success, in terms of the ratings, is from these cast changes? A lot of it's because A&E came onto the scene and gave them a whole new audience. Most people still look at the A&E stuff as *Law & Order.*..."

That experience is shared by Richard Brooks. "It's almost as if I've never been off the show.... I would say I'm definitely more popular than I was then. People are still discovering it. Most people don't know I'm not still on *Law & Order*, even in the industry. I go to auditions and producers say, 'Is the show on hiatus?'"

Even George Dzundza, gone since the early 1990s, finds the A&E resurrection of his series character a bit odd. "I feel like I'm still doing the show. People don't know I ever left."

The various cast changes on *Law & Order* have been endlessly debated by the press and the public, although few outsiders are really aware of the seismic shifts beneath the show's surface. Enormous transformations took place when those charged with producing and writing *Law & Order*—many of them in Los Angeles—migrated in and out of positions of power.

Writer Ed Zuckerman left in the first season under awkward circumstances, returned after a year, was later promoted to co-executive producer, then remained on the job until late 1996. "My take on it? I was working in New York under David Black, with a guy named Robert Nathan. It's possible there was competition between me and Robert for what was really one job, and I lost that competition. [But] Robert was instrumental in getting me back on the show a couple of years later."

David Black gave notice after two seasons, but then returned in 1997 as writer and supervising producer. "Universal [TV] asked me to take a reduction in fees. The first year, I believe, I wrote and produced all or part of eighteen hours of TV, including nine of the first thirteen *Law & Orders*. That's enormous. The second year it wasn't quite that much, but close to it. Universal had it in their mind that, because I was in New York, I wasn't pulling my weight. I don't know how much more I could have done.... So I left, with great regret, and struck out on my own."

Robert Nathan, who went on to write for the TV series *ER* (1994–), quit at the end of the fourth season (1993–94). "I was happy to go out with [Episode 88:] 'Old Friends' [Moriarty's final episode]. At that point, I had done four years, and written or co-written thirty or so episodes. There comes a moment when you want to do something new. Michael's leaving crystallized it for me.... I needed new challenges."

Finally, after three very productive years, why did Joe Stern decide to call it a day? "I felt that I had done all that I could do and I wanted to start my own theatre when I came home to Los Angeles," he explains. "I also thought that the show was going downhill a little bit. Things were getting sloppy. We were falling behind in the scripts. I didn't want to just go through the motions. I felt that a sanitation of the show was coming as well.... [T]here was a sense of moving toward this white-collar thing. We had done it. We had made three great years of television. I thought the show wasn't going to be as good."

Nathan believes Stern always pushed for perfection. "If we hadn't given it enough, or gone far enough, he would remind us that we would have to live with this for the rest of our lives. 'This show will run forever—somewhere. Don't turn on your television in four or five years and wish you did better. Do it now.' That was his pursuit of excellence, which made the show what it was."

IN WITH THE NEW

When Joe Stern went West, Ed Sherin moved into his executive producer slot and launched some new initiatives. "I don't think people knew what the show was exactly," he says. "It takes several years before a show develops its identity and you know how to produce it. I think Joe did a very, very good job. Where I think the show failed was in the preparation of scripts.... That was one big area that I thought was probably, at worst, chaotic; at best, it was undetermined."

Sherin suggested to *Law & Order*'s head honchos "that the [California] writers come East, that one key writer shepherd the script through. Well, that was met with some concern. Some people thought it was foolhardy to spend that kind of money on travel and housing people."

He also instituted "the prep reading of the script. We would read through a script and stop at the end of a scene and ask if anybody had any comments." Sometimes those comments were nihilistic. "I understood the difference between deconstructing a script and helping a script," Sherin says. "My intention was not to write the script; it was to fulfill what had been written.... I had no desire to make less of anyone. I wanted to make more of them. In order to do that, certain things had to be very clear: It was our objective to help the writer fulfill his vision, not to impose our vision."

Jill Hennessy, hired to play ADA Claire Kincaid when Richard Brooks (ADA Paul Robinette) was dismissed at the end of Season Three, and Sam Waterston, assuming Law & Order's **EADA role as Jack McCoy after Michael Moriarty's (EADA Ben Stone) angry departure in 1994.** *[courtesy of Photofest / Copyright ©1996 by Universal City Studios, Inc. Courtesy of Universal Publishing Rights, a Division of Universal Studios Licensing, Inc. All rights reserved.]*

Over time, Sherin saw the process blossom. "The beauty part is that it involves location managers who get a much clearer insight into the environment because we constantly discuss it in those terms. It involves the production designer talking about the ambiance, the ethos, the mise-en-scène, the leitmotif—things that are never discussed in television, to my knowledge. All of these are subtle contributions to the script."

As a director, Sherin ushered in the "one-er," a way of capturing several viewpoints in a single shot as the camera circles the action.

Writer/executive producer Rene Balcer welcomed the new era on *Law & Order*. "In the first couple of years, there was more hysteria. There weren't read-throughs, so script problems weren't addressed until late in pre-production and sometimes on the set. Whether by design or by accident, there was a sort of hysterical attitude: 'We have to get the writer right away and where is he?'"

Now script problems are more readily solved, according to Balcer. "In the first two or three years, there was a deliberate move to keep the writers separate from the actors and never let them talk to each other. It was very territorial."

Under Sherin, local talent was tapped. "We made a concerted effort to hire New York directors," remembers Lewis Gould, a producer on the program who also directs. "A lot of TV shows that shoot in New York fly in their directors from L.A. We used to do that. You have to fly them in first class, put them in a hotel, give them a per diem, and it adds a lot of expense to the show."

People started coming up through the ranks. "Ed developed directors amongst us, which was great for us personally but also great for the

Carey Lowell (left), who took over as ADA Jamie Ross in Season Seven when Jill Hennessy (ADA Claire Kincaid) quit, seen here with Sam Waterston (EADA Jack McCoy) and guest star Patti LuPone in Episode 160: "Navy Blues" (Season Eight).

show," Gould says. "Then you have people directing who really understand the style and the characters. The other thing that has been nurtured here—I have to take my hat off to Ed—is that he's developed a depth in the crew."

Sound mixer David Platt, who periodically directs, calls it "the Ed Sherin tutorial." Suddenly, there was more upward mobility. "I wanted to utilize more skills of the people who were doing the show," Sherin says. "I knew for a fact, having worked with the company as a director, that there were many people on the crew who were very bright, had good solid college education.... It seemed to me to be a waste of resources."

At one time, Constantine "Gus" Makris was the show's only director of photography (DP) and Christopher Misiano was the sole camera operator. "This work is so exhausting and people get ill or just run down, and it's always safe to have a backup for any of the key positions," Gould says. "So we started to give Chris a chance to DP, which kind of happened hand-in-hand with Gus directing. When Chris began to DP, we got a new operator at those times, Richard Dobbs. Last year he, too, made the leap from operator to DP because there was a period when neither Gus or Chris could do it."

Martha Mitchell, one of the few women to direct *Law & Order* episodes, credits both Ed Sherin and Joe Stern for helping her career progress. She is unequivocal in her praise: "*Law & Order* changed my life. I had been a script supervisor for twelve years [including other shows], and now I've been directing [on a freelance basis] for four years.... It's very hard to get that kind of break as a woman and a New Yorker. My relationship with *Law & Order*, and more specifically with Ed Sherin, made that possible."

The flow was certainly democratic, but ill will emerged from loyalties to one "era" as opposed to another for both personal and artistic reasons. "I've tried to watch the new shows," Chris Noth says. "I think it's incredibly derivative. It's so f***ing stuck in its habits. I look at it and go, 'Oh, there's the Ed Sherin one-er.' I anticipate what they're doing before they do it. It's just so f***ing old.... That became the signature *Law & Order* shot, which I find to be dull as dishwater now. It was very innovative when we first did it, but now it's the rule. Now it's f***ing McDonalds for Chrissakes."

He does give Sherin credit for instituting the roundtables, the term everyone uses for the weekly script meetings that give the show's actors an opportunity to have a say. "The cast at that time probably got along well enough to do this. We didn't have them till Jerry Orbach was on board. Having a roundtable with Dzundza would have been a complete disaster."

Gene Ritchings, *Law & Order*'s production coordinator, does not see the Stern/Sherin divide as a choice between better and worse. "It's a distinction between two different periods and two different personalities that defined the workplace.... For Joe, it was a one-man show at the executive producer level. He dealt with the writers directly on the development of the scripts. If the actors had questions, problems, suggestions, they came to Joe."

Just as Sherin does now, Joe Stern previously hired all the show's directors: "A good many he knew from television in Los Angeles, so he flew them in. Established people, very talented people. There's a whole list of people who don't work with us anymore because Ed changed to a system he was more comfortable with. But I think the approach of the show, that combination of the police-procedural storytelling and a reality cop show with documentary-style photography and the courtroom drama, is the same."

The changes that Sherin made "had more to do with broadening the participation, now that the foundation was established, of a great many more people working on the show," Ritchings says. "Ed opened the process up and brought people along—which, I think, creates more of an emotional investment in the work."

Ritchings believes that "Joe kept the show on point and did not let it stray into what Hollywood calls 'character,' which tends to be overly sentimentalized. *Law & Order* was regarded in its early years as rather emotionally cold and very male-dominated, but I think that's because it stuck to structure and basic drama."

If you compare NBC's new *Law & Order* episodes to the reruns on A&E, according to supervising producer Arthur Forney, "it's a different feel. I think it's shot a little warmer than it was in the first three years. It's a little bit more personal in the writing."

Nonetheless, in Chris Noth's opinion, it just doesn't measure up. "If anything, when I watch the show—and I can only watch about five minutes of it—it's very stagnant," he declares. "You lose something very valuable by not taking the kind of risks we did the first few years. You don't get the unexpected at all.... The edges are rounded out. It's a f***ing imitation of itself."

Although less strident, Dann Florek also is disappointed with the current atmosphere in the *Law & Order* TV

Creator/executive producer Dick Wolf (right) with longtime Law & Order **director Ed Sherin, who took over as the New York-based co-executive producer when Joe Stern left at the end of Season Three.** [courtesy of Jessica Burstein]

precinct. "Briscoe is laid back. Curtis is laid back. Van Buren is laid back. Now I see three laid-back people sitting in a room. Beautifully shot, nicely done, but nobody is taking over.... Back then, I sometimes felt those guys were going to kill each other. All of that fed into who the characters became."

While not as disenchanted as Noth and Florek, director of photography Gus Makris does lament losing some of the show's old ways. "The cops could get on either side of an issue and argue it out. That doesn't seem to happen now. It's more *Dragnet.* You know, 'What color was the car, ma'am?' There just doesn't seem to be time anymore."

Cinematographer/director Chris Misiano echoes that mantra: "I look at some of those early shows I didn't work on and I look at the relationships between the cops and I see great stuff there. They had conflict. We don't have time for that when there's so much plot to get in. It would be nice for these guys to be able to play that again. There was great work in those first casts."

David Platt sees a paradox. "As *Law & Order* lost some of that New York edge, the ratings have gotten better and better. This is such a weird show; it's an aberration. I don't know how many shows started out barely hanging on in the ratings, and now it's been going eight years."

Chris Noth offers some uncharacteristic praise: "In the world of entertainment today, *Law & Order* is probably still way above most things."

Even George Dzundza musters up some kind words: "The bottom line is the show's still on the air, it is employing a great many people, and it's bringing pleasure to countless millions."

The longevity of *Law & Order* makes Dick Wolf purr. "This organization after eight years runs like a Swiss watch." Ritchings is equally effusive about the show's inner dynamics. "It's very gratifying to work with people who are skillful, technically accomplished, competent—and to see this enormous collaboration reach the point when everything is ready and the director, in that quiet moment, says: 'Action!' Everybody's contribution leads to that moment again and again. There's something really magical about that I've always loved."

THE WORDS

*Anyone who says that the artist's field is
all answers and no questions has never
done any writing or had any dealings
with imagery. An artist observes, selects,
guesses and synthesizes.*

—Anton Chekhov, 1888

As FAR AS Dick Wolf is concerned,
the ideal *Law & Order* segment has yet to be written. "The perfect
episode is where all six of the regulars have different viewpoints on the
same case and they're all right," he says, invoking the *Rashomon* scenario.
"That's the joy of the show. It's the writing. Somebody said, 'How long
can it run after the eighth year?' I said, 'I'd like it to go fifteen more years
and beat *Gunsmoke* [1955–75] and there's really no reason it couldn't, as
long as the writing stays at this level."

He credits wordsmiths Rene Balcer, Michael Chernuchin, and Walon
Green, among others. "There's a whole litany of the best writers in the
business who've been with the show," Wolf says. "And they have been vastly underappreciated. It's not the touchy-feely stuff that wins Emmies, but
it's incredibly difficult to write. It requires unbelievable discipline and talent to pull off on a weekly basis. To give what is essentially a very dry procedural so much intellectual spin and so much character spin every week
is really a testament to the written word."

Producer Joe Stern believes that, during his era, Robert Nathan and
Michael Chernuchin drove the show's high quality. "They wrote most of
the scripts. They were the mules. Between the two of them, they were

Los Angeles-based co-executive producer Rene Balcer, a writer with Law & Order *since Season One.*

[courtesy of Rene Balcer]

responsible for two-thirds of it because a lot of the rewrites which were uncredited, they did. I think they're the real heroes of *Law & Order.*"

Nathan began on a temporary basis in Season One. "They gave me one script to write, since they were short of staff," he recalls. "It was a lot of fun, and then they gave me another one. Dick asked me if I wanted to do this for a while. I told him that maybe I would for six or seven months, then go back to Los Angeles and finish the novel that I was in the middle of. But it was so much fun that I stayed for four years."

He felt that there was "something exciting about making this show because the form was new for its time. The style was different than any other police show that had ever been done on television. This was a writer's show because it featured wall-to-wall dialogue. There were no action sequences or pauses in the dialogue. This was a writer's dream because it was all about words."

For co-executive producer Ed Sherin, thoughts about writing inspire various beastly images. "The writers are under enormous time pressure to deliver material....Sometimes it doesn't get done quickly because you've got a tiger by the tail. The actors have learned that the writers are human, that they try to put these things together with a rapidity that is inhuman."

Ask David Black what attracted him to *Law & Order* and he responds without hesitation: "I was happy to be writing quality. I was working with Dick [Wolf]. He creates a safe place for writers to be able to do the best they can do, which is not always true on shows. Dick has drawn a magic circle within which the writers can work safely."

Robert Palm, who worked for the show during the first two seasons, echoes that sentiment: "As writers, since we were all new, there was less scrutiny [than] there would be now. There was a naive, blithe, what-the-f*** attitude. We just did what we wanted. And Dick was our great defender."

Black suggests that it might be the trickiest show on television to write. "We kept learning our craft as we went along," Black says. "It stretches us. The conflict comes not out of good guys and bad guys, but out of the collision of realities—which always gives you an interesting subtext. That collision of realities creates the core of the drama."

Palm suspects that "the television medium is a black-and-white world these days, but on this show we got to pull off an ambiguous picture where heroes are tainted and the guilty characters have mixed motives."

Rene Balcer was hired as a writer during Season One, at about the same time as Michael Chernuchin (who left six years later). In a long-running TV series often marked by personality disputes, this duo seems to have functioned as a sort of John Lennon-Paul McCartney scriptwriting team. Make that "the Lerner and Loewe of the show," says Chernuchin. "We usually divided the story into cops and lawyers, and I took the back half and he took the front half. . . . He liked twists and turns and forensics evidence, and I go for the big issues and the legal part at the end. That's why we worked so well together."

Former co-executive producer Michael Chernuchin, an attorney who became a Law & Order *writer beginning in Season One.* [courtesy of Michael Chernuchin]

Balcer agrees. "The collaboration worked beautifully. Some of the best shows I've done—I hope he thinks they're some of the best he's done—are ones we wrote together. What was funny is that we'd beat out the stories and then he would go write one half and I would go write the other half. And—boom!—they meshed."

One of their first joint projects was the second half of the two-parter, Episode 16: "Torrents of Greed," in the first season. "I think we rewrote it looking at the same computer screen and just trading lines," Balcer says. "It was a very fruitful partnership. Michael brought a unique take on the law and way of manipulating the law—very interesting legal theories. There's really no one who has stepped in to do the same kinds of things."

Since Chernuchin's departure, Balcer has had to rely much more on his own intuition. "Because of my ignorance of the law, I'll come up with

Jeffrey Hayes, a producer and unit production manager who began working for Law & Order *in Season One.* [courtesy of Jessica Burstein]

these ideas and theories that normally a lawyer would dismiss right out of hand. I push our legal advisor, Bill Fordes: 'Well, what if? Isn't there any case law?' Then he'll find the case and, lo and behold, 'Yes, you can do that. You can certainly argue it and, depending on the judge, get it by.' Working with Michael, I learned a lot about the law."

Fordes compares West Coast story sessions to "partner meetings in a law firm, where they're ranting and raving. Rene is the head writer and show runner; if you didn't know, you couldn't guess who is the attorney in the room. I call it the Dick Wolf School of Law. We'll have this incredible argument, then look around and ask, 'Hey, did anybody write that down?' Because there's our scene. All we have to do is boil down the argument we just had. Remarkably often, that's how scenes are born."

As evidence of the show's efficacy, Fordes mentions that they've devised legal theories "about which law professors have called us and asked what our references are for that. People from the Soviet Union asked if we could send them tapes because they want to show how an American courtroom is done."

Dick Wolf is proud that "there's no exposition and nothing is repeated," as he told the *Houston Chronicle* in 1992. "Legal philosophy, legal nuance and legal language—and there's plenty of it—are never explained. The viewer is simply thrust into the complex and often opaque world of lawyerly subtleties, legal wranglings and bizarre (at least to the uninitiated) loopholes."

From an actor's perspective, "it's a question of whether a particular show and a particular situation is well or badly written," suggests lead Sam Waterston. "That's all anybody cares about: Did they write it right? Then it will [support you]. A tremendous amount of effort is put into keeping it good. We have an extraordinarily complicated story to tell in a short amount of time, so you can't mess around."

Certainly, nobody working for *Law & Order* does mess around. Production coordinator Gene Ritchings explains that "the standards here are very, very high. It's an incredibly hard show to write because the research that goes into the scripts, to make them as accurate as possible for the world that you're portraying, is really extensive. A lot of work goes into making sure that, when the show appears, if it's watched by someone who knows that world, they will say, 'That's the way it is. They got it right.'"

Ritchings, who co-wrote Episode 111: "Pride," points to the complicated themes in many scripts. "It's not just a matter of the police and how the judicial system works. We've done shows on quantum physics, we've delved into politics, we've delved into the military, all these different worlds. We've gotten complaints from people who disagreed with the point of view that we took on that world, but not about its accuracy."

The effort can be maddening. "When you think in terms of literary standards, there's a high degree of naturalism and authenticity. . . . The scripts take a long time to develop. I can't see anybody pounding one out in a couple of weeks," Ritchings says.

Legal advisor Fordes believes that the key is "understated realism, a lack of melodramatic fireworks, which in one sense limits *Law & Order* in that we'll never have the histrionics of other shows that get bigger ratings. As intellectual property, it makes us very proud to look at it. You view an episode that is as close as you can get [to the criminal justice system] yet still conveys the emotional underpinnings of the piece."

Years before she was hired to portray Lieutenant Van Buren, S. Epatha Merkerson would become transfixed watching *Law & Order.* "The first thing that got me was the fact that Ben Stone lost a case. Television, to me, was always [about] the good guys. And here was a good guy who lost. Good guys don't lose; that's what I'd been told. It was so real to me that, even though he may have been right, it just didn't work out that way."

Writer Robert Nathan was intent on always avoiding the way "traditional law and police shows had the heroes winning all the time. When Stone started to lose cases regularly, and accurately reflected the real percentage of felony convictions in New York, it made the show much more absorbing for the audience. They could see that the criminal justice system worked on an abstract level, but it didn't work in always getting convictions."

Michael Chernuchin suggests that "you have to be realistic, even to the point of showing that you don't always win. I think we are one of the first law programs to demonstrate that. Audiences love that aspect of the show because they never know what'll happen in the last five minutes."

Gene Ritchings also loves the show's surprise conclusions. "It's much better to leave the jury hanging and leave the case unresolved on screen, and let the audience vote in their hearts for what they think is right. Then you've given them something that extends beyond 11:00 p.m."

Others echo that viewpoint. "I love the fact we don't know if we're going to win or not. And we don't always, even when we're right," says producer Jeff Hayes.

"They present a situation with no solution; that's what I like," says William H. Macy, a colleague of playwright David Mamet with an Emmy nomination for his recurring character on the TV series *ER* (1994–), an Oscar nomination for best supporting actor in the film *Fargo* (1996), and a guest star in both the *Law & Order* pilot episode in 1988 and Episode 39: "Sisters of Mercy." "I love that they don't win sometimes. That's brave writing. That's Mamet. That's Chekhov."

Although proud of *Law & Order*'s high standards, creator Dick Wolf remains a bit more cynical: "Yeah, we're down here every week doing *The Cherry Orchard.*"

THE ISSUES

True and false are attributes of speech,
not of things.

—THOMAS HOBBES, *Leviathan* (1651)

"**W**HEN the show first came on the air the critics really loved it, but the audience response was quite underwhelming for a while," Dick Wolf recalls of the start of *Law & Order*. "It was one of those arguments between the show not doing that well and the NBC sales department camping in [network president] Brandon Tartikoff's office, [wanting] to take it off the air. We had $800,000 in advertiser pull-outs on the abortion clinic bombing episode [Episode 12: 'Life Choice'] . . . half a million dollars in pull-outs on the assisted suicide for AIDS victims episode [Episode 3: 'The Reaper's Helper']."

The controversial subject matter, though rather thrilling for viewers of network television, gave NBC a headache. "I mean, every week there was a drum roll of hundreds of thousands of dollars," Wolf says. "If it hadn't been for Brandon [Tartikoff] and Warren [Littlefield], the show would have been taken off the air. They believed in it and they stuck with it."

Littlefield still believes in it. "Rather than come up with too many rules—like, 'You can't go there'—we would just kind of build in a certain amount of advertiser defection from the show. We can live with that. Sometimes, once it was on the air and life as we know it did not come to an end, then there would be less of a problem the second time around [for reruns]," he recalls.

With another *Rashomon* angle on the show, producer Jeff Hayes recalls that Littlefield's statement wasn't always the case. "For a while, we had the highest advertising drop-out rate. Some of our best episodes were never rerun because they were too controversial," he says.

"Advertisers are sheep. You can't blame them," declares Wolf, who spent a decade laboring in their ranks. "If it was my money, I'd probably feel exactly the same way."

He persevered in the face of all that first-season backlash. "I certainly never expected them to abandon the show in the droves that they did initially. Millions and millions of dollars of pullouts," he muses.

"My dream for every *Law & Order* show is that it presents issues the country is trying to deal with, moral issues," says writer/supervising producer David Black. "It presents both sides equally strongly and when the show goes off the air, people start arguing with each other. It's good for the civic dialogue that a country must have to remain free. No one side should corner the market on righteousness, for dramatic reasons and for the health of the republic."

Black believes the show has always been "so exciting to write because we get to explore our hearts on these issues. The power of the writing comes not only from the research we do of the external world; it allows us to really go deep in ourselves.... That's what keeps the writing alive and urgent. It's not just a gig. It's not a vocation. It's a calling."

Actor Richard Brooks told the *Los Angeles Times* in 1992 that "[t]here is always the potential for *Law & Order* to be making political statements that are uncomfortable. It's the nature of the show. The title alone glamorizes the subject. But for the most part, we play in a gray area."

Fellow actor Paul Sorvino, interviewed for the same article, also appreciated the grays. "It's totally rational. No philosophy. And no politics. Not right, not left. It can't take a wrong position. All it does is uphold the law."

Executive producer Wolf, whose paternal grandmother was a Marxist, maintains that the show's viewpoint is indeed universal. "I don't think *Law & Order*'s sensibility is limited to Manhattan lefties or the children of lefties. Conservatives like it too. It presents an idealized sense of the justice system; everybody on the team is trying to effectuate justice, as opposed to just winning a conviction or slamming it to somebody."

He senses that the balance comes from "a feeling of humanism that runs through all the writers. We present a no-excuse situation. A constant theme over eight years is the fact that, more and more in this country, nobody is willing to take the responsibility for what they do.... [I]f you had to boil down one of the core ideas and ideals of the show, [it would be] that actions do have consequences, that there is no excuse for killing somebody."

According to Wolf, the guilty must pay for their crimes, but, "at the same time, we're dealing with a legal system that can be manipulated—which is why certain people on this show get away with it."

He approves of the ripped-from-the-headlines promotion that the NBC network uses to plug *Law & Order*, but draws the line at presenting a real crime verbatim. "We take the headline, not the body copy, because the first half of the show is a murder mystery and the second half is usually a moral mystery.... [I]t's not supposed to be the actual case."

Although over the years some articles on *Law & Order* have pointed to the front page of the *New York Times* as the chief source of story ideas for the show, Wolf insists it has always been the *New York Post*.

"In the early days, it was stories [taken] from *New York Post* headlines. You would see something in the *Post* and, two weeks later, there was a script and we were shooting it," remembers longtime extra and stand-in Spike Finnerty.

Rene Balcer thinks perhaps another tabloid, the *New York Daily News*, had been touted as the *Law & Order* bible. Regardless, "Now the bible is almost really anything," he says, adding that topics are determined by the requirements of art rather than by social concerns. "We're not going to do a subject just because it's controversial; we're going to do a subject if we have a new angle, a new approach to it."

Producer Ed Sherin sums up the essence of what makes *Law & Order* so savvy in topical matters. "Life is very chaotic," he says. "You can't really make head nor tail of it as it flies by. The stream of activity is too intense. But drama allows you to literally elongate that moment, to view it from many sides. What the show does with issues is to pull them apart. The best shows are those when our heroes are on opposite sides. When you tackle the reality of an event, you're going to bump headlong into the opposite."

To bump headlong into opposite sides of any thorny issue makes for gripping primetime television, as producer Jeff Hayes points out: "They think we need the headlines.... It's really just a gimmick. You can invent any crime you want, although the real ones are sometimes more bizarre. Tackling themes is what makes it interesting. Most of the crew and production team probably wouldn't be doing this show if it weren't really terrific and intelligent. *Law & Order* is smart and has high production values."

Producer Lew Gould figures the series took a while to catch on because "it doesn't have flash.... I don't think there's a show on TV that has more of a topical bite. We go after the issues more than anybody, but it's done with an intelligent bent.... [It's] kind of like a PBS program. The audience finds it and they stick with it and they tell their friends."

Production coordinator Gene Ritchings insists that "there's no such thing as positive role models on our show. We don't deal in black and white, and we're not interested in projecting role models that people can admire."

This aversion to a politically-correct line comes from the show's aim for naturalism. "It goes wherever it needs to go and there's never a consideration that maybe we should lighten the character a little bit because this group or that group won't approve," says Ritchings, who is convinced that "all writing is about creating tension, suspense, mystery. And once you resolve the tension, you either don't have a story anymore or you quickly resolve it in a way that creates more tension. Positive role models get in the way of that.... Who the hell wants them cluttering up a good story?"

CHAPTER 6

THE GRIT

Oh, let us love our occupations, Bless
the squire and his relations, Live upon
our daily rations, and always know
our proper stations.

—CHARLES DICKENS, *The Chimes* (1844)

CONSTANTINE "Gus" Makris sometimes finds himself thinking like the social conscience of *Law & Order*. The accomplished cinematographer, who also directs about five episodes a year, has been with the show since the middle of the first season. A two-time Emmy winner, he is largely responsible for the glorious images that accompany the often superb writing, acting, and directing.

Yet this native New Yorker is critical of the route the TV show has taken in recent years. "I haven't been to a crackhouse in ages," Makris says wistfully. "People only want to see the rich and famous. I've heard that our audience is more interested in blueblood crimes....I don't know why. I believe the word is demographics. They'd rather see that than what might affect them more directly, like subway crime, just a plain old guy walking down the street and getting bashed in the back of the head, drugs."

Makris values salt-of-the-earth situations for their larger implications. "What's great about those [earlier] shows is they would open up an entire new subject: illiteracy, abortion. I'm more fond of the scripts that were done in the first two or three years, like [Episode 17:] 'Mushrooms.' We never do stories like that anymore. The discovery, when Moriarty nails this child on the witness stand for killing a boy by mistake because the kid couldn't read, to me was unbelievably powerful."

In fact, a number of *Law & Order* veterans point to this episode, written by Robert Palm and featuring S. Epatha Merkerson (later to take on the regular role of Lt. Anita Van Buren) as a bereaved mother, as an example of an exquisitely conceived and executed episode.

"All those writers—the Robert Palms, the Robert Nathans, the Michael Duggans, the Michael Chernuchins—they're all gone," Makris continues. "Without trying to demean anybody else's talent, I just feel that there were really compelling stories in the first three seasons."

He cites Episode 9: "Indifference," another Season One script by Palm. "That to me was just brilliant. It brings out other questions: adoption, child abuse, wife abuse. It opens up the social welfare system. They're taxed and overworked; they don't have enough money. It's not just a simple whodunit and how are we going to get the guy thrown in jail. It forces you to think about bigger problems than that specific crime," Makris says.

"Last year we did the department store sisters who killed," he adds with a laugh, referring to Episode 142: "Family Business." "There's nothing wrong with that stuff. It's entertainment. But the best ones hit bigger issues, bigger problems...."

Makris imagines how things might have been different on a Season Six trilogy that everyone refers to as the three-parter (Episode 149: "D-Girl," Episode 150: "Turnaround," and Episode 151: "Showtime"), which took the show to Los Angeles and back a few times. "I'd rather have reached for *The Battle of Algiers*," he says, becoming the second *Law & Order* person to reference the Pontecorvo film as a point of comparison. "I wish it could have been filmed in all five boroughs and ended at a huge garbage dump on Staten Island with the gulls circling above, instead of at a glitzy L.A. hotel."

Rene Balcer tallies up the grit-versus-no-grit installments over the seasons and then concludes: "I beg to differ with Gus. If it's changed, it's changed by maybe ten to twenty percent. As far as the network wanting more upscale stories, Gus is right. They feel it plays more to their audience. By the same token, the studio doesn't like us to do more upscale shows because it's more expensive."

Nonetheless, Balcer could foresee adding a little arthouse fare to future scripts: "Do *The Battle of Algiers* on *Law & Order*? That would be a great idea. Maybe that'll be the *next* three-parter."

Although he returned to L.A. after leaving *Law & Order*, Joe Stern also mourns the diminished New York edge. "I think it's more intellectual, less emotional now. It misses [writers] Robert Nathan and Michael

Chernuchin. The writing is not as good. It feels like the old show and the new show. More white-collar, less gritty. It's still a very good show. . . . I just don't think it has that consistency of every week saying, 'Holy sh**!' So many people feel like the A&E episodes are one era and this is another era."

"It was kind of like being in the Old West," explains actor/stand-in Spike Finnerty. "I've been in New York since 1983 but there are places I've been with this show that I would never have gone, especially at three or four o'clock in the morning. There have been crackhouses, murders nearby, police actions, and stuff. In one scene, we were taking a body out of the water and, not too far down the river, there was a real body being taken out."

Chris Noth (Logan) and George Dzundza (Greevey), searching for witnesses to a murder in Episode 17: "Mushrooms" **(Season One)** [courtesy of Photofest / Copyright ©1991 by Universal City Studios, Inc. Courtesy of Universal Publishing Rights, a Division of Universal Studios Licensing, Inc. All rights reserved.]

Writer/producer David Black has a literary comparison. "I like to see New York as Dickens would have seen London, from the gutter to the penthouse. The more class conflict you get, the stronger the show is," he says.

"We try to shoot two or three issue-oriented shows a year, but they don't do as well," acknowledges creator Dick Wolf. "The public does want more upscale crime. With grit, that sophisticated audience really doesn't want to go there at ten o'clock. You've seen it even on *N.Y.P.D. Blue* [1993–]. The perpetrators aren't quite as scrofulous-looking now. Adults like our storytelling but ask, 'Do we have to look at these unattractive people at the same time?' They want a pleasant environment. They want the grit too, but 'just don't show it to me all the time.'"

Not so for former producer Joe Stern. "They made it more upperclass. Now they have very few black stories. Regarding demographics, I believe the network overreacted. . . . I think people love those A&E shows; those are the minority shows that increased the audience. To tell you the truth, I think it's bullsh**. I don't agree that the demographics were affected by the fact we did stories about minorities."

Actress S. Epatha Merkerson believes *Law & Order* is making a social statement by moving away from grittier episodes. "My own personal bent on it is they're saying they don't want to see too many black people on TV.... If you're going to deal with the city, you have to deal with the texture of the city. If you candy-coat it, you might appease some people but you're not going to please the crowd. Most people who watch the show enjoy the grit and like seeing those issues played out. It also gives a lot of black actors work."

Sound mixer David Platt is of the old school: "I think it was down-and-dirtier, grittier, with more of a documentary feel in the early days. It was almost cinema-verité but, as years progressed, it's gotten slicker, gone a little bit more into mainstream perhaps."

That doesn't necessarily please the crew. "We all got hooked on the shows dealing with those issues," Platt says. "Even when we were shooting fourteen, fifteen hours a day the first couple of years, we were jazzed because we were dealing with some real issues. It's kind of dived into white-collar crime, rich yuppie people. And I think it got a little boring for a bunch of us who work on it.... I don't think we're ever going back, week in and week out, to that kind of urban crime that we once used."

In 1992, Chris Noth told *People* magazine that he was already becoming disillusioned with the artistic direction *Law & Order* had taken. "I'm not a big fan of the white-collar homicides we're doing. You know, the socialite murders. Let *Murder, She Wrote* do that. I care about reflecting what's happening in this city because of drugs, because of poor schools, because kids have guns. If we cut back on what's happening with minorities in New York, well, it's chickensh**."

Actor Sam Waterston is of two minds on this topic. "It seems to me as long as the episodes have the ring of truth and they take place in New York City, they'll have the requisite amount of grit.... Of course, it's disappointing if we shy away from telling wonderful stories for fear that some few people will miss the Armani suits."

After a pause, Waterston decides that "maybe I'm more of a cynic. There's a [William Butler] Yeats poem Ed Sherin recommended to me, 'Lapis Lazuli,' that has a wonderful line in it: 'Though Hamlet rambles and Lear rages.... It cannot grow by an inch or an ounce'—referring to the amount of grief, tragedy, pain. There's just this much of it in the world and you can't add to it or subtract from it. It's just there. So, Sam can ramble and Gus can rage, but the network is going to do what the network is going to do."

CHAPTER 7

THE PLACE

*The only credential the city asked was
the boldness to dream. For those who
did, it unlocked its gates and its
treasures . . .*

—Moss Hart, *Act One* (1959)

It's surely no accident that so many
of *Law & Order*'s key players, both behind and in front of the camera, hail
from the Big Apple. Some have chosen to settle in California, but only in
New York City can you really take the kind of "walk on the wild side" that
rocker Lou Reed sings about. In L.A., nobody even seems to walk.

Dick Wolf, who considers his hometown another character on the
show, is a native son transplanted to Hollywood. So why isn't *Law & Order*
about the police and prosecutors of Los Angeles? "The light in California
is different. It doesn't have that gritty, grainy quality," Wolf explained to the
New York Times in 1995, adding that he loves it when the camera captures
glimpses of high-rise buildings through the windows in various scenes.

"The way Gus [Makris] or Chris [Misiano] shoots an exterior, you get
these long, raking shots where you see all the way down Madison Avenue
and all the way up. You get all that wonderful vertical upthrust of the
buildings," he said in 1997, referring to the show's photographers. "So
you know you're in New York and get a real sense of the city."

In addition to skyscrapers, Wolf wanted weather. He likes the variety
that the East Coast can offer, unpleasant as a deep freeze or a blizzard
might sometimes prove for those working in it.

The current six-member Law & Order ensemble cast with the seventh star of the show: New York City.

Take, for instance, Episode 19: "The Serpent's Tooth." Spike Finnerty, a day player with the show since the beginning, remembers a bitter truth about the New York climate: "One day, it was thirty-five degrees below while we were doing an exterior scene. All the cars were running with their heaters on full blast. We dove inside the cars to stay warm every time they said, 'Cut!'"

George Dzundza told *People* magazine in 1996 about one memorable day on the set five years earlier: "We worked twenty-four hours in a seventeen-below windchill.... I said to the policeman doing security on the set, 'Do you realize that if we were dogs, you'd shut this company down?'"

Those dog days of winter are just fine with sound mixer David Platt. "It sounds different here. Especially in the wintertime, the sound is more brittle; it's shriller. When you're looking at a winter scene, you're hearing a winter scene as well. It has a crackle to it," says the *Law & Order* technician. "When we're filming on the streets, the energy of New York City is still there no matter how much you try to control it. The soundtrack vibrates with New York. You can see it in the light as well. When you watch *N.Y.P.D. Blue*, you can tell it's not New York because the light's not right."

When it comes to *Law & Order*'s New York authenticity, former police officer and technical advisor Mike Struk knows it from the inside out. "They shoot it in the streets of Manhattan. The detective squad on the set looks like places I've worked in. Some of my *tchotchkas* and memorabilia are hanging on the walls there. Some old plaques I had. The sets are great. It's the real deal; it's really very close."

Producer Jeff Hayes scoffs at the notion that New York is a nightmare. "There's television happening here now that never would have been before *Law & Order*. We showed you could do it. Executives in L.A. are always afraid of the same thing: traffic. They ask me, 'Don't you get caught in traffic jams?' The answer is we've never been stuck in a traffic jam. If you live in New York, you know not to cross midtown at rush hour and expect to get there.... Even if you are stuck in traffic, if you're only going a mile, how bad is it? We never travel very far. There, they've got [to use] a freeway."

California's freeway-obsessed moguls also worry about security. "They think there's a mugger on every corner waiting to knock off crew members and cast. We shoot all over the city. The only problem we ever had was some minority organizations hitting us up for jobs; extortion, really. They tried to intimidate us by showing up with clubs once. We called the police."

However, disturbances sometimes did occur. In 1992, a mugger on the lam from New York's real-life finest hid under actor Paul Sorvino's trailer parked at a *Law & Order* location in Times Square. "We go to very dangerous areas, with drug deals going on right near us," Sorvino said that same year. "One time we were downtown in the Wall Street area and heard two shots. Turns out that a guy shot at a policeman, didn't kill him.... It was within one hundred feet of us. There's a lot going on in the streets of New York."

What's going on can sometimes be a swirl of friends and lovers. "Last season, we were shooting down in the Village and Jill Hennessy walked by because we were in her neighborhood. Once Sorvino walked by the crew at the courthouse exterior [on Centre Street]. We've bumped into Chris Noth too. We run into our girlfriends and wives. We're always shooting in somebody's neighborhood. Manhattan's a small town," says producer Jeff Hayes.

It annoys Merkerson that *N.Y.P.D. Blue* "always puts so much graffiti on the buildings. New York does not look like this, people! They're shooting in California so everything they do [with the cast] has to be up close. On our show, you notice everything going on in the background and it's like, 'Holy Moses! Look at all this.'"

Chris Noth thinks "there are so many shows that are derivative. I don't like *N.Y.P.D. Blue* because it tries to pretend it's a New York show. You know it's shot in a Hollywood backlot. Also *Brooklyn South* [1997–98]. It's so L.A., so un-New York.... They all try to talk New York. They all sound stupid. *Law & Order* is one hundred times more authentic."

To writer/producer David Black, "New York encompasses so many worlds. Los Angeles does too, but the dominant world there [Hollywood] swamps the others. In no other city on the globe do you get this kind of mix of cultures. Maybe in London one hundred or one hundred fifty years ago you had that. So New York is now Dickens's London. You read Dickens and you think his characters are cartoons but they turn out to be real portraits. You walk down Broadway and you see characters. I remember walking with my daughter when she was about seven and we saw a six-foot-tall, albino, transvestite hooker. A good character."

Black finds it "fun to get the changing sociology of the city. Because the show was always so austere in terms of plot, a very pure procedural, the language became very important, the distinct tones, the differences in how people talk. Language reveals character. It's like writing poetry. We became very attuned. . . . I used to wander around and eavesdrop. I'd sit in the subway and eavesdrop."

One of the advantages of living in New York is "you stay in touch with the city, and the city has changed a lot in seven years," Black insists. "I think it's valuable—Dick, are you paying attention?—to have somebody here who can walk out on the street and find new stuff."

Wolf is listening. "You can't duplicate New York," the California-based executive producer says, but his own personal New York experience can no longer be duplicated either. "Forty or forty-five years ago, New York was a different place. I rode the subway from 42nd to 86th Street every day when I was seven, eight, nine, wearing grey flannel shorts, knee socks, a blue blazer, a tie, and white shirt. I would not put a child on the IRT [trains] anymore alone, dressed like that. Then, I could go anywhere in the city."

New York-born George Dzundza was less than thrilled to be back. "Part of my problem with the show was that originally they told me it was going to be done in Toronto. I had no problem bringing my family to Toronto. But I did have a problem, because I grew up in New York, bringing my family there. . . . It had advantages, yes, but not for raising children."

Wolf, whose old Tudor City neighborhood on the East Side near the United Nations periodically shows up in an episode, should have the last word on this topic. "The reality is that New York seeps into film in a way that no other city in the world does, with the possible exception of Paris," he told TV talk show host John McLaughlin in 1991. "It becomes another character in the story. New York is symbolic of so many things. Anything that happens anywhere on the planet can happen in New York."

CHAPTER 8

THE DIRECTION

I shall tell you a great secret, my friend.
Do not wait for the last judgment. It
takes place every day.

—ALBERT CAMUS, *The Fall* (1960)

W ITH SO MANY producers and crew members who direct, *Law & Order* has a significant network of talented people taking turns at the helm. Although each person brings a different sensibility to the job, the show's template is so well-developed that a seamlessness generally prevails from week to week.

For producer Joe Stern, the late E. W. Swackhamer (1927–1994) "was really the heart of *Law & Order* that first year. He did seven of them. His were always the edgiest, the most hand-held. He was very fast and he moved; sometimes that was great, sometimes it wasn't."

There was an unpredictability to the first two seasons. "Swack did a third of the shows and he was a wild horse out of the barn," Stern says. "His shows were a little bit more radical than the others. I had some trouble reining him in. After the first season, he did only one more show and I didn't hire Swack anymore."

(Producer Ed Sherin did, however. Swackhamer returned in Season Four to direct Episode 70: "Profile.")

During *Law & Order*'s early years, production elements started to evolve. "I began to believe the second half of the show should be more muted, not as hand-held, that it didn't need to have the same texture,"

Stern says. "So we softened that a bit, made it not quite as frenetic. We stopped putting the camera on our shoulders in the courtroom and we put it on the sticks. We felt that if we just calmed it down a little bit, the show would become more accessible to the audience. I'd say half of that was conscious and half of it was that you just find your way."

Although he was finding his own way as an executive producer after Stern left the show, Ed Sherin already had three solid years of *Law & Order* directing experience. "I think I'm on the cutting edge of a style here," he says. "I wish the other directors would take more risks. I don't think coverage is important. You've got to really find the emotion in the scene and get that camera there. You've got to muscle that camera to that point."

He is proud of his approach. "It's one that I brought to the show and one that Joe subscribed to and why they kept asking me back. I never use cranes, for example. I think you've got to be right in the sweat of the action. You cannot be afraid of conceiving of a complicated one-er, as they've come to be called," he says of the technique that encompasses much of a scene in a single camera movement and leaves little room for editing. "If you can see it, don't be afraid of doing it."

Producer Lew Gould supports another of Sherin's innovations. "We have observers who come in and follow us around and see what it's all

Producer/director Lew Gould, positioning a scene. [courtesy of Jessica Burstein]

about and learn how the show is done. Most of those people are directors in other mediums, like soap operas, theater, independent films. Some are less experienced than that. We've brought in some of those guys and gals to direct after they observe for quite a while. It's an unusual process."

For Martha Mitchell, the climb from script supervisor to director was difficult but quite natural. "I always wanted to direct even before I started [working for *Law & Order*]. Ed Sherin was an enormous influence on me....I had been talking to him for about two years before I directed my first episode in the fifth season [1994–95]. I guess I wore him down. He knew I understood enough about story and camera angles, and there's a supportive crew. It was both thrilling and frightening. The script supervisor is more of an obsequious position; when you direct, it calls for a sense of authority."

On his first episode as director (Episode 99: "Guardian"), Christopher Misiano was "relatively confident about all the camera stuff because I was so familiar with the show and had assisted so many directors as camera operator and DP. I had never directed actors before, but I'd studied acting for five years. Still, my fear was I wouldn't know what to say to the actors. The regular players, in large measure, take care of themselves because they know their characters so well. But there are a lot of day players, so what do you

Co-executive producer/director Ed Sherin (right), pointing out something to Dick Wolf on a Law & Order *set.*
[courtesy of Jessica Burstein]

say to somebody the first time you think they've made absolutely the wrong choice? But, in fact, I found it incredibly comfortable."

Misiano's boyhood friend and partner in on-set merriment, director of photography Gus Makris, directs about five *Law & Order* episodes a season. "It's a different language. As a cinematographer, I collaborate with and support a director. I try to visualize the scene with light. It has its own purity. But there's a language that actors speak with directors and directors speak with actors that I'm still learning."

For Makris, silence speaks volumes. "There's a shorthand a director has with a good actor. In episodic television, time is a big factor. One of the main things I think I have going for me is I try not to talk a lot. I find the more you talk about something, the more convoluted and confused it gets. But I think I'm a good listener. If I hear a scene, I can tell whether or not the truth of it is revealed to me. I trust my instincts enough to say, 'That sounds right.' If it doesn't, how to fix that without disturbing the confidence of an actor is a tough thing."

CHAPTER 9

THE LOOK, THE STYLE

Do not leave my hand without light.

—MARC CHAGALL, 1977

L*aw & Order* can count minimalism among its greatest aesthetic strengths. The dialogue, the direction, the cinematography, the acting, the editing—all the components seem to subscribe to the less-is-more theory of art. Although it goes against the grain of almost everything else on television, this show rarely underestimates the value of leaving much to the viewer's imagination.

"One of the things that NBC executives (not Brandon Tartikoff or Warren Littlefield) always tried to improve about the show is its minimalism. They said, 'We should really know what Chris Noth is feeling. He should come up and kick some garbage cans.' The cops have never fired their guns, except for [S.] Epatha [Merkerson]," series creator Dick Wolf recalls, referring to Episode 94: "Competence," a Season Five (1994–95) segment, in which Van Buren shoots a teenage boy who tries to steal her money at an automatic teller machine.

However, Wolf struggled to retain the show's unique documentary-fiction sensibility. "In the pilot, there was only one setup on sticks, on a tripod," he says. "The entire show was hand-held. It was sixteen millimeter, which was very deliberate...to get a documentary feel. Now it's the norm. No one else was doing it at the time and not for several years after.

Emmy-winning cinematographer Gus Makris (seen here directing Episode 166: "Burned" from Season Eight, with guest star Robert Vaughn) is largely responsible for Law & Order's distinctive images.

[courtesy of Jessica Burstein]

Now you have to fight to be able to shoot in thirty-five. We also desaturated all the color. There are a lot of people who think *Law & Order* is in black-and-white. You tend to remember it in black-and-white, not in color."

Producer Jeff Hayes tells of the first six episodes, before Ernest Dickerson left to continue making movies with Spike Lee, and Gus Makris took over as director of photography, when "we used smoke in there for a photographic effect. Then we changed cameramen and didn't use smoke."

In the early days of the program, he continues, "every setup was a negotiation about whether it was [going to be] hand-held or not. It seems so easy now to know which shots should be hand-held and which shouldn't be, but back then it was a process of finding our way, defining a style, and then trying to make it work. It wasn't a question of right or wrong. I remember the negotiations: 'We just hand-held that one. Can this one be on the dolly?' It was really trying to focus on what the show should look like."

In assessing *Law & Order*'s concise quality, producer Lew Gould considers the financial perspective. "Since it costs time and money to shoot it, if we think we're not going to use it, we don't shoot it. It also has to do a lot with the pacing of the show. A lot of TV shows don't move as fast. We have a lot of short scenes. We very rarely start a scene with a greeting, a 'How ya doin'?' or whatever. You come into the scene, you're in the middle of it. And very often, when we close a scene and there's no real end to it, it's like—baboom!—and we're on to the next thing."

While on the subject of "baboom!" *Law & Order* moves things along at a nice clip with the help of two mysterious notes or noises between scenes. "[Y]ou hear: 'BEE-bing!' Or is it: 'BAH-bong!' or maybe 'BEE-bong!'? Anyway, there's a pungent little hiccuping sound, and the show is off and running," concludes a 1992 Associated Press story.

Mike Post, who composed the minimalist music to match *Law &
Order*'s abbreviated style, discussed with *Entertainment Weekly* what he calls
"The Clang" and what TV critic Ken Tucker refers to as an "ominous
chung CHUNG." It was synthesized electronically, "combining six or seven
different sounds to get the right deadbolt effect," Post says, noting that
the interlude incorporates the sound of five hundred Japanese men
stamping their feet on a wooden floor.

The production team has developed not only the style but the personnel to follow through on the style, producer Gould says. "Going back
to the early years of the show, we would average somewhere around 108
to 110 hours to shoot an episode. Last year, we were down to ninety-eight
hours. That's a big, big reduction and it all comes from just being aware
of how to make it happen."

To make that possible, "we do less coverage. That's why we do a lot of
one-ers. Whenever the scene is relatively short and we can get away with it,
we try to do it in one shot. So we're not hung up on being on everybody's
face for every line they speak. We feel the audience is intelligent enough to
follow the story without having to cover everything," Gould says.

A significant portion of
time is spent on lighting. "The
look of the show is so beautiful; we don't want to sacrifice
that," he explains. "[I]t looks
like a movie. You need a little
time to light, so you make up
that time by being succinct in
the shooting."

Gould elaborates on *Law
& Order*'s breathless technique.
"We'll take an action sequence
that, if you did it in a movie,
you would probably have thirty,
forty cuts. We'll do it in four.
The audience is fine with that.
They don't need forty angles to
get excited. There's a quasi-doc-
umentary feel.... When everything happens quickly, you feel
you're there with these cops,
you're there with these DAs,
and you're experiencing it as
they are," he says.

**Law & Order's minimalism and crisp cine-
matography, evident in this Season Two
shot of Chris Noth as Det. Mike Logan.**

Sound technician David Platt thinks that producer Ed Sherin's impact has been immense. "He added to the original concept by designing shots that would be these very complicated one-ers, a kind of ballet, that help distinguish the show in style. It truly has evolved," he surmises.

"In the first thirty seconds, you discover a dead body and I try to create a mood, a source," says cinematographer Gus Makris. "My experience came out of movies, so I try to shoot the show, within reason, like a picture, as a one-camera show except for the court scenes. We, as a crew, have developed ways of keeping up with a brutal pace. If you shoot a two-and-a-half page scene in one day on a movie, you're really kicking ass. We do that and then we shoot seven more scenes. We've become adept at finding ways to do things very rapidly."

Makris points out that "directors on our show have to be inventive enough to kind of twist a scene so you're not shooting every possible angle, from everybody's point of view. The way we work, it gives you the impression you're watching a real event."

That quest for realism is exacting. "We often do huge shots, traveling down the street, into a doorway, around the corner, into another room, stuff you don't even see on some ambitious movies. We do some things that are so ambitious, if you saw them on a feature you would be impressed. There's a choreography between the actor and the camera.... It's a real dance. And then trying to light the damn thing! It becomes visually interesting and striking when we're good. When we're really good, hopefully you're not even paying attention to that because the words and the story are so compelling. But it doesn't hurt to have the great shots," Makris says with a smile.

"I could light for hours," he vows. "Luciano Tovoli, the Italian cinematographer who shot [the film] *Reversal of Fortune* [1990], told me: 'There's only one thing on the screen and that's cinematography.' What you see is a moving photograph."

As producers, writers, and directors have left the show over the years, however, Makris figures some aspects of the style have gone with them. One example of this is in Episode 9: "Indifference," a Season One (1990–91) segment by Robert Palm in which a young girl dies from child abuse. There is a chilling courtroom scene in which Moriarty circles the witness silently. "We can't actually afford to do that as much as we used to, to have cinematic moments without dialogue," Makris says. "This show is always wall-to-wall talking and basically if they don't talk, you don't shoot it. I know that the shows are shorter because they get in more commercials."

CHAPTER 10

THE PERFORMANCES

On the stage he was natural, simple, affecting; 'Twas only that when he was off he was acting.

OLIVER GOLDSMITH, 1774

Iɴ ᴛʜᴇ early years, producer Joe Stern was faced with a dilemma. "The scripts were so spare that they were really, to a great extent, legal tracts. The characters were not so three-dimensional. I felt that, in the acting, I could provide a piece to elevate it. That was my background. The actors could bring something that was not necessarily in the scripts; they could provide a certain emotion."

Consequently, series creator Dick Wolf "allowed me to do anything I wanted. He trusted me. And I was the only [producer] in New York; everybody else was in L.A. I had the ability to change ages and gender and race, and I frequently did with the lawyers, the judges, and the denizens. I saw a tremendous opportunity to hire minorities, although they weren't necessarily written that way."

Stern cites a recurring defense attorney played by Elaine Stritch, who won an Emmy for Episode 53: "Point of View." "Initially, she was written as a contemporary of Ben Stone's. We asked them to make her an older woman and [Michael] Moriarty's ex–law professor. That happened many, many times. We began to lure in theater people who had not done much television," he says.

George Dzundza, as mini-mart owner Gordon Feester in the short-lived Open All Night *(ABC, 1981–1982).*
[courtesy of Photofest]

Chris Noth, as the bearded action hero of Jakarta *(1987).*
[courtesy of Photofest]

Paul Sorvino (right), in a previous police incarnation as Detective Ike Porter on The Oldest Rookie *(CBS, 1987–1988).*
[courtesy of Photofest]

"One thing I will take credit for, and it was there in the scripts, is a kind of documentary acting style," Stern adds. "Ours was the first minimalist acting. I believe *N.Y.P.D. Blue* was influenced by *Law & Order*. [Producer Steven] Bochco's shows were well-acted but they didn't have that minimalist flavor."

Stern developed a four-tiered theory about casting for *Law & Order*. "First, all the single-scene parts, the denizens of the New York streets, were written in a very exotic, idiosyncratic manner—you know, the doormen kind of roles. I felt the writing was so strong that you could get people who were limited as actors perhaps, but were

Jerry Orbach, about to fall for Jane Alexander (wife of Law & Order *co-executive producer/director Ed Sherin) in* 6 Rms Riv Vu *on the New York stage.*
[courtesy of Photofest]

types, and all they had to do was show up.... The writing was so picturesque, they would just embody those characters," he suggests.

"Secondly," Stern continues, "what I thought was very important for the show was the actors' sounds. So, I cast people with regional accents in the small parts, because you don't hear a lot of New York accents in the big parts."

The third rung of casting that Stern devised was more elusive. "We knew there were no backstories for the leads, so it was very important just to get actors with a sort of star quality. They weren't going to get the big speeches, so they had to have a kind of charisma. Even though they could all be replaced, they all had tremendous presence. They didn't have anything else to get the audience with. They didn't have any big arias."

In the opinion of former cast member Dann Florek, the lack of arias sometimes led to heated oncamera exchanges. "Often, we picked up in the middle of a scene... [when] the conversation is at a full boil. There was so little writing and we would cut into something quickly; there were only a few sentences and we were out of the scene. So I think a lot of people felt, to use a baseball metaphor, you have to go with your fastball. 'I've

Benjamin Bratt, as Captain Ramirez in Clear and Present Danger (1994). [courtesy of Photofest]

Dann Florek, posing with a pooch and actress Rose Marie for the sitcom Hardball (Fox, 1994). [courtesy of Photofest]

S. Epatha Merkerson, with the dreadlocks hidden by a wig on Law & Order. [courtesy of the Everett Collection]

Richard Brooks, navigating the jungles of Vietnam in 84 Charlie Mopic (1989). [courtesy of Photofest] only got eight lines in this scene, so let's get to the f***ing heart of it right now.' But when you see it, you think that's a little relentless."

Stern viewed the storyline lawyers and judges "as all involved in a ritual of ideals. Nothing really was dramatized. These are people who do this every day for a living. They just negotiate, so they very rarely become emotionally involved with any of the issues. They're written with a certain amount of wit, so there's no reason to act," he says, adding that the roles required "people who can just sit there and rattle off stuff, without trying to embroider it."

The fourth of Stern's tiers involved guest stars. "I thought they had to be the virtuosos, because they had to play the notes that weren't in the scripts. They had to improvise the emotions.... *Law & Order* scripts are dry and we would try to lift them and give the characters behavior. The actors would do that."

One such guest was Felicity Huffman, a longtime member of the Atlantic Theatre Company founded by playwright David Mamet and Huffman's actor husband, William H. Macy. "They're very respectful of actors," says Huffman, a veteran with two appearances, first in Episode 50: "Helpless," and then in Episode 148: "Working Mom." "They give you the time. They give you the quiet. The directors understand the craft."

David Pittu, another player in the Atlantic troupe, remembers what is was like when he appeared as a banker questioned by Briscoe and Logan in Episode 90: "Coma." "The acting was so downplayed. I was amazed at the way [Jerry] Orbach and [Chris] Noth spoke. I could barely even hear them.... [The writers and directors] want to make sure there's no theatricality. They want you to be you. It's really stripped down. There's an unadorned quality. In a way, it's sort of perfect for Mamet."

Huffman is pleased that the theater community benefits from the series. "Because *Law & Order* shoots in New York, it feels more like a play. Just about every actor I know has been on the show. It's a wonderful source of work."

Law & Order has indeed proved to be a tremendous source of work for veteran talent Jerry Orbach, who, according to Dick Wolf, inhabits a role specifically conceived with him in mind. "We didn't audition anybody else. Jerry said, 'What do you want me to do with this?' I said, '*Prince of the City* [1981] will be just fine.' That's one of my favorite movies. Women *du certain age* see Jerry and it's like people seeing Mick Jagger. Older women just go nuts."

Orbach, that Rolling Stone of stage and screen, divulges the secret of his craft: "Years and years ago, I was doing a Kojak," he says of the 1973–78 CBS detective series that was briefly reincarnated in movie form on ABC in 1989. "Telly Savalas would come in and say, 'What scene are we doing?

Jill Hennessy, toting a mean-looking weapon in her role as Dr. Marie Lazarus in RoboCop 3 *(1983).* [courtesy of the Everett Collection]

Carey Lowell, a pistol-packing James Bond Girl in License To Kill *(1989).* [courtesy of the Everett Collection]

Michael Moriarty, participating in a massacre as SS officer Erik Dorf in Holocaust *(NBC miniseries, 1978).* [courtesy of Photofest]

Sam Waterston, sporting an anti-death-penalty button in the John Waters comedy Serial Mom *(1994).* [courtesy of Photofest]

What do I say here?' I'd ask, 'Telly, you didn't study this last night?' He'd say, 'I don't have time. I read it once.' I thought that was really laissez-faire."

However, Orbach came to understand that the method Telly Savalas had advocated could work for him here. "I realized that most of these scenes are comprised of, oh, six or eight speeches at the most. We have the script meeting to figure out the logic and any changes we might want, then I don't look at it again. I have no plan. I'm flying by the seat of my pants....And maybe the director has an idea. I learn the lines while they're lighting— that's the easy part," Orbach

Steven Hill, as the tormented son of a famous movie star in Paddy Chayefsky's classic film, **The Goddess (1958).** *[courtesy of Photofest]*

says. "Coming in cold, I find I'm wide open to stimulus from whoever the other actors are. It's very fresh for me that way."

Executive producer Ed Sherin, who has a vast theater background, brought some well-articulated ideas about the craft to his roundtables. "With the actors, it became a question of inviting them to visit those areas in their personalities and their intellects that were unhappy about a given thing. And initially it was not easy because they didn't take enough time to consider the material, so their first responses were off the top of their heads. It didn't necessarily reveal a careful assessment of what the writer was doing," he says.

On the other hand, Sherin is convinced that occasionally "these writers simply don't have that notch on their belts [of knowing the characters as well as the actors]. They haven't gotten there yet. That's certainly not true in the case of our main writer, Rene Balcer, who knows the characters well. But even Rene is aided, sometimes largely, by the actor's contribution."

Cinematographer/director Chris Misiano combines a thespian background with a crew perspective. "I love actors. I just love their process," he says. "I know the cast, Sam [Waterston] in particular, loves to rehearse. Jerry [Orbach], on the other hand, wants to learn his lines five minutes before we're about to start and keep them fresh that way."

When it comes to the acclaimed minimalism of *Law & Order*, Misiano cautions that "this is touchy territory. The actors want more to do. Jerry [Orbach] and Ben [Bratt] like to interrogate people individually, rather than together.... You can see them get a little more juiced because usually those are slightly more intense scenes. There is something about being tethered together; in a show that's so plot-driven that can get a little redundant. So when they get something else to do, they shine."

Chris Noth, who managed to do so much on the series with, basically, so little, found that "you had to have your own inner evolution going on. The trick for me was to speak without the lines. I made sure there was always something going on with Logan. There's a constant inner dialogue. You don't always need a line. Just sitting there and thinking real thoughts can be a powerful experience on stage or screen."

His successor, Benjamin Bratt, recalls, "I always joke about how the challenge for me is how to make it unique and different each time I ask the question, 'What color was the car?' Sometimes in read-throughs I ask, 'Wait a minute! Didn't I say that line about, like, three episodes ago?'"

"I don't think there is much evolution of character," Sam Waterston says of *Law & Order*. "That would be true of television series in general. They're very parsimonious in spending the arc of character because once it's gone, it's gone. Whatever it is he's struggling with at the inception of the series, if he resolves it by Christmas, then what do you do? I think most characters on TV are sort of preserved in aspic."

Waterston believes that this television program "is not about an examination of a crisis that changes a character's life, except some of the guest characters. A perfect example is that Adam Schiff lost his wife. It was an awful event but it didn't change the way he came to work. Insofar as there's a philosophical point of view to this show, it's that people die, people are born, relationships happen or don't—and you show up for work."

Producer Jeff Hayes has a long-range view of *Law & Order*. "As the actors are finding their characters, the writers are finding it too. And you don't want to stand still, which is why I think all the cast changes have worked for us. It sort of shakes things up."

When Hayes participates in casting an episode, he finds the process exhausting. "It's three intense sessions. When I'm in a three-hour casting session, seeing about twenty or twenty-five people, towards the end I have to kick myself to concentrate. I get bleary-eyed. But New York has got such a bunch of talented people. We rarely see a bad actor."

Just ask Sam Waterston. "It's a nice show for a nice pool of talent in this city.... Here, there's an opportunity to eat a piece of scenery that they haven't been allowed to eat before."

CHAPTER 11

THE PERSONAL

There is properly no history; only biography.

—RALPH WALDO EMERSON, 1841

SOME love it. Some hate it. For years, the show resisted network pressure to send the characters on tangents not directly related to crime in the crackling workaday worlds of *Law & Order*'s police and prosecutors. More recently, some outside elements have begun to creep in.

For the last installment (Episode 134: "Aftershock") of Season Six (1995–96), both *Homicide: Life on the Street* crossovers, and the 1997 three-parter set largely in L.A., the onscreen characters were allowed to explore dimensions that had little to do with their careers. These diversions included an extramarital fling and temptation to participate in a second for Rey Curtis; a backslide into alcoholism and a troubled father-daughter relationship for Lennie Briscoe; and the long-rumored affair between Claire Kincaid and Jack McCoy that becomes most vivid when she's killed in a car crash after missing a date with him because McCoy was busy getting drunk.

All this ongoing angst comes from the characters witnessing an execution, once New York State brought back capital punishment in real life and, in turn, on the show. Is it wise? Producer Jeff Hayes doesn't think so. "I am very conservative about that sort of thing. I was very uncomfortable with those shows. I thought we did an okay job but I didn't like the whole concept. Believe me, a lot of us here felt that way. The writers want to try different things. If you let them do everything they want to do, they'd kill the show because they don't want to be writing the same thing over and over again."

The spartan nature of *Law & Order* that ensnared TV viewers in the first place now gives the show's writers gray hair, Hayes suggests. "They're frustrated with the format. I was against breaking the format to that extent. I didn't like more than one person drinking, for instance. What's the point? Let's have everybody dealing with [the execution] in their own way."

In Episode 157: "Terminal," at the end of Season Seven (1996–97), Adam Schiff's wife dies. "That was on the edge for me and yet I liked it, because we didn't beat them over the heads. It was his own crisis and he kept it private. He's such a great actor; he just did it with his eyes," Hayes reflects.

The outcome of character Claire Kincaid's fatal car crash was apparently not such a sure thing. "We didn't know until the next season whether she was going to be dead or not. We were actually shooting an episode she was supposed to be in—in which case she wasn't going to be dead. But, at the last minute, [Jill Hennessy] decided not to do it, so then Claire was dead."

Writer/producer Rene Balcer sticks to his guns, despite disapproval from those he considers purists. "The audience likes it and I like it, so the hell with what those guys think. When they run a show, they can do whatever way they want. . . . In [Episode 80:] 'Censure,' Hennessy was involved with a judge. [Chris] Noth was involved [unwillingly, in his childhood] with a pedophile priest in [Episode 108:] 'Bad Faith.' We've always done, every now and then, stories with personal angles. There's nothing really new there."

Advisor Mike Struk, who keeps *Law & Order* faithful to police procedures, is another "purist" with a penchant for the plot-driven approach. "That's why I think the show has been so successful and extremely popular in the law-enforcement community, as well as with attorneys. . . . There are many entertaining shows, like *N.Y.P.D. Blue* and *Brooklyn South*, but they're a lot deeper into the social and behind-the-scenes crap—you know, who's screwing who. That's life, but when you want to see something from the investigative point of view, from the crime to the prosecution without all the other [stuff] mixed in, *Law & Order* is the cat's meow."

However, one cat's trash is another's treasure. "We've definitely gotten into personal stuff a bit more in the last year or two, which makes the actors happy," says John Fiore, whose ubiquitous character of Det.

Anthony Profaci has been recurring on the show since the pilot. "There's more for them to do. Prior to that, it was pretty much a just-the-facts kind of show. . . . "

Actor Sam Waterston sits on the fence. "It's a fine line. If the show is life, then the show and life are not particularly interested in your troubles. Life wants to know if you can fill your position, if you can continue to function. As long as it's perfectly clear that this is the demand of the show, then you can pile on terrible disasters and see how much a person can take. As soon as it becomes just about personal life, that's another thing," he says.

"If you can't perform your function, people will be very sorry but, just like in life, they will replace you," Waterston adds. "That bitter pill gives this show its acidity and sense of realism. I compare it to *M*A*S*H* [1972–83]. You know, the chopper and the music at the beginning and the end of *M*A*S*H* is a reminder there will always be another crisis and there'll always be another patient. Nobody's going anywhere, so it's all about how you cope."

The personal angles have been a given during Carey Lowell's time on the show as Jamie Ross, although she appreciates them much more when they're subtle. "Anything they've shown in terms of my character, it's been in glimpses. I think that's one of the extraordinary things about *Law & Order*, that you can reveal so much about a character by saying a minimum. You don't have to even show it," she says.

Longtime series regular Steven Hill (Adam Schiff) speculates, "I think the personal world is not as interesting to audiences as the crime itself, the solution of the crime, and the justice that's going to be administered in the end. . . . The personal story just does not match up to the crime story, the law story, and the morality story. But I don't see it as objectively as the audience sees it, so I'm really no judge."

Jerry Orbach is pleased that Lennie Briscoe's character got a full backstory, as it's called in the entertainment world. "That's a good thing, but it's tough because *Law & Order* sticks close to the case; it's almost *Dragnet*-like. But we try to warm it up a little bit emotionally. We all have little problems, so that it's not quite so cut and dried."

In fact, Orbach says, "the personal stuff is much easier for an actor. My big joke when Chris Noth was leaving the series was, 'Can we have him die in my arms? Let me cry a little bit.' I know it's not really *Law & Order*. It's more soap-opera-y. We can't do it often but, every now and then, we should. These things happen in life. And those are the episodes you remember. Those are the powerful moments. You don't remember saying, 'What color was the car?'"

His co-star, Benjamin Bratt must also ask such questions, but his Rey Curtis alter ego sets out on a new path at the end of the sixth season

(1995–96) as the entire cast reacts to the oncamera capital punishment. After Curtis witnesses the execution, this very married man gets to kiss a girl he has just met. "It just makes it more interesting. Also, on a selfish level, I enjoyed it as an actor because it gave me a chance to do something else—to be the romantic guy with another woman, to show another aspect to that character," he says.

"As I have received publicity for being on the show and it takes a certain slant, I think that, even subconsciously, it informs the writers on how to approach the character," Bratt suggests. "In other words, if a magazine article is sexing me up, I think the writers seize upon that and they, in turn, sex the character up...."

As a result, in his third season (1997–98) on the show, Bratt finds "there's more of a physical awareness of Rey Curtis as someone to be looked at, to be gawked at. It's kind of odd. I've also noticed a big difference in real life the way people on the street, women especially, treat me as opposed to before. They sexed the character up. They had him in these tank tops—all this stuff that we never really saw on *Law & Order* before."

CHAPTER 12

THE
RIGHT STUFF

*Scenery is fine but human nature is
finer.*

—JOHN KEATS, 1828

CASTING

ONE CRUCIAL component of *Law & Order* takes place in a fairly nonde-script office on prestigious Park Avenue in New York City. "When I start-ed [over] seven years ago with the first episode, I was putting in ten hours a day," casting director Suzanne Ryan recalls. "It's down to eight hours now, though I do get calls at home."

Her casting chores include "everybody who speaks, except for the lead characters. So we turn the pages and go: 'Please, don't say a word.' When they have a little kid in the description, I'm like: 'Don't open your mouth!'"

When they do open their mouths, wonderful things sometimes emerge from the most unlikely performers. "Casting against type is kind of just the magic of it," Ryan says. "You also trust a body of work for an actor.... People like to spread their wings. It's nice to use someone in a fresh way. We have an opportunity here to actually do something innov-ative once in a while."

For her, the difficult part of the job is "the volume on this show [which] is much more than most any other [TV] episodic show, as far as number of characters. There's never a day when you can come in and just coast. As a woman and a mother, it's a nightmare."

However, the sacrifice is creatively worthwhile. "What I like about it is, the show has a lot of integrity," Ryan acknowledges. "I like the fact that it's not about the beautiful people. A lot of casting can be very frustrating because it doesn't matter who's a better actor, just who's prettier. This is an opportunity to cast something that has some texture to it and that is rewarding. I'm a girl from the Bronx. I should be working on a show like this. It seems only fitting."

LOCATIONS

"I came from doing movies," explains location manager Moe Bardach. "You tell people, 'Al Pacino wants to do a movie here.' Or Martin Scorsese. You bring those names into the mix and people get pretty excited. When this show was younger, no one [in the Big Apple] really knew what it was. That part has gotten easier now that *Law & Order* is so well known."

The location team must interact with the public and, for a show that takes to the actual streets, that means reaching into several strata of New York City life. There are posh scenes set in posh penthouses, of course, but "buildings we might use on the Lower East Side have squatters living there who are sometimes helpful, sometimes hostile," Bardach says.

In some areas of town, things can get a bit dicey. "We have lots of police who work with us, especially in so-called bad neighborhoods," he explains. "That's one of the incentives to filming in New York—the police that work with us are free. That's very unusual. All our permits are free too. Very few cities can say that. You usually have to pay for streets."

Bardach says that the labor unions once made it prohibitive to shoot in New York, but "the city turned it around. It came out to be a pretty good deal. We get city buildings and city offices for free. That's one of the main reasons Dick Wolf was able to convince the studio to let *Law & Order* be done here."

Bardach's dream-come-true location is more of a confluence of appropriate sites. "We use hubs," he says. "A hub can start with a very unique or difficult location to find, something you don't have on every block. Or a hub can be where we have a lot of work, almost a whole day's work, maybe five or six pages worth of work."

The purpose of a hub is to lower the number of times the company must pack up the equipment trucks to move to another spot. For example, a script might include scenes in a bar, a hardware store, a hotel, and a park. It's more efficient if all those elements can be found in the same neighborhood.

Law & Order uses no establishing shots on the program. The camera does not film a building exterior or street before the detectives knock on the door of an apartment there. "It's not the style of the show. Instead, we 'black card' them," Bardach says, referring to the words that pop up on the screen to indicate where the action is supposed to be taking place.

"Most of the time they are not actual addresses," he points out. "Sometimes we use a real name, sometimes not. It depends on the content of a script. A location might really want their name used but if we're finding a dead guy in the hotel or the store, then they probably don't want that."

Although the body count could prove a deterrent, Bardach has avoided physical damage to on-location sites. "We never had an insurance claim and we've used some beautiful mansions," he says. "They always invite us back. The set dressers do a wonderful job. We bring in our own furnishings. We take Polaroids of everything in its place, so it can go back exactly the way it was. The people who live there will look at it afterwards and say, 'Omigosh!' "

DESIGN

"You prep," says Bob Thayer, with a deep sigh. "That's kind of my life. I prep always."

He is describing his job as production designer. "We have to visually tell the story in the most economical fashion.... We try to make everything on the set appropriate to the character and the story, even though a lot of it goes unseen. It's the overall impression. Sometimes, the details are bang-on; sometimes, it's a fudge."

In Season Eight (1997–98), "the biggest bear for us on [Episode 166:] 'Burned' was the Anderton house," Thayer recalls, referring to a fictitious palatial home at an upscale location on Manhattan's Park Avenue and 68th Street. "There was a cocktail party the night before and breakfast for seventy-five people the morning we shot there. An hour before the crew arrived, that living room/dining room was set for breakfast. We had an army of set dressers standing by in the room next door, having loaded everything in the day before, and—bang, bang, bang—as soon as the breakfast people finished, our guys were right behind them."

"By the time the crew got there, we were just tweaking it," he says. "We try not to do that every time. But that was the best location, both in terms of the look and where it was in the city for the other things we had to do in the day. So, we decided we would work around the nightmare of the logistics."

Thayer feels that all the episodes "have their little wrinkles. For [Episode 138:] 'Survivor,' we needed a coin-and-antiquities shop....It was a little more than we'd ever done on *Law & Order*, but it was early in the season and we were all kind of fresh and it was a great challenge. The four gilded-wood panels on the door that looked like they might have come from a fourteenth-century Spanish church—well, they did. It was the kind of richness that we don't often get to do....We had a ball."

CENTER OF THE *LAW & ORDER* UNIVERSE

Gene Ritchings is at the controls of command central. "The office is a service organization first, last, and always," explains Ritchings, the inordinately calm production coordinator for *Law & Order*. "Other departments have specific areas of expertise. We have to service the entire show. People who work for me have to be very committed, work long hours, not be that concerned about the compensation (which is adequate but by no means generous), and have a spirit of helpfulness and awareness about what's going on."

Law & Order *production coordinator Gene Ritchings, who also wrote a Season Five script, Episode 111: "Pride".* [courtesy of Jessica Burstein]

What's going on is a tangle of actors, directors, writers, producers, crew members, and other personnel buzzing along with the single-minded purpose of creating a weekly television drama. "We book airline tickets, book hotels rooms, find lost equipment, order birthday cakes; sometimes we do transportation if the Teamsters are short-handed," Ritchings says of his operation. "It's a catch-all where anyone who needs help can come....We're concerned with what is best for the show. That's the universal ethic."

All of that is just the fun stuff. In addition, the production office handles an array of clerical matters, while also "coordinating pre-production, production, and post-production constantly because, unlike the usual sequence of doing one after another in a lineal way, on a show like this we do all three at once. There's always a crew prepping; there's always a crew shooting."

The list of weekly production tasks is enervating to contemplate. "We try to ward off the occasional feeling of being beleaguered and overextended and overworked because that's the life we chose," Ritchings says, with typical *Law & Order* pluck. "We are all basically a part of the same effort. Everybody makes a contribution to that eventual moment when something appears on the screen. Our work is often invisible and taken for granted, particularly when it's working well. The office is the town square of this little community we have, the one space where everyone is allowed."

CHAPTER 13

THE COASTS

This land is your land,
This land is my land.
From California,
To the New York island. . . .

—WOODY GUTHRIE, 1956

L*aw & Order* is something of a schizo-phrenic organization. Most of the writers, top producers, and editors are in Los Angeles, but the production team, cast, and crew are based in New York.

"It works very well," series creator Dick Wolf contends. "I like it even though it's a pain in the ass sometimes. It gives everybody some distance. In the same city, people get upset with each other. There's a very clear-cut chain of command in both operations, a sort of military command structure."

In terms of the editing process, "Arthur Forney, who has been the supervising producer since we started, and Billy Fox run post-production flawlessly in L.A. There are financial reasons to do it in California because we're getting a better deal with the studio than if we had to find the facilities in New York. It drives [executive producer] Ed Sherin crazy, but everybody has their own set of frustrations," Wolf says.

The frustrations for a director of photography on *Law & Order* are sometimes monumental. "It's hard to keep the look of the show long-distance," says Gus Makris, after a spasm of too-dark episodes in Season Eight had Internet fans commenting unfavorably. The normally crisp images and colors were replaced by shadows that partially obscured the actors. Apparently, a processing decision, or an accident, had taken place on the West Coast, resulting in what Forney calls a "chiaroscuro" look. But nobody ever thought to inform the East Coast of this development. Makris complained and, by mid-season, viewers were still waiting for the show to inch back toward preserving its usual award-winning cinematography.

"Episodic directing is not like even movie-of-the-week directing," Wolf suggests. "The artistic vision is pretty much set. This show is shot very efficiently too. At this stage, the actors don't need eight takes to get into it. There is a rhythm to the show that the editors know. Even Ed, underneath, knows the show usually comes out pretty damn well."

Does he? "The only problems I have with the West Coast are budgetary and not very many of those anymore," Sherin explains. "They usually bother me at the beginning of a season when they see shows coming in maybe one-half of one percent over [budget]. Then they leave me alone. There's an enormous advantage of being here. They can't walk into my office. And you can quote me on that."

The long-distance editing is not generally problematic because "we shoot very tightly now. The way our style has developed, particularly in the first half of the show, there's not so much editorial choice. We do a lot of one-ers. And the smarter directors shoot it the way they want it edited. . . . There's a lot of ways you can shoot it that guarantee it'll be cut the way you want," producer Jeff Hayes says.

Supervising producer Arthur Forney explains that "sometimes the director flies to L.A. and works along with the editor but, in television, it's a producer's medium. The producers take over, move scenes around, take lines out. The key is to tell the same story with less film."

For Rene Balcer, "the editing brings an emotional texture to the show. For example, Jill Hennessy didn't have much to do in the courtroom except look concerned. But she always gave you a great read on the emotional temperature of the scene, so the editor would cut to her to clarify or reflect what was going on. She was great for improvising that level. We didn't write, 'Claire Kincaid looks concerned. Claire Kincaid furrows her brow.'"

CHAPTER 14

THE BUCKS

Money is like a sixth sense without which you cannot make a complete use of the other five.

—W. SOMERSET MAUGHAM, *Of Human Bondage* (1915)

As THE MAN most in touch with the purse strings for the show, series creator Dick Wolf spotlights *Law & Order*'s thrift by discussing the refreshments available for cast and crew. "How many movie sets have gallon jugs of soda instead of cans? We ain't living in luxury here. But we always manage to get enough money to do it the right way. An average hour-show costs about a million six. We're somewhere between a million and a half to two million an episode," he acknowledges.

"When you're not prepared with a script, that's when the production costs soar," says executive producer Ed Sherin of the show's early years. "You get out on the floor to shoot a scene and the actors ask, 'What the hell is this about? I can't say that.' Well, it's a nice time to come up with that one but there was no place for them to come up with it before, nor did they really look at the script until the night before. Or, in some instances, that morning."

In those situations, a scene that should be staged in ten minutes is staged in an hour and ten minutes, Sherin adds. "That turns a twelve-hour day into a fourteen- or fifteen-hour day. It turns a show that should be done in under a hundred hours to a show that's done in a hundred and twenty-two hours. The difference in the budget is enormous. The overages, at the end of the season, can be in the hundreds of thousands or millions of dollars."

This bothers Sherin, as someone with a foundation in regional theater, "where you had to take a dollar and literally stretch it around the block. We now have control. We know down to the tiniest element or detail what will cost us more and what we can do for less. We're constantly modulating the script to the budget without impacting negatively on the show."

Producer Jeff Hayes recalls that "it was a fight to keep *Law & Order* in New York because it was [so] expensive. There was talk of bringing it to Canada or Los Angeles after the second season. Universal was getting nervous [because] it cost so much [to produce on location], and they said we had to cut $50,000 or $100,000 an episode. We met with all the unions and got concessions that truly did cut out $50,000 [per segment]—and that became the boiler plate [episode cost model] for all television in New York."

Cinematographer/director Chris Misiano does not believe that "on the floor, we make a lot of creative decisions differently than we did four years ago or because of the budget. We may be a bit more adept at doing it. We may be a little more skilled in knowing what you can get away with and knowing that there's a time pressure."

One consequence of Sherin nurturing people within the company is that "everybody is acutely aware of the style of the show and what you can do," Misiano suggests. "I don't really think we consciously adjust the style to meet the budget. In the course of the day, you may look at your watch. When I get my sides [a portion of the script with the day's scenes] in the morning, either as the director or as the DP [director of photography], I get them with a breakdown of how many hours have been budgeted for each scene so I can know when I'm ahead, when I'm behind."

To which the show's chief director of photography, Gus Makris, adds, "Under the right circumstances, you can create brilliance on a shoe-string."

CHAPTER 15

THE CLAN

*Accept the place that divine providence
has found for you, the society of your
contemporaries, the connection of
events.*

—Ralph Waldo Emerson, 1841

"THERE WAS a real bond between us all," recalls producer Joe Stern. "That was instilled from the beginning. I tried to create that environment.... It was a family. That's what we tried to build. It was a very, very close group. It was the greatest experience of my life, without any question."

Although later alienated from *Law & Order*, Chris Noth also cherished that original acting experience. "In the first three years, it felt very communal. There was a feeling that we had a mission, that we were onto something, that everybody had a part in it."

However, there was another view of the series. "I didn't find camaraderie on the show," counters George Dzundza. "That's why I left, amongst other things. The difficulty of the circumstances did not warrant the kind of effort that it took."

Beyond the first season's wrenching battles in 1990–91, director/cinematographer Chris Misiano is realistic about the ongoing bond among those working for the show. "There are going to be times when this kind of company becomes a dysfunctional family. It's like you are at Thanksgiving dinner with your Italian family all day long, every day."

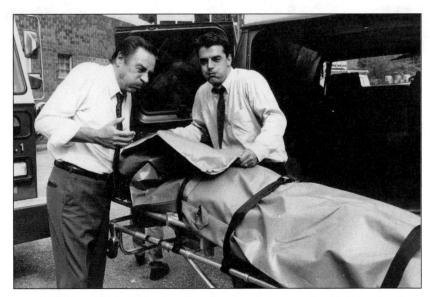

Jerry Orbach and Chris Noth, clowning over a body bag at a Law & Order ***location for Season Five's Episode 89: "Second Opinion."*** *[courtesy of Jessica Burstein]*

Nonetheless, he always has had a good rapport with the crew. "Because I was a grip and a camera operator and I'm a DP [director of photography], they know I understand their problems. With Gus [Makris], we have such a shorthand with each other because of our particularly close relationship and we have both done these jobs on this show," Misiano points out. "I feel like Gus is another brother."

The two met while Misiano was still a teenager and his older brother Vincent, who has directed episodes of *Law & Order*, roomed with Makris at Brooklyn College. The trio even began making amateur films together, including one that starred Jerry Seinfeld, Misiano's pal from Massapequa High School on Long Island. In Misiano's estimation, Makris has "a kind of fatherly quality, a patriarchal quality for the entire crew. It has a very familial feel. When I say it's a dysfunctional family, I mean it in the best of ways. It can get ugly but you still go out to drink together."

Makris also speaks of a "non-verbal shorthand that Chris [Misiano], Richard [Dobbs, the show's current camera operator], and I have. We can just wave our fingers, without disturbing the actors," he explains, demonstrating the gesture. "It may look mysterious but it's not at all.... People on this job care about each other, which is nice to know because I see them much more than I see my wife and kids."

According to production coordinator Gene Ritchings, producer Joe Stern always made the point that the real star of the show is the crew. "They so believe in what they're doing. There's a strong fraternal sense. It's one of the most gratifying aspects of working here. Usually at the end of a season, I can't wait to get out because I've just had too much of it. By the time the hiatus is over in the spring, I can't wait to get back among friends," Ritchings says.

"From the day I walked onto this show, I felt very much at home here," recalls actor Jerry Orbach. "I never felt like the new kid on the block."

Jill Hennessy, who portrayed ADA Claire Kincaid, is very enthusiastic when talking about the people she left behind when she quit the TV series. "The crew and the cast became my staunchest supporters. I felt like they were always watching out for me. I had family. I had personal therapists. I had a lot of people who were always there to share a story or tell a joke."

Hennessy could share a joke but she also shed many a tear: "When Michael Moriarty left, I cried. When Chris Noth left I remember trying not to cry, but crying. Some people in the crew and I decided to shock him right in the middle of his last take. We dropped our pants. They weren't wearing anything; I was wearing men's briefs over my nylons. 'We'll miss you, Logan' was written on our rearsides. I had the Logan on mine."

After three years on *Law & Order*, the actor who replaced Noth, Benjamin Bratt, concludes, "I'm not bored yet and I think a good reason for that is I really do enjoy the people I work with. Epatha [Merkerson] and Jerry [Orbach], we're very dear friends. Jerry and I especially spend a lot of time together. I always tease him that I share more meals with him than he does with his own wife because we lunch together every day we're working."

The friendship has proved to be deeper than an ordinary

Carey Lowell and Steven Hill share a laugh while shooting one of the show's episode-ending "tag" scenes.

[courtesy of Jessica Burstein]

workplace association, according to Bratt. "On a personal level, me being much younger than him and having not really been involved with my own father in the last ten to twelve years, he has sort of taken on that role, not even by decision. It just sort of organically has happened that way. Jerry is one of the most gentle, honest people I know. He treats me like a son and he has two sons of his own right around my age."

"And Epatha," Bratt continues, as a smile spreads over his face. "I always say, 'That's my girl.' When the three of us get together, we just laugh all day long, sometimes right up until they say, 'Rolling!' Sometimes right up until they say, 'Action!'"

After eight years with *Law & Order*, actor John Fiore (who plays Det. Anthony Profaci) doesn't appear in every episode, but "I'm very attached to these people. They're the best. They were nice in the past too. Now, they're just mellower and mellower."

THE CENSORSHIP

I cannot and will not cut my
conscience to fit this year's fashions.

—LILLIAN HELLMAN, 1952

ALMOST more than any other episodic TV series, *Law & Order* has found itself over the years caught up in the ongoing brouhaha about small-screen censorship. Series creator Dick Wolf has frequently spoken out against such proposed measures as the content-based rating system and the V-Chip, both geared to prevent children from watching programs with material deemed inappropriate for them. Alone among the major networks, NBC has consistently refused to accept these restrictive concepts.

"From day one, NBC has basically never balked at doing anything we wanted to do," Wolf recalls. "There's never been a story line that has been turned down; there's never been an area where they said, 'You can't do this.' And a lot of the time they lost money. If it's a story we think is important and we can put a really good spin on it, nothing has been off limits. We've never had problems over the language."

Even so, occasionally the network does voice "concern," as with the original script for Episode 86: "Nurture." In this case, a woman's role eventually replaced that of a male pedophile that the writers initially created to parallel a well-known abduction case on Long Island. "We probably would have made that change anyway because it was too close to the real story," Wolf suggests, in explaining the show's acquiesence to the network's qualms.

"That sort of thing happens rarely. Usually, everything comes together like a puzzle," producer Lew Gould says.

"We had a number of episodes each year that caused significant advertiser fallout and, in a way, we kind of built that into the series," NBC's key programming executive, Warren Littlefield, has explained.

Producer Jeff Hayes believes that "thorny issues make it more interesting for everybody but it's a fight sometimes to get it on television...."

Director of photography Gus Makris remembers one instance of a network mandate. "On [Episode 136:] 'I.D.,' we had a naked body on an elevator. I directed that. Dick happened to be here. He said, 'Look, I want to go as far as we can go.' I asked, 'How far is that?' He said, 'I'm going to find out from the network.' So he laid out what we would and would not see. It sounded like more than I thought we would see. We could see the woman's derrière but not the working parts. Obviously, no frontal nudity. We could see virtually all the breast but not the nipples."

Then, after the scene had been shot, "it turned out somebody at the network thought we were seeing too much breast. They said it would have been okay if the body double's breasts weren't quite that big, but since they were, it was no good. So we had to shoot an alternate shot, building the inside of the elevator in the studio while we were in the middle of the next episode.... It wasn't as graceful as it once was," Makris says.

Producer Ed Sherin is clear about the issue of violence: "I do not like to have anyone shot on our show. I've had arguments with Dick [Wolf] on that. By and large, I win that one. I don't think it's appropriate. But we do see somebody dead on the ground as the result of a violent act or see somebody shot in a way that is archetypical."

While avoiding battles with the network, Dick Wolf has given a significant amount of time to defending all popular culture against the onslaught from censorship-minded members of Congress. He has appeared on numerous talk shows, debating the likes of Senator John McCain, a Republican from Arizona. "I was on a panel with Edward Markey [Democratic Congressman from Massachusetts] and I told him I really don't think America wants *Forrest Gump* [1994] blocked," Wolf recalls. "He said, 'Well, the V-Chip wouldn't block *Forrest Gump*.' And I went, 'Really? In other words, a movie in which body parts are blown thirty feet in the air in Vietnam and a woman has unprotected sex and dies from AIDS, that's fine? That wouldn't be V-Chipped?'"

Wolf is certain "that it would be V-Chipped, the same way *Schindler's List* (1993) would be V-Chipped. My argument is that, in many instances, people's only exposure to controversial issues is on shows like *ER, Law & Order, N.Y.P.D. Blue.* A lot of these issues deserve and need a public forum."

CHAPTER 17

THE VIEWERS

When fortune is on our side, popular
favor bears her company.

—PUBILIUS SYRUS, First Century B.C.

THERE IS little doubt that NBC has reaped the benefits of the A&E network's decision to broadcast daily reruns of *Law & Order* in recent years. As a consequence, the ratings for NBC's new episodes have jumped. As once casual viewers became hard-core fans through tracing the early years of the show, they began tuning in the weekly first-run installments of the drama.

"It had just the additional klieg-light of publicity," says Warren Littlefield, the peacock network's president of Entertainment. "It was kind of an eye-opener for us. We used to think when we had a show on the air for a number of years that everybody would know about it, but there are so many choices. Cable brought audience attention to *Law & Order*. They got hooked and then realized there were more originals to find over on NBC."

A&E's vice-president of programming for Daytime Specials, Michael Katz, remembers how his company made the decision to air *Law & Order*. "We were getting out of the stand-up comedy business in the 11:00 P.M. eastern time slot....We wanted something to replace that. Brooke Johnson [vice-president and general manager] said, 'If we can find a recent, off-network, high-quality drama, it would probably work in that time period.' She recognized *Law & Order* as the perfect syndicated property because it's so plot-driven. If you look at certain classic British mysteries, from Agatha Christie on down, that's what drives it. It's the puzzle. And it was right for our image."

Katz says he and Johnson "were confident that, when you take a program like this and strip it five nights a week, an audience will find it. It was a big risk for us. . . . It did better than we had anticipated, frankly. To say that we were pleased is an understatement. We've heard Dick Wolf has actually said that, when A&E started running the show at eleven o'clock, a whole new audience went looking for *Law & Order* on NBC."

Better yet, Wolf himself channel-surfs to see the old episodes. "People do become addicted to this show. It's quite gratifying. I still watch it. If I'm at home, I put it on at eleven on A&E," he acknowledges.

For cinematographer/director Gus Makris, "there are times when I've read the script and then I'll see it on the air and I'll say, 'What? Who are they talking about?' It's not the kind of show you can go get a sandwich while it's on. If you miss sixty seconds of this thing, you're at a great disadvantage because the stuff is so rapid-fire. It can really throw you for a loop and I can't believe sometimes that people stay with it. . . . All that legalese in the second half! The complex legal terms don't seem to faze the audience."

As an actor who has to master the tongue-twisting legalese of *Law & Order* on a weekly basis, Sam Waterston feels that "it's like doctor talk. You know they're on about their business. You don't necessarily know what it is. It's also true that people do like the familiar. . . . They know they can tune in and we will give them something they will recognize as a *Law & Order* show. There's some reassurance in that. I think we have an appetite as human beings for the retelling of stories."

He thinks "it's really a result of that reassurance, like a child who says, 'Read me the same Beatrix Potter story.' So I can go through the same anxiety but this time knowing that the bunnies will be safe. And then again, so I can rehearse and rehearse the arc of my own feelings. . . . How else to explain so much storytelling. Isn't that amazing?"

CHAPTER 18

THE FUTURE

It takes a long time to bring excellence to maturity.

—PUBILIUS SYRUS, First Century B.C.

THE ACCOMPLISHMENTS of *Law & Order*—better and better ratings, rave reviews, a 1997 Emmy for best drama—are remarkable in the pantheon of American television success stories. In a medium that values glitz, the show offers no big stars, no sex, and only marginal violence. In addition, it is full of mind-boggling legal terms and complex tales that attempt to comfort the afflicted while afflicting the comfortable, to borrow a phrase from legendary journalist Joseph Pulitzer.

The Emmy Award win was very sweet. According to producer Lew Gould, "The fact that we're in New York, politically, goes against us. It's not the place to be if you want attention from the TV industry for getting awards. We were kind of shocked that we got the Emmy because of that."

"You go out to the Awards and you don't know anybody," Gould continues. "Everyone else is shaking hands. Our group goes out there, six years in a row. This year, we're all sitting there and it's long and kind of gets a little slow and we're coming up to the big award. I can tell you for a fact that not one of us expected to win.... It was like, 'Okay, let's wait till this is over and go eat.' So when Glenn Close called out our name, it was a shock."

"I was the most stunned person in the auditorium," series creator Dick Wolf says. "I thought it was a mistake. Everybody went nuts. The most gratifying thing was when we got on stage, it was like a standing ovation, a sense of completeness almost. Everybody in the room was happy for us, with the exception of people on the other four nominated shows."

Gould reports that "it was very surreal when we got up on stage. I was trying very hard to hear what Dick had to say. The way the speakers are, all the sound is going out toward the audience. We're standing behind him and I could not hear a word. I asked, 'Dick, what did you say?' He said, 'I have no idea.' Dick Wolf is not a man to be at a loss for words. He is a master of the media. But there was a moment there when he was speechless."

Once again loquacious, Dick Wolf comes up with a little bit of tomorrow-the-world enthusiasm when asked what the future holds for *Law & Order*. "The show airs in forty countries now, but we're playing around with the idea of doing it in Germany with Germans and the German legal system, in Japan with the Japanese legal system. France and Spain and England. Nobody's ever had this kind of franchise. It works wherever you put it."

Wolf even foresees taking one issue and letting it ripple around the globe. "That would make an interesting night of television. Use the same case in the American version, in the Japanese version, in the English version, and get different verdicts in every country."

Back in New York, with Energizer-Bunny-like determination, *Law & Order* just keeps going and going and going. "After the end of the second season Joe Stern told me, 'You've got a five-year show here, kid.' And I thought he was out of his mind," Gould says. "All of us never had a job longer than a movie before this."

Writer/producer Rene Balcer thinks the scribes can make the show fresh "if every week we can keep the audience off balance as to what kind of story they're going to get....As long as we keep mixing it up from week to week, I think that they'll keep tuning in. And as long as the criminal element does their share in committing more unusual crimes every month, we'll never run out of material."

So, where is *Law & Order* heading? "If it's not fresh, it's going to die anyway," says producer Jeff Hayes. "Otherwise, I'd have moved on. I'm a little skittish on the more personal stuff. We're already doing things that I think are too much right now. With this show, if you keep it pure, to me you keep it fresh."

Series costar Benjamin Bratt feels "blessed to have this job. This has been one of the happiest circumstances I've ever been in. But to be invited to New York to become part of one of the most respected shows on television was a dream come true. The Emmy is just icing on the cake."

As far as Bratt is concerned, the cake can stay fresh indefinitely. "In this society, we're fascinated with the macabre and with life-and-death situations. The subject matter's constantly changing. Also, cast changes have something to do with interest being maintained."

Former series detective Chris Noth has a more satirical slant on *Law & Order*'s future. "They ought to have a show where all the old characters come back. F***ing Paul Sorvino in a wheelchair. Moriarty with his shrink next to him. I think they could only do it on *Saturday Night Live.* Joe Stern? We'd have to f***ing have him in a straightjacket. And we'd have Ed Sherin after he got electroshock treatment, with me administering the shocks," he says in a breathless profusion of ideas, before adding, "I hope I didn't give too dour a portrait. I'm not bitter at all, in retrospect, when you put all the pieces together."

Perhaps no one says it better than actor John Fiore, whose recurring role as Det. Anthony Profaci is a staple in the precinct. "It seems to me the show could go on indefinitely. It's like a new show in a way. It's the same and yet it's new," he suggests. "The sad thing is there's more weird stuff happening in the headlines. It seems as if that whole thing could never dry out."

Law & Order's creator and guiding light, Dick Wolf, is more succinct: "How do you keep it fresh?" He repeats the question, then answers without hesitation: "The front page of the *New York Post.*"

CHAPTER 19

THE PLAYERS

The scripts are so good and, on every level, there's such power, not the least of which is the cast . . . probably the greatest cast assembled in any TV series in the history of television.

—Paul Sorvino, 1992

Famed Russian stage director and producer Konstantin Sergeivitch Alexeyev Stanislavski believed that great theater required "the conception and birth of a new being—the person in the part."

Half a century later, *Law & Order* fostered the conception and birth of a new forum for television: a realistic, almost documentary-style series in which actors would reach for some spare, vital essence of drama. The person in the part coexists with the part in the person.

The show's shifting company of indelible performers has always included strong personalities who sometimes crashed into each other with a resounding thud. Yet each actor who departs from *Law & Order*, for whatever reason, has left a glowing trail in the television cosmos. "It's the closest thing to a repertory company in series TV," suggested a 1992 story in Toronto's *Globe and Mail*, "The *Law & Order* Players."

THE POLICE

Benjamin Bratt
Det. Reynaldo Curtis (1995–)

JUST THE FACTS

Bratt: Born on December 16, 1963, in northern California; mother, Eldy, a Peruvian Quechua Indian from Lima; father, a sheet-metal worker of German and English descent; one of five children; parents divorced in 1967; received BFA degree with honors from the University of California at Santa Barbara; master's program at San Francisco's American Conservatory Theatre; professional debut at Utah Shakespearean Festival.

Curtis: Part Quechua, part German-English descent; devout Catholic; married to Deborah; three young daughters.

THE REST OF THE STORY

"I love New York—I really love it," says Benjamin Bratt, sounding as if he's doing one of those promotions for the city with its own catchy theme song. "A dream of mine, since I was young, has been to come to New York City and take it on. That's been the big challenge."

While right at home in the Big Bad Apple, the California-born actor finds it ironic to be playing Rey Curtis. "For some reason, and to this day it remains inexplicable, I keep getting hired as the man in uniform," he says. "Most of those roles have been a cop in one form or another, either a park ranger who carries a gun in *The River Wild* or the sidekick in *One Good Cop* or a futuristic cop in *Demolition Man*. In *Blood In, Blood Out*, I start as leader of a gang and become a cop. I don't know if it's something in my personality or what."

His real personality is very much at odds with what *Law & Order* demands of him for the fictitious TV part. "The one danger in taking on a role like this was that I might be some sort of mouthpiece for The Man," Bratt says, using the colloquial term for the white male power structure. "Dick [Wolf] said, 'No, don't worry....I want someone from Generation X who is righteous, moral, upstanding, who believes in the system, believes in good and evil.'"

Although some viewers and critics have been wary of just how righteous, moral, and upstanding a guy Curtis can be at times, Bratt himself comes across as exceedingly sweet-natured, funny, and way beyond liberal. "The role did surprise me at first because, in my own personal life, I tend to be far left of center. Being a man of color, I'm aware of injustices in our country and some of the mistakes [America] has made, not only with other countries but with native peoples that lived here before."

Bratt's mother is descended from the Incas, the Quechuan people whose ancient empire flourished in the Andes until the Spanish conquest of Peru in the 1500s. "I think it was smart of Dick to bring in someone from another culture, American through and through but representative of so many other millions of us that come from backgrounds other than European."

Instead of spotlighting Curtis's biculturalism, the writers have concentrated on his

Benjamin Bratt, the show's straight-laced Det. Rey Curtis since Season Six.

marriage, in good times and bad. On the good side, he's devoted to his wife, Deborah, and their three young daughters. On the bad side, he slept with another woman at the end of Season Six and, later, was tempted by a Hollywood babe in the show's 1996 three-parter. Recently, Deborah has been diagnosed with multiple sclerosis.

Despite all that's going on in his backstory, Bratt knows that the show must focus on the crimes and the trio of cops trying to solve them. "But when you bring flesh-and-blood individuals to the roles and respective baggage from their personal lives to an acting setting and they flesh the characters out, a lot of fireworks go off."

Those fireworks, of the friendly variety, have helped Bratt, Jerry Orbach, and S. Epatha Merkerson to bond even as their fictitious characters of Curtis, Lennie Briscoe, and Anita Van Buren grow ever closer. "Epatha is a woman, outside of being Anita Van Buren, that I love. I hold her so dear to my heart," Bratt says.

"Lennie's a veteran cop and he's been doing it for years and years. And I'm still fairly new to homicide investigation, so there will be times when we disagree with each other. But we now and forever have each other's trust," Bratt says, before adding, "unless he goes astray."

When it comes to going astray, Rey Curtis has been naughty. "It's very tricky to have someone who is so conservative and yet be appealing to women on a pure physical level. What I've found is that they've started to write more situations where women that I come into contact with make remarks to me. They give me a look, a once-over. There's more flirtation going on."

Does this serious actor with a theater background mind becoming a sex symbol? "I don't mind," Bratt replies, his eyes flashing with amusement. "What, are you kidding?"

SELECTED CREDITS

FEATURE FILMS
One Good Cop (1991), *Bright Angel* (1991), *Bound by Honor* (1993), *Demolition Man* (1993), *The River Wild* (1994), *Clear and Present Danger* (1994), *Follow Me Home* (1996)

TELEVISION
REGULAR: *Nasty Boys* (1990) as "Eduardo Cruz," *Law & Order* (1995–) as "Det. Reynaldo Curtis"
MOVIES: *Chains of Gold* (1991), *Shadowhunter* (1993), *Texas* (1994), *Woman Undone* (1995)

George Dzundza
Sgt. Max Greevey (1988, 1990–91)

JUST THE FACTS

Dzundza: Born on July 19, 1945, in Rosenheim, Germany; Ukrainian ancestry; grew up on Manhattan's Lower East Side; attended St. John's University; studied acting with Stella Adler and Harold Clurman; married, with three children; lives in California.

Greevey: Catholic; married to Marie, with whom he has three children; former partner of Capt. Donald Cragen.

THE REST OF THE STORY

So effective was his portrayal of a streetwise New York City cop that George Dzundza impressed even a genuine streetwise New York City cop. "George was a guy I could see myself riding in a detective cruiser with," says veteran detective Mike Struk, *Law & Order*'s technical adviser on police matters.

"He had a pretty good flair for playing a cop. He's a regular guy. I always felt very comfortable around him."

Some of Dzundza's other colleagues were far less comfortable around him. Dann Florek believes that Dzundza "thought it was going to be the Greevey show. Then he realized that, at the very least, it was going to be an ensemble drama."

Dzundza will not go into many specifics but what he does say sounds somewhat remorseful: "It was a long time ago for me. The show was in New York; I lived in Los Angeles, where my family is. I was commuting back and forth. It was a very difficult, hard job for me to do. I'm not perfect. I make mistakes, but so do a lot of other people."

While there may have been difficulties with Dzundza the man, not a single soul denigrates the way he played Greevey. And Dzundza now seems a lot more appreciative of the

George Dzundza, who performed in the 1988 pilot and left after one unhappy season on Law & Order as Sgt. Max Greevey.

show and what it did for his career. "I'm proud of my work on it," he says. "I'm proud of the show and I was happy to go back to my family, and I'm fortunate enough to still be making movies. I don't think a lot of that would have been possible had I not done *Law & Order*. It was a great step for bringing me to the attention of America."

For him, Greevey was "a guy who had been in the service for a long time and who was, in some ways, shaped by the job he was doing. . . . I had no preconceived notion about how to do it. I had an overall blueprint. It wasn't rocket science. The [suspect] is either a bum or he's not a bum. The rest of it is dictated by the script."

Given his current enthusiastic endorsement of *Law & Order*, it's hard to believe that Dzundza was ever so disgruntled with the show: "There weren't many opportunities to show those [personal] points of view but, as a concept, the show worked. It's still working. As it progressed, it was pretty solid. What's the competition now? It doesn't really have it. If you want a serious police drama that's not about naked people, you don't have any other choice really."

What, if anything, did he learn from the series? "Not to do one," Dzundza replies without hesitation. "It was the beginning of a long road I've been taking over the last ten years. I'm one of the luckiest guys on Earth. I've learned more about myself, about my relationship to God, about my relationship with my family, and a lot of that had to do with the fact that I was able to leave the show."

The people he quarreled with in New York may disagree, but Dzundza suggests he "tried to be a gentleman. My only concern was an artistic expression and truth. I take television very seriously as a medium. You can do things on television that you can't do on film. You can change the world through television."

He didn't change the world in his single *Law & Order* season, but Dzundza did garner some nice reviews, such as the 1991 (Toronto) *Globe and Mail* piece that suggested he "invests the role with flawless ordinariness. He's a cop from his plain, doughy face down to his heavy, sensible shoes." Or, as another story in the same newspaper proposed a few months earlier, the show's cops "dress as badly as Bible salesmen."

SELECTED CREDITS

FEATURE FILMS
The Happy Hooker (1975), *The Deer Hunter* (1978), *Honky Tonk Freeway* (1981), *Streamers* (1983), *Best Defense* (1984), *No Mercy* (1986), *No Way Out* (1987), *The Beast* (1988), *Honor Bound* (1988), *White Hunter, Black Heart* (1990), *The Butcher's Wife* (1991), *Basic Instinct* (1992), *Dangerous Minds* (1995), *Crimson Tide* (1995), *That Darn Cat* (1996), *Species II* (1998)

TELEVISION
REGULAR: *Open All Night* (1981–82) as "Gordon Feester," *Law & Order* (1990–91) as "Sergeant Max Greevey"
MOVIES: *Salem's Lot* (1979), *A Long Way Home* (1981), *Skokie* (1981), *The Face of Rage* (1983), *The Lost Honor of Kathryn Beck* (1984), *Brotherly Love* (1985), *One Police Plaza* (1986), *The Ryan White Story* (1989), *Cross of Fire* (1990), *What She Doesn't Know* (1992), *The Enemy Within* (1994), *The Limbic Region* (1996)

Dann Florek
Capt. Donald Cragen (1988, 1990–93)

JUST THE FACTS

Florek: Born May 1, 1950, near Detroit; studied theater arts at the University of Michigan and Eastern Michigan University; left school before graduation to move to New York City; worked with The Acting Company at the Juilliard School; married to Karen.

Cragen: Irish Catholic; recovering alcoholic; married to Marge, a flight attendant; teenage child; frequently says "bupkes," "squat," and "diddley," as in *nada* or nothing; former partner of Max Greevey; leaves the precinct to head the N.Y.P.D.'s Anti-Corruption Task Force.

THE REST OF THE STORY

Captain Cragen lives in a modest, single-family house with a swimming pool, as we discover in Episode 22: "The Blue Wall," but the actor who inhabited that role for four years once dwelled along the canals of Venice, California. That's where Dann Florek first got word that he'd been hired for the *Law & Order* pilot.

He remembers: "Cragen had very little to do; I think there were two scenes. I told [producer] Joe Stern, 'There's no role here.' He kept insisting, 'It's going to be more.'" Indeed, after a wait of almost two years, there was more. In all, Florek spent three seasons with the show.

In the beginning, he warned friends about the unique nature of this TV series. "I told people, 'It's very challenging. You must pay attention. This is not *Matlock* [1986–96]. This is not *In the Heat of the Night* [1988–94]. This is real, adult stuff. This is television for people who don't watch television,'" he says.

"It seemed a little chaotic," Florek recalls. "We were figuring out what we were doing but there was definitely a sense of adventure, almost like a mission. We were all involved in the shaping of the show. [Sometimes] there was a sense of, 'We can't do that. That isn't honest. We created something and we've got to stay on track. We can't become *Murder, She Wrote* [1984–96].' There was a great deal of integrity."

However, there was still not a great deal for him to do and

Dann Florek, whose favorite words during a three-year **Law & Order** *stint as Capt. Don Cragen were "bupkes" and* **"squat."** [courtesy of the Everett Collection]

he was commuting to New York. "I would say, 'Why are you flying me in? I only have two scenes in the office.' Also, Florek was given almost no pointers about his character. "It wasn't until the sixth or seventh episode when all of a sudden they said, 'You're an alcoholic.' And I said, 'Well, thanks for telling me.'"

So Florek had to decide who Cragen really was. "I thought he would have a dry, witty sense of humor. I used to kind of improvise a little bit and they would almost always go, 'That's a good idea.' That kind of helped shape the character, so it was this guy cracking wise."

The current incarnation of the show rarely makes the grade in his estimation. "We've joked about it—I think with [Chris] Noth, maybe. We refer to it as *Law & Order Lite*. It's on cruise control, virtually all white-collar crime."

Florek began to observe that "Epatha [Merkerson] is Cragen in a dress and it doesn't work. That was just my take on it. She's a very talented woman and everything, but they were writing the exact same character. Now they've changed that. They give her more women's issues and things like that."

When he was recruited to direct his first segment, Episode 76: "The Pursuit of Happiness," Florek bumped into Merkerson for the first time. "She almost started stuttering, I think. I said, 'S., call me D. We should be on a first-initial basis.' She said, 'This is so weird.' I told her, 'Don't worry about it. You had nothing to do with it. I had nothing to do with it. I want you to feel comfortable if we're going to work together.'"

Florek was initially reluctant to return to the set in New York. "I was back home [in Los Angeles] and Ed just called me: 'I'd like you to come direct.' I said, 'I don't want to be anywhere near those idiots.' He said, 'I understand you're upset and emotional right now, but this is a wonderful opportunity.' So I thought about it for a few days and then called back to tell him he was right," Florek recalls.

The onscreen chemistry between Noth and Florek, who periodically called Logan "Mikey," reflected their real friendship. "It was almost like a father-son thing. I knew Chris a little before [*Law & Order*]. When he was a student at Yale, I played some leads at Yale Repertory Theatre. Then we did a couple of stupid episodes on some [soap] opera I can't even remember. We would always have fun. My biggest joy of the entire thing was working with Chris."

As another wounded veteran of the show, Florek sounds like Noth while expressing anger, regret, and nostalgia. "I hated to commute from L.A. I hated all the down time. I hated not having enough to do. I felt I was underused, underpaid, and underappreciated. But the actual work itself was spectacular. Every episode, it felt like we were doing a movie."

SELECTED CREDITS

FEATURE FILMS
Sweet Liberty (1986), *Angel Heart* (1987), *Sunset* (1988), *Moon Over Parador* (1988), *Flight of the Intruder* (1990), *Getting Even with Dad* (1994), *The Flintstones* (1994), *Hard Rain* (1998)

TELEVISION
REGULAR: *L.A. Law* (1988–90) as "David Meyer," *Law & Order* (1988, 1990–93) as "Capt. Donald Cragen"
MOVIES: *Alex: The Life of a Child* (1986), *The Trial of Bernhard Goetz* (1988), *A Nightmare Come True* (1997)

S. Epatha Merkerson
Lt. Anita Van Buren (1993–)

JUST THE FACTS

Merkerson: Born on November 28, 1952, in Detroit, Michigan; youngest of five children; father, a factory worker; mother, post office administrator; graduated from Wayne State University, Detroit; has dreadlocks in real life; resides in Manhattan and Clinton, Maryland; married government social worker Toussaint L. Jones in 1995 after two decades as sweethearts.

Van Buren: Husband owns hardware store; two pre-adolescent sons; worked in narcotics before homicide; has been passed over for a promotion to captain in favor of a less-qualified white woman.

THE REST OF THE STORY

In the mirthful *Law & Order* company, S. Epatha Merkerson ranks among the wittiest. Her playfulness is punctuated by a booming, infectious laugh. During the shooting of Episode 167: "Ritual," Merkerson warbles some high-pitched, operatic notes between takes in Van Buren's office. After the third such piercing musical exercise, sound mixer David Platt says, "Epatha, you're killing me."

"That's four years of not smoking," she boasts.

In the make-believe squad room where the production team is assembled, wardrobe assistant Rosie Wells asks, "Anybody got a cigarette?" Director Brian Mertes shouts out, "Epatha, everybody's lighting up out here."

S. Epatha Merkerson, who has portrayed the show's no-nonsense Lt. Anita Van Buren since Season Four. *[Copyright ©1997 by Universal City Studios, Inc. Courtesy of Universal Publishing Rights, a Division of Universal Studios Licensing, Inc. All rights reserved.]*

Back in Merkerson's tiny dressing room, she hits a more serious note. "I've been an outspoken person most of my life and I probably won't change. . . . No one in this company has lived black and a woman. I have. . . . [B]eing an all-male group, they don't know what to do with the women. It was absolutely like breaking a male domain when I started and it's still like that. . . . They don't know me. They don't know women. They don't know black people. But they're learning and it doesn't matter how old you get, as long as you learn something."

She is referring to the way that *Law & Order*'s writers have not, in her view, always crafted scripts that accurately represent either an African-American or female perspective. "I think it's the way they were raised," she suggests. "I have to exist in this world with white people. They don't [have to exist with blacks]. Y'all don't. If you don't choose to, then there's something you don't know. . . . And that's where I become very important to this group, in terms of my slant on things."

Merkerson's slant on things is precise. "Why am I in a position of authority yet you rarely see me on screen? . . . It's all relative. I can hear Ben or Jerry saying, 'Geez, we're not even in the script this time.' And I think, 'Huh? Huh?' In an episode, they might get, like, twenty scenes and I've got only four."

She wants to see Van Buren have "a more significant role in the investigations. When something goes wrong, let Van Buren deal with it, not the guys. Cragen got to interact much more with the DA's office but he's a tall, white man. You can write stories for me without them necessarily being about a black issue, but it never happens that way."

Executive producer Rene Balcer wants to write Van Buren "not as just a conveyor of information but as someone who is...I would use the word 'sassy.'"

Merkerson does not relish the perception that she has been given an earth-mother image on *Law & Order.* "I think that's why Van Buren has been made black and female; [earth mother] is another role we tend to find ourselves in: 'Come and tell me the problems and I'll help you out.' You know, 'Come sit on mammy's knee.'"

Her perspective was shaped by an early awareness of how racism has transformed the American landscape. Hers was the first black family in a neighborhood where so-called white flight was taking place. Merkerson and her brother had a game, predicting how many new "For Sale" signs they would be able to count on their way to school each day.

Although she's been a regular cast member since 1993, Merkerson actually began her association with the show during the first season as a guest star in Episode 17: "Mushrooms." "I was doing *The Piano Lesson* on Broadway. Joe Stern came to see the show—he was the executive producer then—and I got called in for an audition."

Less than a year after she began playing Van Buren, Merkerson married and became a long-distance commuter. "My husband works for the Washington, D.C., government, such as it is, so I'm the one who does the commuting. I thought it would be a problem but that train ride from D.C. to New York and back is really quite nice."

She has just returned to the set after more than a week's absence, in fact, and one by one the cast pops in to say hello. Carey Lowell (Assistant DA Jamie Ross) beckons Merkerson into her slightly larger dressing room for a closed-door tête-à-tête. "They all miss me when I'm not here," Merkerson explains with a dimpled smile. She may wish to forego the earth-mother role, but her warmth, sassy or not, lights up the *Law & Order* world.

SELECTED CREDITS

FEATURE FILMS
Jacob's Ladder (1990), *Loose Cannons* (1990), *Navy SEALS* (1990), *Terminator 2: Judgment Day* (1991)

TELEVISION
REGULAR: *Pee-wee's Playhouse* (1988) as "Reba, the Mail Lady," *Mann & Machine* (1992) as "Margaret Claghorn," *Here and Now* (1992–93) as "Ms. St. Marth," *Law & Order* (1993–) as "Lt. Anita Van Buren"
MOVIES: *It's Nothing Personal* (1993), *A Place for Annie* (1994), *A Mother's Prayer* (1995), *An Unexpected Life* (1995), *Breaking Free* (1995)

Chris Noth
Det. Mike Logan (1988, 1990–95)

JUST THE FACTS

Noth: Born on November 13, 1956, in Madison, Wisconsin; father, died when he was ten; mother, former CBS reporter Jeanne Parr; two brothers; raised in Connecticut, England, Yugoslavia, and Spain; bitten by the acting bug in the mid-1970s at Vermont's Marlboro College; dropped out six months before graduation; studied with Sanford Meisner in 1978; graduated Yale Drama School; lives alone in Greenwich Village in New York City.

Logan: An Irish Catholic background with alcoholic parents; father, a cop; physically abused as a child by his mother and sexually molested by a parish priest; drove a cab to pay his way through college; single, favors plaid ties and a worn brown leather jacket.

THE REST OF THE STORY

Three years after Chris Noth's somewhat shocking eviction from *Law & Order*, fans have yet to let go. On the Internet, there's more chatter about him than about any other character on the show, past or present. "I read recently that the reason Chris Noth was replaced by Benjamin Bratt was the producers' desire to attract more Generation X viewers to the show," wrote someone named Catherine in December 1997. "I find this curious since I am twenty-five years old and much prefer Chris Noth, who I think is extremely attractive."

Has Dick Wolf's strategy backfired? The chiseled perfection of Bratt does not appear to have captured the public's fancy. For many fans, his buttoned-up Detective Curtis is tame compared to the unpredictable, always edgy Logan. Viewers like a bit of danger in their heroes. Costar Paul Sorvino once described Noth as "a handsome class clown in a leading man's body," and many Noth fans seem to agree.

After spending a year in Indonesia, following the shoot for *Jakarta* (1987), Noth was doing regional theater and Shakespeare when his agents told him about the very first *Law & Order* script in 1988. "I was struck by the fact that it did not read like TV-pilot-land. There was a credibility to it and a starkness that I liked," he recalls.

"When we came back in 1990 with that series, with that cast, in this city, you have to believe we all thought we were doing something special," Noth says. "But the pilot and the first few...when I look at them now, I cringe. I was working too hard.... It was over-the-top naturalism."

As things evolved, however, few would contest Noth's uncanny ability to use *Law & Order*'s much-vaunted minimalism to his own advantage. Noth provides a quick overview of Logan's attributes: "I liked that he was, on one hand, a mixture of rebel and traditionalist at such a young age. Which is why I put a flag pin on him. There's something really square about Logan and, at the same time, something can come out of left field that you never expect. He's full of contradictions and those are always fun to play.... You don't know what to f***ing think. But you really get a sense that this guy is a true-blue cop."

While mourning the departure of executive producer Joe Stern in 1993, Noth gave Ed Sherin "a lot of sh** in my time. I was very vocal. I was a thorn in

Chris Noth, the show's volatile and charismatic Det. Mike Logan who was demoted to Staten Island beat cop at the end of Season Five. *[courtesy of Chris Noth/Copyright ©1993 by Universal City Studios, Inc. Courtesy of Universal Publishing Rights, a Division of Universal Studios Licensing, Inc. All rights reserved.]*

the press to Dick Wolf and, on the set, to Ed. I'm responsible for my departure. In the third year, I already knew. Ed and I went nose to nose a lot. I was at the time also in a very crazy relationship [with model Beverly Johnson].... There were a few times when I was a mess. There was no doubt in my mind that Ed was behind the idea of me leaving, and I wasn't giving Dick Wolf any reason [to keep me]."

While Dick Wolf did not opt to keep him on *Law & Order*, surprisingly, in the winter of 1997 Noth was busy planning for a two-hour Detective Logan movie on NBC called *Exile*, for Wolf's production company, no less! Noth maintains he would not consider the project "if I didn't think we could do something interesting and different. And frankly, I didn't realize how popular the character was. I don't own a computer or anything [to see the Internet Web sites] but I get boxes of f***ing mail. I don't want to go back to the show as a guest artist. But I thought, 'If I can do this on my terms, why not play to my strengths?'"

His strengths were also recognized in January 1998 by Warner Bros. Television, which signed a development deal for Noth to star in programs that he will also create and co-produce, no doubt providing much future fodder for the already fruitful *All Things Noth* Internet Web site.

SELECTED CREDITS

FEATURE FILMS
Smithereens (1982), *Off Beat* (1986), *Apology* (1986), *Baby Boom* (1987), *Jakarta* (1988), *Naked in New York* (1993), *The Confession* (not yet released)

TELEVISION
REGULAR: *Law & Order* (1988, 1990–95) as "Det. Mike Logan"
MOVIES: *Killer in the Mirror* (1986), *At Mother's Request* (1987), *I'll Take Manhattan* (1987), *Someone's Watching* (1993), *Where Are My Children?* (1994), *Born Free: A New Adventure* (1996), *Medusa's Child* (1997), *Exile* (not yet released)

Jerry Orbach
Det. Lennie Briscoe (1992–)

JUST THE FACTS

Orbach: Born on October 20, 1935, in the Bronx, New York; grew up in Waukegan, Illinois; son of ex-vaudevillian restaurateur; attended University of Illinois and Northwestern University; studied with Herbert Berghof and Lee Strasberg; married since late 1970s to actress Elaine Cancilla; has two sons and two grandchildren.

Briscoe: Jewish father, Catholic mother; from Upper East Side of New York City; twice divorced; two daughters; a recovering alcoholic.

THE REST OF THE STORY

A master of misanthropy, Det. Lennie Briscoe gets some of the snappiest lines that *Law & Order*'s writers can devise. He's streetwise and sarcastic but somehow always lovable.

Benjamin Bratt, who plays the prim Curtis to Orbach's sardonic Briscoe, says of his costar: "A friend of mine who watches the show said: 'You just turn a camera on Jerry, let it roll and then, in putting the scene together, cut over to Jerry for a simple reaction—he doesn't even have to be saying anything.' You get so much of the way he's feeling just by looking at him because, in reality, he's lived so much life."

In the course of living that life as an actor since a stint in summer stock at age sixteen, Orbach has great stories. Ask him why he decided to join the cast of *Law & Order* and you get a wonderful snippet of television history: "Back in the early '60s, my pal David Janssen was doing *The Fugitive* (1963–67). He used to come home eight, nine o'clock at night, having gotten up at five in the morning, have one drink and boom! He'd fall asleep on the couch and we'd carry him to bed. I told myself, 'I will never do an hour drama. It's just too hard.' But then, as you get older..."

Once his own show, *The Law and Harry McGraw* (1987–88), a *Murder, She Wrote* (1984–96) spin-off, was canceled in 1988, Orbach "realized then the tremendous odds against a) getting in a series, b) getting it on the air, and c) staying on the air."

In 1991, when he made a guest appearance on *Law*

Jerry Orbach, as Det. Lennie Briscoe, flashing his don't-mess-with-me **Prince of the City** *look on the* **Law & Order** *set.*

& Order as a defense lawyer (Episode 24: "The Wages of Love"), Orbach remembers Paul Sorvino raving about the quality of this TV show. "'I've jumped on a winning horse,' he told me. I said, 'Boy, you are lucky and you get to stay in New York.'" When Sorvino split the scene and Orbach took over, "I saw him two weeks afterwards and said, 'My family thanks you. My children thank you. My wife thanks you. My ex-wife thanks you. We all thank you.' Because this is not about a decision to spend a lot of hours and work hard—this is a great job."

It's also a job for which Orbach was considered twice before, in 1988 and 1991. George Dzundza and Sorvino, respectively, were hired instead, but three proved to be Orbach's lucky number. "They'll really have to shoot me to get me out of here," he told the *New York Daily News* in 1992, and columnist Matt Roush trumpeted that "Orbach's arrival signals a welcome new layer of grist to an already substantially entertaining mill."

In a *Law & Order* dressing room filled with golf memorabilia, Orbach is pleased to have that mill still churning. "This is, for me, what we used to call 'the f***-you fund' or the annuity. I'm socking away the life savings and I'm in no hurry to leave that. I love it."

In that Orbach seems to wear Briscoe like a second skin, does he see similarities? "I'm not as sarcastic as Lennie and I don't carry a gun around with me and I'm not as tough as Lennie, but when I want to think funny—and I think funny most of the time—I can have the same kind of humor. But it's not quite the gallows humor that Lennie has. Cops see terrible things all the time."

Orbach's humorous side is balanced by a savvy, tell-it-like-it-is attitude, not all that different from Briscoe. "In *Prince of the City* [1981], my character throws a guy's desk over and knees him in the groin," Orbach says. "Anybody who comes up to me and mentions that movie says, 'Oh, you know the scene I love?' Well, of course I do, because that's the one scene where the cops get even with these people that are browbeating them so badly. So, when we have something like Episode 139: 'Corruption,' with a guy calling me crooked and I had to clear myself, the audience hates to put up with that kind of thing. They love it when somebody gets even."

They also love his character. "I think they like his humanity. If somebody believes, 'That's how I would feel if that happened,' that's the universal appeal of any art. If you look at a painting and you say, 'Oh, yeah, I can see what he meant by that,' then it communicates to you."

Orbach communicated to the crowd in the summer of 1997, when he walked out on stage for a brief stand-up routine at Montreal's annual Just for Laughs festival. "I came out with a uniformed cop. The band played the theme from *Law & Order*. I arrested two guys for bad comedy."

SELECTED CREDITS

FEATURE FILMS
Cop Hater (1958), *Mad Dog Coll* (1961), *John Goldfarb, Please Come Home* (1965), *The Gang That Couldn't Shoot Straight* (1971), *Foreplay* (1975), *The Sentinel* (1977), *Underground Aces* (1980), *Prince of the City* (1981), *Brewster's Millions* (1985), *F/X* (1985), *Someone to Watch Over Me* (1987),

Dirty Dancing (1987), *Crimes and Misdemeanors* (1989), *Last Exit to Brooklyn* (1990), *Beauty and the Beast* (1991, voice of "Lumiere"), *Mr. Saturday Night* (1992), *The Adventures of a Gnome Named Gnome* (1993), *To Wong Foo, Thanks for Everything! Julie Newmar* (1995), *Aladdin and the King of Thieves* (1996, voice of "Sa'luk"), *Beauty and the Beast: The Enchanted Christmas* (1997, voice of "Lumiere")

TELEVISION
REGULAR: *The Law and Harry McGraw* (1987–88) as "Private Detective Harry McGraw," *Law & Order* (1992–) as "Det. Lennie Briscoe"
MOVIES: *An Invasion of Privacy* (1983), *Out on a Limb* (1987, miniseries), *Broadway Bound* (1991), *Quiet Killer* (1992)

Paul Sorvino
Det. Phil Cerreta (1991–92)

JUST THE FACTS

Sorvino: Born on April 13, 1939, in Brooklyn, New York; graduated from Lafayette High School; went on to the American Musical and Dramatic Academy in Manhattan; divorced Lorraine Davis in 1988; three children, including Academy Award-winner Mira; lives in a six-room penthouse apartment on Manhattan's Upper East Side with second wife, Vanessa.

Cerreta: Italian, Catholic; served in the military; married to Elaine; five kids; headed the investigation into Detective Greevey's shooting death; transferred to precinct as partner to Logan; transferred back out for a desk job after being shot himself.

THE REST OF THE STORY

"Television is notorious for being mediocre," proclaimed Paul Sorvino in a July 1992 *Us* magazine story about the show. "But *Law & Order* is becoming notorious for wonderful acting and writing. There is no finer dramatic show on television."

As he was leaving the series later that year, Sorvino complained to *New York Newsday* about the sixteen-hour days of shooting in every kind of weather: "The schedule on the street is very, very hard. It's not human; it's not right; it shouldn't be done this way."

Sorvino's brief tenure on this TV show brought a certain elegance to the precinct, as Det. Phil Cerreta proved more even-tempered than either his predecessor, Sgt. Max Greevey (George Dzundza), or his brash partner,

Paul Sorvino, whose elegant Det. Phil Cerreta was transferred to a desk job after being shot by a crazed gun dealer in the middle of Season Three. *[courtesy of Photofest / Copyright ©1992 by Universal City Studios, Inc. Courtesy of Universal Publishing Rights, a Division of Universal Studios Licensing, Inc. All rights reserved.]*

Det. Mike Logan (Chris Noth). In turn, Cerreta was far less world-weary than Det. Lennie Briscoe (Jerry Orbach), the cop who replaced him early in Season Three (1992–93).

"Cerreta's a smart guy who uses his head more than his hands, a guy who's seen it all, a detective sergeant on whom people would rely," Sorvino says of the character. "He enjoys life. Some police are extremely well-educated, cultured people. So I didn't want to do a standard, 'Yeah, wadda ya want?' It just didn't make any sense to me."

Yet, after a mere twenty-nine episodes, Cerreta was out of the picture. "I needed broader horizons," Sorvino says of his desire to leave the show.

He expressed his complaints in operatic terms for a 1992 *Los Angeles Times* story: "The cops have no arias. All the drama is in the *Order* section." A tenor, Sorvino quit the show to preserve his vocal cords for singing opera, a career he had launched in 1981 in a Seattle Opera production of Johann Strauss Jr.'s comic operetta *Die Fledermaus.*

Sorvino studied singing while still a teen but asthma made it problematic for him to continue. The trauma of his parents' stormy relationship (they would remain married for sixty-two years) reportedly triggered Sorvino's first asthma attack at age ten, when his mother moved all three children to California. Their father, Ford, reclaimed them two years later and Sorvino would not see his mother again till he was seventeen, another tragedy of his youth. He maintains that, in his twenties, he was cured by yoga breathing exercises.

The the failing health of his mother, a piano teacher named Marietta, was one reason Sorvino decided to join the *Law & Order* cast in the first place. She died, at age eighty-three, in 1991, not long after he assumed the Cerreta role.

"The quality [of *Law & Order*] is so close to the best movies...that you can't really call this a television show," Sorvino proclaimed in 1992, just as he was about to quit. "It's singular. There's no category for this....It was a very involving and very deep experience, second to nothing I've ever done before."

Half a decade later, he still has kind words for *Law & Order*. "The formula works. It has had the most exceptional actors in it and very high-quality writing. But it's not for nothing that all those actors are gone....They really didn't need me. You want to feel your contribution is necessary. I felt that any good actor could do it."

Sorvino cites other television detectives, like *Kojak* (1973–78, 1989–92) and *Colombo* (1971–93), who made "significant contributions, created very rich characters. But *Law & Order* is not that, it's an ensemble piece that's bifurcated, so there's not enough for anybody. If you want to do that for six or seven years, God bless you if you can. I couldn't. I just have too much bursting inside that needs to be expressed."

SELECTED CREDITS

FEATURE FILMS
Where's Poppa? (1970), *Made for Each Other* (1971), *A Touch of Class* (1973), *The Day of the Dolphin* (1973), *Panic in Needle Park* (1975), *Oh God!* (1977), *Lost and Found* (1979), *Bloodbrothers* (1979), *Reds* (1981), *That Championship Season* (1982), *Off the Wall* (1983), *The Stuff* (1985, with Michael Moriarty), *A Fine Mess* (1986), *GoodFellas* (1990), *Dick Tracy* (1990), *The Rocketeer* (1991), *The Firm* (1993), *Parallel Lives* (1994), *Nixon* (1995), *William Shakespeare's Romeo and Juliet* (1996), *Love Is All There Is* (1996), *Most Wanted* (1997, with Jill Hennessy), *Dead Broke* (not yet released, with Jill Hennessy), *Bulworth* (1998)

TELEVISION
REGULAR: *We'll Get By* (1975) as "George Platt," *Bert D'Angelo, Superstar* (1976) as "Bert," *The Oldest Rookie* (1987–88) as "Ike Porter," *Law & Order* (1991–92) as "Det. Phil Cerreta"
MOVIES: *Tell Me Where It Hurts* (1974), *Dummy* (1979), *A Question of Honor* (1980), *Chiefs* (1983, miniseries), *Almost Partners* (1987), *Without Consent* (1994), *Escape Clause* (1996)

THE PROSECUTORS

Richard Brooks
Assistant District Attorney Paul Robinette (1990–93)

JUST THE FACTS

Brooks: Born on December 9 (though thirtysomething, he declines to give the year) in Cleveland, Ohio; does theater, film, television; sings.

Robinette: African-American, Catholic; grew up in Harlem in New York City; eschewed offers from Wall Street to work in the DA's office; presumably single; plays tennis with DA Ben Stone.

THE REST OF THE STORY

"Usually we think of black as one thing and the system as another," Richard Brooks told the *Los Angeles Times* in 1992. "And we think of them as in conflict. Robinette is able to bring it all together. *Law & Order* shows that anyone can work within the system and not be an outsider."

Although his character was still working within the system, Brooks became much more of an outsider when he returned to the show in Season Six (1995–96) for an appearance in Episode 125: "Custody." It was his first time back on the set since he and Dann Florek were replaced by Jill Hennessy and S. Epatha Merkerson two years earlier. In this segment, Robinette is a defense attorney defending a crack-addicted mother accused of kidnapping her son from the people who adopted him.

During his entire stint on *Law & Order* in the DA's office, Robinette did lots of investigative work but never got to argue a case in court. His return in this episode finally gave him that opportunity, this time for the opposing side. Brooks informed *Us* magazine in 1992 that playing second banana to Michael Moriarty means "I have to take myself down to a real zero place and go into a numb state or else it would be unbearable. I just try to stay calm, stay in control, and not take things too personally."

For the show's producers and writers, Brooks thinks his return was a way of saying, "'Let's give Richard and Robinette a chance to really shine, the moment that we never gave them before."

Back in the early 1990s, according to *Us*, Brooks was flattered by the attention that television fame had brought him: "It's cool to be recognized after so many years of struggling."

His professional struggles began at a very young age. "As a kid, I started doing fashion shows for my mom," Brooks explains. "I would emcee when I was, like, three or four years old. . . . My mother was really active in the night scene and the fashion world; she was a hairstylist. She would take me to the clubs with her when she didn't have a babysitter. She dressed me in costumes that were almost like hers, little fancy clothes."

During the sixth grade, he saw his first play and the rest was indeed history. Brooks acted in school productions, did community theater, and received a scholarship to attend a prestigious arts camp. From there, he went to New York City. "I managed to get right into Circle in the Square theater school. I was the youngest— maybe still one of the youngest—to go there. I was seventeen."

On *Law & Order*, Robinette was always recognizable for the hip flattop he sported, believing that it would help young black viewers identify

Richard Brooks, went from 1988 pilot through the end of Season Three as Law & Order's *ADA Paul Robinette.* [courtesy of John Cocchi Archives/Copyright ©1991 by Universal City Studios, Inc. Courtesy of Universal Publishing Rights, a Division of Universal Studios Licensing, Inc. All rights reserved.]

with his character. For his guest appearance in Episode 125: "Custody," Robinette sports a shorter hairstyle, one that Brooks describes as "kind of a *GQ* look."

While auditioning for the pilot in 1988, he had dreadlocks! The famous flattop "came a little bit from the [*Law & Order*] hairdresser. He wanted me to do something cool: 'You've got a lot of times when you're just standing there, without saying anything. You need a look. We could say a lot with your look.' So we tried it and I started to like it," Brooks says.

(Brooks also sings and he is putting out a CD, *Smooth Love.* "I have my own company, Flattop Entertainment, because of the flattop I used to wear on *Law & Order.*" In early 1998, he was also producing, directing, and starring in an independent film, *Johnny Be Good.*)

As the only African-American in the Law & Order cast at that time, "when there was a black or race show, I would have to step up to handle the complexity of those situations.... And I had to actually tie the two [halves of the show] together, go right in with the cops and bring it over to the DA's office. I was the glue."

He's proud of his work. "Maybe even now in the greater picture of the '90s, I think Robinette has helped a lot of black actors get better roles, helped society in a way." In addition, given the recognition he still gets thanks to A&E re-runs, Brooks enjoys a sort of perpetuity with *Law & Order*. "I perceived that the show could have that kind of life.... That's why I wanted to always do my best work, to give classic performances. No one really put too much of a lid on how good we could be. I can watch [the earlier shows] and say, 'Wow!'"

SELECTED CREDITS

FEATURE FILMS
Teen Wolf (1985), *The Hidden* (1987), *84 Charlie Mopic* (1989), *To Sleep with Anger* (1990), *Listen Up: The Lives of Quincy Jones* (1991), *Machine Gun Blues* (1995), *The Substitute* (1996), *The Crow 2: City of Angels* (1996), *Wings Against the Wind* (not yet released), *Johnny Be Good* (not yet released)

TELEVISION
REGULAR: *Law & Order* (1990–93) as "Assistant District Attorney Paul Robinette"
MOVIES: *Badge of the Assassin* (1985), *Resting Place* (1986), *A Special Friendship* (1987), *Memphis* (1991), *The Wedding* (1998)

Jill Hennessy
Assistant District Attorney Claire Kincaid (1993–96)

JUST THE FACTS

Hennessy: Born on November 25, 1968, in Edmonton, Alberta, Canada; identical twin sister, Jacqueline; younger brother, John Paul; parents divorced in 1982; mother, Maxine, a secretary; father, John, a sales and marketing executive; grew up in Kitchener-Waterloo, Ontario; started modeling school in Toronto at age thirteen; plays guitar and sings; obsessed with animated TV satire *The Simpsons.*

Kincaid: Agnostic; single; attended Harvard Law School; becomes romantically involved with Jack McCoy, despite his reputation for affairs with co-workers; dies in a car crash.

THE REST OF THE STORY

In real life, Jill Hennessy peppers her conversations with nouveau-hipster lingo: "Awesome, babe!" "The guy was such a skeebie dude." "It's brilliant, man!" Such talk contrasts sharply with her oncamera dialogue during a three-year tenure on *Law & Order*, for which the actress remained rather serious as Assistant DA Claire Kincaid. (Even though there WAS that cool black leather jacket the character sometimes sported while conducting investigations outside the office.)

Despite the challenge of playing it with a straight face when her natural inclination was to laugh, she relished her TV series role. "I kept begging them. I'd suggest comedic lines. They'd say, 'No, we can't do that. Are you crazy?' One time, I actually smiled in a scene and they said, 'Cut. Let's do that again. Jill, don't smile.' It does create an acting style that's great to watch. As a viewer, I wouldn't want them to change it an iota to be very honest. It works so well," Hennessy says.

"My origins are in improv comedy," she explains. "I studied at Second City in Toronto. [On *Law & Order*] the whole art is finding the depth within a character who is not really allowed to smile or crack jokes and who does not have a lot of dialogue to reveal her personal feelings."

Off camera, Hennessy had oodles of warm, personal feelings for her colleagues. "To be with people who inspire you, who are so supportive, so

Jill Hennessy, whose ADA Claire Kincaid brought a bit of glamour to the all-male district attorney's office on Law & Order *in Season Four.* [Copyright ©1995 by Universal City Studios, Inc. Courtesy of Universal Publishing Rights, a Division of Universal Studios Licensing, Inc. All rights reserved.]

protective—I felt like I had a solid family who really saw me through a lot of rough times," she says. "It was wonderful to know you have that security to go back every day, to work on a character and fight for this character and, in doing so, learning a lot about the legal process, about writing, about directing, about the way actors communicate. That was very important, especially for this twenty-four-year-old person surrounded by these guys between the ages of thirty-five and sixty-five."

When Hennessy auditioned, her initial perception was that the part would call for surprising maturity and a certain sparkle. "I had never seen [*Law & Order*] previously. I thought they were looking for a new character in addition to the existing characters. I was reading the lines of a character named Robinette. I was so psyched.... I thought, 'This is great. This is going to be somebody who's got a voice, who has an opinion, who communicates, and who is very active.'"

But when the writers actually developed Claire Kincaid, Hennessy saw that the character would be standing a bit more in the shadow of her boss. "I began to discover the character they had initially conceived was very much an acolyte to Michael Moriarty's character, somebody who Michael could teach.... It worked very well on the show, I have to say. Personally, I was a little disappointed because I just loved Robinette's fire," she says.

In her first *Law & Order* season (1994–95) with Sam Waterston, she found that "it was so satisfying to finally voice opinions, to make her a lot more dimensional, to have her come out. In the first season, I saw her as always sort of lurking in the shadows, desperately wanting to say something. You could see she had an opinion but was never really given a chance."

Some of Hennessy's opinions met with disbelief at the highest levels during a script meeting for 1994's Episode 89: "Second Opinion," in which McCoy lectures Kincaid for sounding like a feminist. "Originally they had me just ignoring that comment," Hennessy recalls. "I said, 'Let's *make* her a feminist.' Dick [Wolf] said, 'What? You're making her a feminist?' I said, 'Well, Dick, I'm just curious. What's your perception of what a feminist is?' He said, 'Angry, angry. They hate men and they're all lesbians.' I said, 'Are you serious? Dick, man, I must disagree at this juncture. I think we should go for it. It gives Claire a strong voice. A feminist doesn't have to be man-hating or angry.'"

Despite such victories in the name of sisterhood, when Hennessy's three-year contract expired, she chose not to renew it. "I could have stayed. They were very generous and nice and made me a lot of offers. As an actor, I needed to go off and do other things that I knew are in my potential. I loved Claire but I need to play other characters. I need to be in films," she says.

Luckily, as a New York resident, Hennessy can stay in touch. "I go back to the set as many times as I can. I love these people so much."

Her love for the people blends with some nostalgia for the quality of the show, now that she's back out in a world of uneven opportunities. "I read other [film] scripts sometimes and think, 'I wish the *Law & Order* guys could see this. They'd die laughing.' They really perfected something. They created so many beautiful gems."

SELECTED CREDITS

FEATURE FILMS
Dead Ringers (1988), *RoboCop III* (1993), *The Paper* (1994), *I Shot Andy Warhol* (1996), *Most Wanted* (1997, with Paul Sorvino), *A Smile Like Yours* (1997), *Dead Broke* (not yet released, with Paul Sorvino)

TELEVISION
REGULAR: *Law & Order* (1993–96) as "Assistant District Attorney Claire Kincaid"

Steven Hill
District Attorney Adam Schiff (1990–)

JUST THE FACTS

Hill: Born on February 24, 1922, in Seattle, Washington; real name, Solomon Berg; founding member of New York City's Actors Studio, same class as Marlon Brando and Montgomery Clift; lives in Momsey, New York, with his wife; they have nine grown children.

Schiff: Jewish; his wife, Bea, died at the end of Season Seven (1997); a son, Josh; a grandson who plays Little League baseball.

THE REST OF THE STORY

Jill Hennessy recalls that, "On the set of *The Paper* [1994], Robert Duvall said to me: 'So I hear you work with Steven Hill on that *Law & Order*. He's the best working actor today, bar none.'" Hennessy adds, "I was so in awe of this guy."

William Fordes, *Law & Order*'s legal advisor and a veteran of the Manhattan district attorney's office, explains how the writing team devises Steven Hill's dialogue on the show: "Then we realize, 'Okay, give these lines to McCoy and those lines to Ross. Throw Schiff in for some acerbic wit.'" Schiff adds, "I throw in the practical wisdom of Robert Morgenthau, who is the real [New York City] DA. I sort of figure out what he would say."

Try talking about his legendary status and Hill shrugs that classic Adam Schiff shrug, then offers a short history lesson: "I was one of the

Steven Hill, a founding member of the legendary Actors Studio and the curmudgeonly DA Adam Schiff on Law & Order since Season One. *[courtesy of Photofest/Copyright ©1996 by Universal City Studios, Inc. Courtesy of Universal Publishing Rights, a Division of Universal Studios Licensing, Inc. All rights reserved.]*

original charter members of the Actors Studio....We were trying to set real precedents of creativity. It was extremely thrilling and exciting. We were privileged. We felt like the chosen of our generation in theater at that time."

In the midst of his distinguished career as a performer, *Law & Order* called on Hill in 1990. "They knew what to demand of me. It was understood that I would bring as much as I could of my experience and ideas...to come up with input that will embellish and bring the material to a higher level than it would seem just from reading the page."

What was the show's appeal? "The thing that intrigued me first, even more than the character, was the implication of the title. At that time, there was a real feeling in the country of bringing back an environment of law and order. It was an extremely apropos title. That is one of its secret powers still."

He hoped that secret power "would naturally spill over into this part. It almost became a commitment to try as much as I could in my small way to help foster the influence of that title. So that was kind of like an incentive for me that has never disappeared."

Hill sees Schiff as something of a standard-bearer. "The way they write that role, it's almost an obligation to see to it that justice to the ultimate is pursued. I try at the same time to conform as much to reality as I can, so it's not a fairy tale of justice, but a very real, connected-to-this-world sense of justice."

Did he foresee the show's longevity? "Not at all. I never dreamed it would go into four, five, six, seven seasons, and now into an eighth. I felt, especially in the beginning, the format was so predictable. I wondered how long people were going to be able to take this. I never was a big detective-story buff; I could really care less. I didn't have the patience for the whodunit puzzle but the audience never tires of it."

The audience never seems to get tired of Schiff's *shtick*, either. His sardonic wit, his impatience with what he considers foolishness, the habit of throwing down his eyeglasses in frustration. And yet, within that framework, there is room for change. "Schiff is much wiser than he ever was to begin with and far more sophisticated than I ever saw him in the beginning. Also much more perceptive. He's also very blunt in so many ways. He would prefer not to go into long dissertations," Hill points out.

He smiles at the suggestion that the character is beloved. "I get a kick out of that curmudgeon business. I used to love to see actors like that, like Monty Woolley. You love those older people who do that deliberately. I get a kick out of doing that. And they [the cast] get a kick out of it too, getting kicked around by me."

How does Schiff view Ben Stone and Jack McCoy? "They're both upstarts," Hill says in a very Schiff-like tone of voice.

SELECTED CREDITS

FEATURE FILMS
A Lady Without a Passport (1950), *Storm Fear* (1956), *The Goddess* (1958), *A Child Is Waiting* (1963), *The Slender Thread* (1965), *It's My Turn* (1980), *Rich and Famous* (1981), *Yentl* (1983), *Garbo Talks* (1984), *Brighton Beach Memoirs* (1986), *Legal Eagles* (1986), *Heartburn* (1986), *Running on Empty* (1988), *White Palace* (1991), *Billy Bathgate* (1991), *The Firm* (1993)

TELEVISION
REGULAR: *Mission: Impossible* (1966–67) as "Dan Briggs," *Law & Order* (1990–) as "District Attorney Adam Schiff"
MOVIES: *Man on a Mountaintop* (1954), *The Sacco-Vanzetti Story* (1960), *King* (1978, miniseries), *Between Two Women* (1986), *Where's the Money, Noreen?* (1995)

Carey Lowell
Assistant District Attorney Jamie Ross (1996–98)

JUST THE FACTS

Lowell: Born on February 11, 1961, in Huntington, Long Island, New York; father, a geologist; childhood spent in Libya, Holland, France,

Texas, and Colorado; began modeling at age eighteen; attended the University of Colorado in 1978; dropped out after a year; studied literature at New York University; married actor/director Griffin Dunne in 1989; daughter, Hannah, born in 1990; divorced Dunne in 1995.

Ross: Catholic; five brothers; divorced from smarmy defense attorney Neal Gorton; young daughter.

THE REST OF THE STORY

When Carey Lowell auditioned for *Law & Order*, she was given Jill Hennessy's lines to read, which was a bit of déjà vu in that Hennessy had tried out for the show three years earlier with dialogue written for Richard Brooks. Such is the nature of the revolving door at the assistant DA's office in a show that has learned to accommodate continual change.

Carey Lowell, who came aboard in Season Seven as the smart, tough ADA Jamie Ross.

"It wasn't like I went in with a part they had already written," Lowell says of her role as Jamie Ross. "I think they were waiting to see who they were going to cast before they developed the character. I am a single mother in reality and I am one on the show, although the child on the show is much younger. I think they drew stuff from my life. They didn't really know that much about me, nor did they ask a lot about me. They gave me five brothers and a Catholic background in the show. I have three sisters and not really a religious background at all."

Rene Balcer, executive producer and writer, explains he was "most involved in creating [the character of] Jamie Ross. I wanted to make her a post-feminist.... For her, Gloria Steinem is old history; she grew up already having absorbed all that. Ross is not afraid to make her opinion known and is certainly not intimidated by Jack McCoy. She loves to give him sh** and kick his ass from one end of the room to another."

In terms of kicking ass, Lowell's entertainment credits proceed from a modeling career while still a teenager to a 1989 gun-toting James Bond girl on screen in *License to Kill*. In 1995, she had just finished making the movie *Fierce Creatures* and was "going on a lot of auditions throughout the entire fall, winter, and spring. I couldn't get arrested. I was enrolled at NYU summer school to study documentary filmmaking. Classes were supposed to start July 1, and then I got the call to go on the *Law & Order* audition."

And that put an end to her academic plans. "I had to withdraw and get reimbursed my tuition. I did that on the first day of class and I started the show two weeks later. It was a very quick thing."

Lowell had been entranced by documentaries since the early 1990s, when she attended the Sundance Film Festival. "I saw *Blood in the Face,* about the Aryan brotherhood, which was startling. It shocked me into realizing the power of that medium and how you can reveal what really is going on."

She has come to believe that "in many ways, *Law & Order* sort of traces that style of filmmaking because it does play so much on reality and what true stories are. Of course, we cast actors to play the parts, but they do cast it to the point where it feels as if they have the actual, specific person there."

The actual, specific Jamie Ross was written out of *Law & Order* at the end of Season Eight, when Lowell quit the show to spend more time with her daughter.

SELECTED CREDITS

FEATURE FILMS
Dangerously Close (1986), *Club Paradise* (1986), *Me and Him* (1987), *License to Kill* (1989), *The Guardian* (1990), *Road to Ruin* (1991), *Sleepless in Seattle* (1993), *Love Affair* (1994), *Leaving Las Vegas* (1995), *Fierce Creatures* (1996)

TELEVISION
REGULAR: *A League of Their Own* (1993) as "Dottie Hinson," *Law & Order* (1995–98) as "Assistant District Attorney Jamie Ross"

Michael Moriarty

Executive Assistant District Attorney Ben Stone (1988, 1990–94)

JUST THE FACTS

Moriarty: Born on April 5, 1941, in Detroit, Michigan; parents divorced when he was eleven; attended Dartmouth College in Hanover, New Hampshire, and London Academy of Music and Dramatic Arts as a Fulbright Scholar; composes, plays jazz and classical piano; twice divorced; one son, Matthew.

Stone: English-Irish, Catholic; father, an alcoholic; grandmother, an Irish patriot; divorced, with one daughter.

THE REST OF THE STORY

Michael Moriarty once described Ben Stone as "a workaholic, a little obsessed with his job, but a crackerjack attorney.... Not a lot of flash, but I wouldn't want to face him in court. Not a lot of razzle-dazzle, but he could be deadly."

Five years later, in 1997, Moriarty was interviewed on Canadian television: "A great dramatic actor is a car accident and people watch it like a car accident and they say, 'I felt like that. Now there's the pain of life.'"

The obvious pain of Michael Moriarty's life seemingly has played itself out in public during the last few years. There is no simple, easy way to address his persona before, during, or after four splendid TV seasons on *Law & Order*. Even the people he worked with closely on the series have different perspectives.

"Moriarty would kick everybody out of the room and do his take to imaginary people because he didn't want to be distracted by the other actors. Everybody says Moriarty's nuts. I say he's not nuts; he's a f***ing egomaniac," insists Chris Noth.

"Michael is from Neptune," suggests Dann Florek. "I say that in a very loving way. He's insane; he's just insane. He's on a parallel reality."

While there certainly were strong hints of that parallel reality during Moriarty's time on *Law & Order*—most notably after he began to denounce U.S. Attorney General Janet Reno—nothing can compare to the changes that have overtaken the actor since he moved to Halifax, Nova Scotia, in late 1996. Moriarty, who declined to be interviewed for this book, has called the United States a fascist country and applied for Canadian citizenship.

The soft-spoken intensity that served Ben Stone so well in interrogating witnesses has now been eclipsed by a gruff, raspy churlishness, albeit still quite intense. Also, seemingly in reaction to Dick Wolf's 1994 remark to the contrary, Moriarty has gone into overdrive to prove he's every bit as sexy as Sam Waterston.

In early 1998, he told a reporter from the (Toronto) *Globe and Mail* that "I've never felt sexier or more alive than I am now. When I walk into a bar I can tell women are checking me out, women who don't even know who I am."

In a downtown Halifax bar, a local woman named Suzana Cabrita checked him out in the summer of 1996 and they have since announced plans to marry. He explains Cabrita's appeal in a January 1997 interview with Christine Nielsen on Canada's CTV network: "She's a natural woman," he says in a

Play it again, Mike? Michael Moriarty, who moved to Canada after quitting his role as EADA Ben Stone and announced plans to open a Halifax bar called Mike's Cafe Americain, à la Casablanca. *[courtesy of Photofest]*

growling imitation of street jargon. "She ain't no feminist.... I come home, she don't sit there and try to debate me."

When Nielsen wonders why he doesn't like women to debate him, Moriarty snaps back: "Well, that's a feminist response. I'm me.... You either love me as I am or let's end this, baby."

He ended his *Law & Order* tenure in a swirl of controversy and contentiousness. His own version of those events can only be gleaned from statements he's made to the media during the last four years and excerpts from his 1997 book, *The Gift of Stern Angels*, which is part diary, part memoir, and part rant. When series creator Dick Wolf invited him to attend a dinner meeting with U.S. Attorney General Janet Reno and assorted television executives, Moriarty asked if the soirée was "some kind of stupid photo op. You know, Attorney General meets Ben Stone and all that stuff. [Wolf] said, 'No, no, no. If she gets her way, shows like *Law & Order* could go off the air.' "

In referring to a discussion about violence on television that had taken place at the dinner, he writes in his book, "I honestly felt, in the

Ulysses S. Grant Suite of the Willard Hotel on November 18, 1993, that I was in the Soviet Union and talking to the KGB."

When CTV network correspondent Christine Nielsen suggested that Reno surely wasn't threatening him in particular, Moriarty demonstrated in his reply just how personally he took the exchange. "Listen, when she says *Murder, She Wrote* is a threat to America, you know *Law & Order*'s got to go with it. After the career I've had, what I've done, and my love of the art, to have a woman get in my face because she's attorney general and can threaten my job, that's tyranny."

In a May 1995 issue of *Variety*, he insisted that he had been blacklisted and that America was now a police state. "I blew my career, blew it right out of the water, by going up against her. She KGB," he tells Nielsen during their interview. Asked if he means America has turned into a Stalinist state, Moriarty asserts, "Increasingly so. Why do you think I'm living in Canada?"

Is he trying to be outrageous? "Well, you can patronize me," he says. "...If I wanted to be outrageous, I could do it other ways. I didn't have to lose my job over it."

He actually lost his job by resigning in January 1994. This action followed some troubling behavior at work while shooting Episode 79: "Breeder" about a week after meeting with Reno. "At the courthouse one day, he became manic," recalls sound mixer David Platt. "His wife was called to take him home. The writers quickly rewrote [Episode 83:] 'Mayhem' to give him time, in case he needed to get himself back together."

The director of this latter episode, Arthur Forney, says that "Michael was walking around, talking to himself. Then, in a courtroom scene, when he came up to question [the witness], he was laughing at every one of his own lines.... When he did that crazy take, you could hear mumbling in the courtroom and I think he knew something was wrong. I don't know if he was off his medications or what...but something clearly was wrong."

Forney tried to discuss the situation with Moriarty. "All of a sudden, I looked in Michael's eyes and it looked like no one was home," he remembers, adding that Moriarty's wife said "she had to take him to the doctor right away."

Moriarty explains things a bit differently in his book, *The Gift of Stern Angels.* "Dick Wolf said I had behaved crazily on the set and claimed *that* is why he felt obligated to talk to Sam Waterston and that it had *nothing* to do with my revealing the details of a meeting with Janet Reno about television censorship."

Insistent that the producers were trying to get rid of him for speaking out, Moriarty contends in his book that "unbeknownst to me they've cut me down to two scenes from the measly three they'd given me in [Episode 83:] 'Mayhem.' I put the script of that episode into my Reno file. Evidence."

Whatever the reality, this was not the first example of Moriarty's apparent psychological difficulties. He acknowledges that, as a graduate student at the age of twenty-two, he thought he saw God in Florence, Italy. "Friends of questionable worth and a meddling school administrator in 1964 escorted me to a car and drove me to a mental hospital just outside London. It was there I spent three months and endured not only heavy drug medication but the experience of ten electro-convulsive shock treatments," Moriarty explains in his memoir.

In 1972, he was hospitalized again after being fired from an off-Broadway play: "Being clapped back into a nuthouse, lied into it by my first wife [Françoise] after eight years of diligent effort to remain 'normal,' proved a simultaneously emboldening and terrifying experience," he writes, adding that he screamed himself into silence in a padded cell.

After resigning from *Law & Order*, Moriarty acknowledged that "I am at times...a functioning manic....If a role or debate or encounter is particularly stressful or challenging, I'm going to go into overdrive....I haven't been depressed in about ten years. I am certifiably *not* bi-polar nor manic-depressive, as it is commonly known. You can't have one without the other. So we're talking style here. Not insanity."

Whatever the case may be, Moriarty also began to drink heavily. "Am I an alcoholic? If I am, it's a recent development. I have spent my whole life afraid of the booze because my parents and sister were alcoholics. I don't care anymore. When you are waging a one-man war against the federal government, you need medication that *you* have chosen. Something not prescribed," he suggests in his memoir.

In the Canadian TV interview, Nielsen asks if he's "a hard-living guy?" Moriarty agrees in a gruff drawl: "Yes, ma'am. I'm a party dawg. I love bars. I love bars." Apparently so much so that, in August 1997, he was arrested in a drunken scuffle with Halifax police after an evening of boozing with Cabrita by his side. After snarling a racial epithet at a black cop, he spent the night in jail and emerged with an apology for the racist remark but was otherwise unrepentant. "I have no desire to stop drinking," he announced to the press.

On a CBC (Canadian Broadcasting Corporation) television program that aired in November 1997, in a voice that was softer but still on a stream-of-consciousness roller coaster, Moriarty announced to journalist Pamela Wallin his rather surreal *Casablanca*-in-Halifax plan to open a nightclub called Mike's Cafe Americain, where he'll hold court as a romantic exile and piano player.

This is a man obviously transformed since leaving *Law & Order*, but who was he before that? Dick Wolf urged him to play himself in playing Ben Stone. In July 1994, Moriarty told *Playboy* magazine, "He's me. We're the same." A 1990 story about *Law & Order* in the (Toronto) *Globe and Mail* described him as an actor who "carries an air of ascetic authority, tinged with a hint of vulnerability that informs all his performances with an irresistible tension."

Unfortunately for the many fans of the show's original prosecutor, Moriarty distances himself from the very notion of such a character. "I'm not the intellectual Ben Stone anymore. I have animal instincts now," he tells Wallin. On the pages of his book, Moriarty surmises: "I feel myself giving up Ben Stone. I feel his persona begin to die in me. It's sad, of course, but inevitable. He really was more of a character than I had imagined. I thought it was just me saying Ben's words but apparently not."

SELECTED CREDITS

FEATURE FILMS
My Old Man's Place (1972), *Hickey & Boggs* (1972), *The Last Detail* (1973), *Bang the Drum Slowly* (1973), *Report to the Commissioner* (1974), *Who'll Stop the Rain?* (1978), *Q: The Winged Serpent* (1982), *The Stuff* (1985, with Paul Sorvino), *Pale Rider* (1985), *Troll* (1986), *Return to Salem's Lot* (1987), *Hanoi Hilton* (1987), *The Secret of the Ice Cave* (1989), *Full Fathom Five* (1990), *Courage Under Fire* (1996), *Shiloh* (1997)

TELEVISION
REGULAR: *Law & Order* (1988, 1990–94) as "Executive Assistant District Attorney Ben Stone"
MOVIES: *The Glass Menagerie* (1973, for which he won an Emmy Award), *The Deadliest Season* (1977), *Holocaust* (1978, for which he won another Emmy Award), *Windmills of the Gods* (1980), *Tailspin: Behind the Korean Airline Tragedy* (1989), *A Good Day to Die* (1995), *Crime of the Century* (1996), *Calm at Sunset* (1996), *Major Crime* (1998)

Sam Waterston
Executive Assistant District Attorney Jack McCoy (1994–)

JUST THE FACTS

Waterston: Born on November 15, 1940, in Cambridge, Massachusetts; studied at the Sorbonne in Paris; graduated from Yale University; lives in

Connecticut; married to Lynn Waterston, a former model, since the 1970s; four children.

McCoy: Grew up in Midwest; father, a cop; attended University of Chicago and New York University Law School; divorced; has a daughter.

THE REST OF THE STORY

As a fellow workaholic, Jack McCoy occupies the demanding workplace that Ben Stone fled. "He loves his work, is absolutely convinced he's doing the right job and that the job is an honorable thing," Sam Waterston surmises. "It suits his personality down to the ground because he's aggressive, confrontational, and a little bit of a know-it-all."

However, the law is a harsh mistress for this TV character with a reputation for romancing his assistants. "McCoy doesn't admit the troubling aspects of his work to consciousness. So, every once in a while you'll see him having a drink, sort of as a way of burying it. But the last chapter in his life has not been written, so we don't know what the cost is. . . . [H]e's probably burying terrible things that will eat him one day."

Waterston agrees that the best *Law & Order* stories might be those that leave a viewer feeling punched in the stomach. "Yes, the ones I like are the ones where it's very hard to conclude what's right. . . . I played Prince Hal a long, long time ago and [*New York Times* critic] Walter Kerr said that the confrontation with Falstaff at the end of *Henry IV, Part Two* was for him the definition of a tragic situation."

The prince, in preparation for becoming king, feels compelled to humiliate Falstaff in public. "You saw the

Sam Waterston, looking casual as EADA Jack McCoy, the role he's inhabited since Season Five.

cold justice of it and the full humanity of it and you just couldn't digest it. Every once in a while, one of these shows does that. . . . You recognize it for truth and you can't stand it. And it's good. Your brain gets excited."

At other times, it is "just a merry chase show, full of narrative surprises," Waterston says, before acknowledging that "I've never liked watching myself, so I haven't seen all the episodes we've made. Once in a while I watch one and think, 'Huh. Not bad.' "

SELECTED CREDITS

FEATURE FILMS
Fitzwilly (1967), *Who Killed Mary What's 'Er Name?* (1971), *Savages* (1972), *The Great Gatsby* (1974), *Rancho Deluxe* (1975), *Interiors* (1978), *Capricorn One* (1978), *Hopscotch* (1980), *Heaven's Gate* (1981), *The Killing Fields* (1984), *Hannah and Her Sisters* (1986), *September* (1988), *Crimes and Misdemeanors* (1989, with Jerry Orbach), *Mindwalk* (1990), *The Man in the Moon* (1991), *Serial Mom* (1994), *The Journey of August King* (1995), *The Shadow Conspiracy* (1996), *The Proprietor* (1996)

TELEVISION
REGULAR: *I'll Fly Away* (1991–93) as "Forrest Bedford," *Law & Order* (1994–) as "Executive Assistant District Attorney Jack McCoy"
MOVIES: *The Glass Menagerie* (1973, with Michael Moriarty), *Oppenheimer* (1978), *Friendly Fire* (1979), *Gore Vidal's Lincoln* (1988), *Lantern Hill* (1990), *The Enemy Within* (1994), *Assault at West Point: The Court-Martial of Johnson Whittaker* (1994), *Miracle at Midnight* (1998)

THE RECURRING REGULARS

John Fiore
Det. Anthony Profaci (1988, 1990–)

JUST THE FACTS

Fiore: Born in Somerville, Massachusetts; graduated from Suffolk University, Boston; lives in Stoneham with his wife and two children.

Profaci: "Profaci? At this point, he's me. I think we're all who we are, at this point on the show. Like a lot of cops I know, he's got a wife and two kids, like I do. He's got a modest house, like I do. He likes to have a few drinks on Friday night. He coaches Little League; soccer on Saturday morning. He loves hockey. He's just a regular guy," Fiore says.

THE REST OF THE STORY

"I don't have a contract. I've never been signed. I pretty much knew it was going to be a sporadic kind of thing. But, when I'm not here, they mention the character's name a lot," says John Fiore, evidently proud that Profaci just seems to roll off the tongue.

"Having the name Profaci has been a big help to keep an ear on," he suggests. "It's so much fun for people to say. Going back to the pilot, I auditioned and Profaci was a relatively small role but, after the lead guys, a steady detective. I would not be here for several weeks and when I'd come back people would say, 'All they talk about is Profaci.' Because it was a fun name to say. It wouldn't work if my name was, like, Jones or whatever.

"....[The cast] would be joking, 'Where's Profaci?' And I wouldn't even be here. Even now when I'm not in the show, the characters mention Profaci. 'That was Profaci. He just called.' People say to me, 'Wow! Your aura.' That's stretching it. I'm almost a *Trivial Pursuit* kind of character."

John Fiore, whose beloved Det. Tony Profaci has been a Law & Order *recurring regular since the 1988 pilot.* [courtesy of the Henderson/Hogan Agency]

From a blue-collar background, Fiore says that "sometimes I consider myself an unlikely actor. It's funny. I have a degree in criminal justice. I started acting at twenty-six; I didn't think it was a manly thing to do. A guidance counselor told me I didn't have the necessary three credits for my speech requirement and said, 'Try acting.' I liked it."

Certain life experiences prepared him for *Law & Order.* "I worked as a district court officer while still in college. It was so boring. And I knew a lot of cops from playing hockey a couple of nights a week."

(Before joining *Law & Order*, Fiore had appeared on such daytime dramas as *All My Children* and *The Guiding Light*, and such TV series as *N.Y.P.D. Blue*. He was in the feature film *Mystic Pizza* [1988]. Later in his acting career he would be in the John Travolta movie *White Man's Burden* [1995].)

In the first season, Fiore appeared in nine or ten episodes. "I did some juicy, insulting little things with Logan. Seems like with Logan, I had more of a rapport [than with the current detectives in the cast]."

Jokes were centered on Profaci's waistline for a while. "I've gained weight on the show. The first year I was really lean. Then I got really heavy. And now I'm kind of like in between. I had a period where I chunked up pretty good there. So people were saying, 'Wow! That's Profaci?' As I started to put on a few, they started writing it into the scripts. It was kind of fun to do in a way," Fiore explains.

"They've been real good to me here," he says. "My fantasy always was to get signed. Short of being signed, it's been good."

Carolyn McCormick
Dr. Elizabeth Olivet (1991–97)

JUST THE FACTS

McCormick: Attended Williams College in Massachusetts, the American Conservatory Theatre, and the Centre d'Etudes Français in France; worked as television news broadcaster in Houston, Texas; married to Byron Jennings, once a guest actor on the show.

Olivet: "She has a basic goodness, a really strong sense of right and wrong. I don't think she plays games. You need to believe she is operating from an altruistic place. She was a beacon of hope there, and a nice energy among all those lawyers."

THE REST OF THE STORY

She was something of a pioneer. "There were all men and I think the network was pushing for them to add a female of some sort in the second season," recalls Carolyn McCormick about her *Law & Order* debut as the only woman, a psychiatrist, among so many male cops and attorneys. "But it was always hard to incorporate much for her because the format of the show is so strong on the police and the law side."

And who was this intruder in their midst? "Early on I remember saying, 'Don't get teary-eyed.' Your first impulse might be to get a little schmaltzy.

She should be thought of as a very good therapist, so you don't know what her personal take is. That's irrelevant," McCormick says.

Then again, asked about the personal dimensions of these characters, McCormick believes that "if there was going to be a liaison, it would be with Ben Stone, not Logan. Michael, I thought he was fabulous, one of the best things on the show. Olivet and Stone had a very interesting thing going on.... There was definitely some sexual tension between those two. He left the show right when it might have started going in that direction."

Olivet's relationship with McCoy, on the other hand, shows less of a rapport. "That was more Sam's doing than mine. His take on McCoy has always been very much to not be a soft, sweet, kind of sensitive guy like Michael Moriarty was.... The vibes he would

Carolyn McCormick, who stuck with Law & Order until Season Eight as the show's police psychiatrist, Dr. Elizabeth Olivet.

send out were not at all like you would get from Stone, who was more intimate. McCoy is rougher and gruffer, so there really wasn't any way to break through that."

Even that much speculation about romance goes against the grain of *Law & Order*'s original premise. "When the show first started, Dick Wolf and Joe Stern really supported the idea that these people are only seen on their professional side, not their personal side. It's nice to let TV viewers imagine again, instead of mapping it all out. That's one of my favorite things about the show: when people are forced to kind of wonder and speculate. It's nice when you have to fill in the blanks. It keeps you guessing. I love not having it spelled out for me."

For the first three seasons (1990–93), "Joe Stern worked really hard to always incorporate me in the episodes," McCormick remembers.

"Under Ed Sherin's domain, there were women [S. Epatha Merkerson and Jill Hennessy], so I was used less and less. They give them the sensitive, delicate things that Olivet used to do. When all the men left, my character's heart was sort of taken away. It was sad for me because I felt the character had so much more to [accomplish]. They never watered the flower."

McCormick made a difficult decision. "It just became psychobabble more and more; it became less profound and complex to me. That's why I went off and did another show. I wouldn't have left *Law & Order* ever but it wasn't enough work for me."

In addition to doing commercials for a product that helps people quit smoking, McCormick began playing the wife of a troubled psychologist on ABC's American version of the British series *Cracker*.

How does she feel about the *Law & Order* shrink who replaced her, Emil Skoda? "He's clearly very gruff. He's not a sensitive Olivet. But I was happy they didn't get a Carolyn McCormick clone. I was glad they didn't get a woman."

J. K. Simmons
Dr. Emil Skoda (1997–)

JUST THE FACTS

Simmons: Born on January 9, 1955; degree in music from the University of Montana; started out as a singer; lived in Seattle, Washington, for several years doing regional theater; moved to New York City in 1983; did a string of Broadway and off-Broadway shows.

Skoda: "I decided I'd gone through a divorce and had kids. In Episode 166: "Burned," we find there's a reference to my kid. So far, we're in happy synchronicity about who we think this guy is."

THE REST OF THE STORY

What does J. K. stand for? "Just kidding," jokes J. K. Simmons, whose wonderfully rubbery face and dimpled smile have made Emil Skoda an interesting replacement for Elizabeth Olivet. "Actually, Jonathan Kimble."

Simmons once did a small part on *Law & Order*, as the TV cameraman who filmed a riot in 1994's Episode 85: "Sanctuary," and then reappeared for the first *Homicide* crossover. "I was the Nazi murdering bastard," he says.

He is glad that "they were willing to bring me back in a different role, which was good for me because the Nazi murderer died, so it's not like he could have come back.... I also did an HBO show called *Oz*, a prison drama that shoots in New York. I'm the head of the Aryan brotherhood in the joint. My mother doesn't understand that at all, how I could play such evil guys."

Simmons's quick wit becomes evident when asked how they decided to cast him as Skoda. "I don't know. Maybe somebody suggested, 'Call the Nazi murdering bastard.'"

He was drawn to the show because "the caliber of the writing is well above average. There's a lot going on in the dark side of this guy."

J. K. Simmons, who started out in Season Eight as Law & Order's *new police shrink, Dr. Emil Skoda.* [courtesy of the Gersh Agency]

Simmons is not concerned that his predecessor disappeared so suddenly. "There hasn't been an explanation in the script at all [for Dr. Olivet leaving]. The show is so plot-driven. Perhaps they don't feel the need to explain.... That's one of the things that makes this show interesting and different and the writing so intelligent."

He's counting his lucky stars. "Thus far, I've been fortunate not to be too typecast," Simmons says. "It's great to be playing a twisted, murdering psycho on one show and a psychiatrist on another."

CHAPTER 20

THE EPISODES

*Injustice is relatively easy to bear; what
stings is justice.*

—HENRY LOUIS MENCKEN
Prejudices, Third Series (1922)

Season One
September 1990–April 1991
60-minute episodes

Production Team:

Dick Wolf (Executive Producer), Joseph Stern (Co-Executive Producer), Robert Palm (Producer), Daniel Sackheim (Producer), Jeffrey Hayes (Co-Producer), Judith Stevens (Co-Producer), Michael Duggan (Supervising Producer), David Black (Supervising Producer), Arthur W. Forney (Associate Producer), Anthony Mazzei (Associate Producer), Robert Nathan (Executive Story Editor), Ed Zuckerman (Executive Story Editor), Lewis H. Gould (Unit Production Manager), Richard Bianchi (Production Designer), Mike Post (Music), Lynn Kressel (Casting), Suzanne Ryan (Casting), Phil Oetiker (Camera Operator), Drake Silliman (Editor), Mark Newman (Editor), Scott Vickery (Editor), Michael Kewley (Editor), Mike Struk (Technical Advisor), Bill Fordes (Technical Advisor)

**Production Team for Episode 6: "Everybody's Favorite Bagman"
(Original Pilot Episode, 1988):**

Dick Wolf (Executive Producer), James McAdams (Co-Executive Producer), Joseph Stern (Producer), Daniel Sackheim (Co-Producer), Peter Runfolo (Coordinating Producer), Diane Foti (Unit Production Manager), Mike Post (Music), Darlene Kaplan C.S.A. (Casting), Lynn Kressel (Casting), Alec Hirschfeld (Camera Operator), Douglas Ibold (Editor), Mark Newman (Editor)

Regular Cast:

Richard Brooks (Assistant District Attorney Paul Robinette), George Dzundza (Sgt. Max Greevey), Dann Florek (Capt. Donald Cragen), Steven Hill (District Attorney Adam Schiff, except in Episode 6: "Everybody's Favorite Bagman"), Michael Moriarty (Executive Assistant District Attorney Ben Stone), Chris Noth (Det. Mike Logan), Roy Thinnes (District Attorney Alfred Wentworth in Episode 6: "Everybody's Favorite Bagman")

Season One Overview

From the start, *Law & Order* would be partly defined and shaped by the adversity in its dramas. The NBC show first previewed on Thursday, September 13, 1990, at 10:00 P.M. with Episode 1: "Prescription for Death" about a prominent surgeon charged with murder after a young woman dies in his hospital emergency room.

With that, *Law & Order* announced to television audiences that no cows would be sacred. The show tackled all the hot-button topics: child abuse (Episode 9: "Indifference"), abortion rights (Episode 12: "Life Choice"), racism (Episode 11: "Out of the Half-Light"), AIDS (Episode 3: "The Reaper's Helper"), vigilante justice (Episode 2: "Subterranean Homeboy Blues"), rape (Episode 14: "The Violence of Summer"), police corruption (Episode 8: "Poison Ivy"), and underworld crime (Episodes 15 and 16: "The Torrents of Greed–Parts One and Two"). Yet it did not exploit these issues for the melodramatic power they might have over an audience. Instead, the series trusted the viewer's ability to grapple with the legal, social, and political issues that color the American landscape.

A minimalist approach, allowing characters to focus strictly on their reactions to the crime, provided *Law & Order* with documentary-style realism. The use of a handheld camera further heightened the immediacy. In the best episodes of Season One, not a scene was wasted on superfluous detail.

Law & Order was broadcast on Thursday nights for the first four episodes, from September 13 to October 11, 1990, when NBC gave the show a regular Tuesday slot. At the time, Warren Littlefield, president of NBC Entertainment, issued a press release that praised Dick Wolf for delivering an "intelligent, provocative drama that not only NBC, but more importantly, the audience has embraced."

A sign of good times ahead? The answer must be yes and no. Season One was both brilliant and inconsistent. Stylistically, the show was still trying to find its own groove, but the adversity expressed so eloquently in the stories was also felt on the set. (See chapter 1: The Momentum.)

Despite the inner-sanctum turmoil, Littlefield was right about the TV audience. According to NBC research analysis based on the Nielsen Television Index, *Law & Order* won its time period against competition on all networks during the two weeks of previews (with an average 13.6 rating and 24 share). Two weeks into the new Tuesday night time slot, *Law & Order* became the second-highest rated new series of the season on any network.

Episode Descriptions

Episode 1: Prescription for Death
Original air date: September 13, 1990
Teleplay by Ed Zuckerman, story by Ed Zuckerman and David Black, directed by John P. Whitesell II, cinematography by Ernest Dickerson

Additional Cast and Guest Stars: Paul Sparer (Dr. Edward Auster), John Spencer (Mr. Morton), Ron Rifkin (Philip Nivens), Erick Avari (Dr. Raza), Maryann Urbano (Nurse Mills), William Roderick (Dr. Abraham), Bruce McCarty (Dr. Simonson), Leslie Goldman (Judge)

Reviewing the Case: When Greevey and Logan investigate the hospital emergency room death of a young woman in cardiac arrest, the alcoholic chief of medicine, Dr. Edward Auster, is charged with malpractice. This episode is a powerful debut that effectively condemns the arrogance of the medical profession, by examining the hierarchy that protects the suspect. The segment depicts how the prestige of an arrogant man's career can override concerns for those who rely on his care. "Prescription for Death" is a classic study of how hospital bureaucracy can protect a killer in a white coat.

Noteworthy Discoveries: It is revealed that Greevey and Captain Cragen used to be partners, and that Cragen was once an alcoholic. Also, Ben Stone mentions that his father was a heavy drinker (in a curious parallel with Michael Moriarty's own life).

Relevant Testimony: ED ZUCKERMAN (writer): "A young woman named Libby Zion, whose father was a prominent journalist, Sidney Zion, died in a New York hospital ten years ago, give or take. There was no drunk doctor involved, but she wasn't watched properly and there was some level of incompetence apparently. [Series creator] Dick Wolf and [head writer] David Black wanted to go after the smug, superior attitude that doctors of a certain ilk have."

Episode 2: Subterranean Homeboy Blues
Original air date: September 20, 1990
Teleplay by Robert Palm, directed by E. W. Swackhamer, cinematography by Ernest Dickerson

Additional Cast and Guest Stars: Cynthia Nixon (Laura Di Biasi), Sam Gray (Judge Manuel Leon), Akili Prince (Darnell Chanault), Lorraine Toussaint (Shambala Green), Dwayne McClary (Michael Jones), Phyllis Somerville (Nurse)

Reviewing the Case: Two young black men are shot in a subway car and the clues lead Greevey and Logan to Laura Di Biasi, a white woman. This episode features one of the longest (and most precisely edited) opening scenes of any to date on *Law & Order*. A train zipping through tunnels is intercut with shots of Di Biasi nervously moving through the cars until the train stops and clears, and the camera reveals the teenagers bleeding on the floor. However, apart from Cynthia Nixon's steady performance, the story line (which uses the infamous Bernard Goetz vigilante shooting as a starting point), is marred by a lot of shouting. The cops and the DAs are so busy screaming at each other, we wonder how they ever manage to work together. Ernest Dickerson's cinematography, which adds graphic vitality to the subway scenes, is overwhelmed by "fog" in the courtroom, as if the trial were being held in a smoke-filled pub.

Noteworthy Discoveries: The talented Lorraine Toussaint is introduced as attorney Shambala Green. She becomes one of Ben Stone's greatest legal rivals, and their future debates are both philosophically exciting and sexually charged.

Relevant Testimony: ROBERT PALM (writer): "Dick [Wolf] said that we should make Bernard Goetz a woman. And he helped me realize that I could change the whole nature of the story by changing the gender of the character. We were right in the middle of a period when a look of unwanted attention could lead to a woman defending herself. So it's more surprising when she turns out to be gunning for those guys. It left more room to create twists in the story."

Episode 3: The Reaper's Helper

Original air date: October 4, 1990
Teleplay by Thomas Francis McElroy, David Black, and Robert Nathan,
story by Thomas Francis McElroy, directed by Vern Gillum, cinematography by Constantine Makris

Additional Cast and Guest Stars: Peter Frechette (Jack Curry), Tom Signorelli (Anthony Holland), Barbara Andres (Mrs. Holland), Jesse Corti (Angel Suarez), Charlotte Moore (Julia Debakee), Steven Gilborn (Trial Judge), Suzanne Shepherd (Arraignment Judge), John Fiore (Det. Anthony Profaci)

Reviewing the Case: Bobby Holland is found dead in his apartment after what appears to be a robbery, but Greevey and Logan trace the crime to Jack Curry, who assists in the suicides of men with AIDS. This episode proves to be one of the best of the season, and demonstrates the show's capacity to delve into controversial social and political topics with unflinching courage. While giving a sense of the anguish felt when someone is diagnosed with AIDS, the story also tackles the issue of mercy killing and Ben Stone's potential for self-righteous devotion to the law. Rather than see the crime as a gay/straight issue, he insists that failure to prosecute would indicate pity for homosexuals, which Stone believes is akin to ridicule. "The Reaper's Helper" refuses to tie all of the problems up into a neat package.

Noteworthy Discoveries: This is the first time Dick Wolf experienced advertisers pulling their ad messages from the show because of an episode's content. Constantine Makris, who later in the season became the regular *Law & Order* cinematographer, makes his debut as director of photography on this episode. John Fiore appears for the first time as Detective Profaci (other than his brief cameo in the pilot segment, "Everybody's Favorite Bagman," which was aired as Episode 6).

Relevant Testimony: ROBERT NATHAN (writer): "We wanted to give Stone the moral dilemma of whether or not he was prosecuting this case for the right reasons, and David [Black] came up with the idea of the defense attorney being tipped with the information that gets her defendant off. . . . We gave it a nice O. Henry ending."

Episode 4: Kiss the Girls and Make Them Die

Original air date: October 11, 1990
Teleplay by Robert Nathan, story by Dick Wolf, directed by Charles Correll, cinematography by Ernest Dickerson

Additional Cast and Guest Stars: Dennis Boutsikaris (Ed Berkley), Marita Geraghty (Rebecca Bourne), Thomas Calabro (Ned Loomis), Priscilla

Lopez (Packard), Rochelle Oliver (Judge Grace Larkin), Jack Ryland (Arraignment Judge), Nandrea Lin-Courts (Elise Brody), Baxter Harris (Mr. Bartlett), Matthew Penn (Mr. Brody), Sarah Fleming (Libby), Troy Ruptash (Steve Feinstein)

Reviewing the Case: When Paige Bartlett, a wealthy young woman, is found almost beaten to death in her apartment, the chief suspect is gigolo Ned Loomis. This segment, with its faint resemblance to the 1988 Central Park murder trial of Robert Chambers, explores the legal problems that can occur in the effort to convict a well-to-do killer. It's also a solid examination of the contemporary psychopath, one with the dashing looks and charm of a Ted Bundy. Unable to put Elise Brody, a woman attacked by Loomis years earlier, on the stand, Stone must find a way to make her testimony admissible without violating the integrity of the criminal justice system. His choice helps him win the case, but the victory is bittersweet. Moriarty beautifully conveys Stone's anguish when he realizes that justice for Loomis won't bring a dead woman's grieving parents another child.

Noteworthy Discoveries: Matthew Penn, who plays Elise Brody's husband, would later return to direct Episode 107: "Cruel And Unusual."

Episode 5: Happily Ever After
Original air date: October 23, 1990
Teleplay by David Black and Robert Nathan, story by Dick Wolf and David Black, directed by Vern Gillum, cinematography by Constantine Makris

Additional Cast and Guest Stars: Roxanne Hart (Janet Ralston), Bob Gunton (Gil Himes), Meg Mundy (Helen Ralston), Philip Bosco (Mr. Schell), Kelly Neal (Willie Tidman), Barton Heyman (Norris), Doris Belack (Arraignment Judge), Steve Gilborn (Judge Marton)

Reviewing the Case: When Alan and Janet Ralston are shot in their underground parking garage, police believe the suspect to be an African-American drug addict until they find out that the crime was instigated by one of the victims. This is not a particularly memorable *Law & Order* episode. Roxanne Hart (former cast member of the TV series *Chicago Hope*, 1994–96) continually hints that her character is the likely suspect, and the story seemingly can't avoid its lapses into melodrama. When Stone assures her that she should fear him, it's reminiscent of those creaky *Perry Mason* (1957–66) shows in which witnesses were intimidated and made to weep. The best work here is provided by Philip Bosco as the defense attorney, Schell, who proves to be a wily fox. Kelly Neal's crack addict also has some reverberating moments, but "Happily Ever After" is happily ever over and forgotten.

Relevant Testimony: ROBERT NATHAN (writer): "That show has in it a sequence that runs over six or seven minutes that is literally one plea bargain scene backed up against the other. Now, nobody had ever seen that on television before because no one had ever seen plea bargaining as an element of the criminal justice system. We never did a six-minute plea bargain scene again. It was a one-time event of the kind we had to come up with every few weeks to keep the show interesting."

Episode 6: Everybody's Favorite Bagman
[Original pilot for the series, filmed in 1988]
Original air date: October 30, 1990
Teleplay by Dick Wolf, directed by John Patterson, cinematography by Geoffrey Erb

Additional Cast and Guest Stars: Roy Thinnes (District Attorney Alfred Wentworth), Trey Wilson (Eddie Cosmatos), Paul Guilfoyle (Tony Scalisi), Dick Latessa (Mr. Wilson), Ron Foster (Jefferson), Marcia Jean Kurtz (Alice Halsey), William H. Macy (John McCormack), John Fiore (Det. Anthony Profaci)

Reviewing the Case: When Councilman Charles Halsey is found beaten in his car in East Harlem, police discover that he's part of a criminal conspiracy at the highest level of city government. This was the pilot episode made for CBS in 1988 but never aired at the time. It became part of the package of six episodes that Dick Wolf gave NBC two years later. This installment serves as a map for the ambitions of the show but it hardly succeeds at carrying out many of those ambitions. Some scenes are forced (an interrogation sequence featuring Greevey and Logan, the latter slapping a suspect) and some are weird

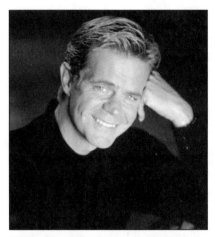

William H. Macy, the Oscar-nominated star of Fargo *who appeared in* Law & Order's *1988 pilot (Episode 6: "Everybody's Favorite Bagman"), and again in Episode 39: "Sisters of Mercy" (Season Two).* [photo by Robert Ferrone/courtesy of Baker * Winokur * Ryder Public Relations]

(Logan slamming the same suspect with a garbage can lid to detain him).
Yet others are underdeveloped (Robinette's disillusionment with his corrupt mentor, Jefferson, is merely a sketch). The episode has the virtue of
firmly establishing the characters so that we know who they are and what
they stand for.

Noteworthy Discoveries: A disclaimer at the end of this episode reveals
that it was inspired by a corruption scandal involving the New York City
Parking Violations Bureau. In this outing Max Greevey is still a detective,
not yet a sergeant. The Masucci Family, mentioned in passing in this
episode, will appear in full force later this season in the two-part segment, Episodes 15 and 16: "The Torrents of Greed."

Relevant Testimony: RICHARD BROOKS (actor): "There we were in '88, as
Jesse Jackson was running for president. It was a time when African-
American men were trying to work within the system. I was a little disturbed, of course, to be tearing down my hero [on the show] but, at the
same time, it really reinforced Robinette's mission to be the good man."

Episode 7: By Hooker, By Crook
Original air date: November 13, 1990
Teleplay by David Black, directed by Martin Davidson, cinematography
by Ernest Dickerson

Additional Cast and Guest Stars: Patricia Clarkson (Laura Winthrop),
Jenny Robertson (Joline), Bernie Barrow (Folger), Kelly Kerr (Jasmine),
Byron Utley (Cookie Molina), Courtney B. Vance (McKee), Patricia
Barry (Mrs. Stringfellow), Brian Smiar (Judge Harcourt), Leslie
Goldman (Trial Judge)

Reviewing the Case: A man named Diamond, found beaten in Central
Park, is tied to a prostitution service run by the wealthy Laura Winthrop.
Loosely based on the Mayflower Madam case involving Sydney Biddle
Barrows, this episode is an effective tale about a blue-blooded woman
who exploits economically disadvantaged girls. Clarkson's role isn't large
enough for her to indicate why Laura Winthrop finds fulfillment running an escort service, but she is otherwise well cast for the part. As
Joline, Jenny Robertson gives a much fuller portrait by suggesting the
blasted life of someone who finds out she has AIDS.

Noteworthy Discoveries: Dick Wolf was forced by network executives to
make three footage cuts in this episode for strong language. The shot of
the courthouse steps under the opening credits of every installment is
taken from the sequence seen near the end of "By Hooker, By Crook."

Episode 8: Poison Ivy

Original air date: November 20, 1990

Teleplay by Jacob Brackman, story by Jack Richardson and Jacob Brackman, directed by E. W. Swackhamer, cinematography by Constantine Makris

Additional Cast and Guest Stars: John Finn (Fredo Parisi), Al Freeman, Jr. (Reverend Thayer), Erika Alexander (Doris Carver), Jack Gwaltney (Davis), Erik King (Silky Ford), Saundra McClain (Mrs. Richardson), Richard Habersham (Abel), Josh Pais (Medical Examiner), Lawrence Weber (Judge Sirkin), John Fiore (Det. Anthony Profaci)

Reviewing the Case: Fredo Parisi, a veteran police officer, shoots and kills an African-American drug dealer who has attended Princeton University. Although the cop then is suspected of corruption, the prosecutors hesitate to go after a veteran like Parisi. If they do, the police brotherhood will be up in arms; if they don't, the black community will be outraged. "Poison Ivy" is an intricate and ingenious episode with great insight into issues of police corruption and racism.

Noteworthy Discoveries: In addition to its other virtues, this episode is also the first one to illustrate how the police can gather evidence through scientific means, such as ballistics.

Relevant Testimony: GEORGE DZUNDZA (actor): "If Americans had the opportunity to spend a week and a half riding around with the police department, nobody would ever leave their house. Most of us take that job for granted or don't understand what it takes to do it. . . . We walk through life with blinders on and then we turn on the television and say, 'Oh, my God, isn't that horrible! Let's do something about it. That should never be.'"

Episode 9: Indifference

Original air date: November 27, 1990

Teleplay by Robert Palm, directed by James Quinn, cinematography by Constantine Makris

Additional Cast and Guest Stars: Marcia Jean Kurtz (Carla Lowenstein), David Groh (Dr. Jacob Lowenstein), John Seitz (Dr. Babcock), Lorraine Toussaint (Shambala Green), Louis Zorich (Trial Judge), Brian Smiar (Arraignment Judge), Blanca Camacho (Ms. Perez), Gordon Joseph Weiss (Rudy Scelza), Sarah Rowland Doroff (Didi Lowenstein)

Reviewing the Case: Didi Lowenstein is a six-year-old beaten by her mother, Carla, who in turn is regularly abused by her husband, Dr. Jacob

Lowenstein. This installment offers a disturbing examination of child abuse and a searing psychological portrait of family dysfunction. Marcia Jean Kurtz's electrifying characterization takes us inside the psyche of a victim who is simultaneously a victimizer. David Groh, as her husband, gives as creepy a performance as can be seen on television in his portrayal of the very embodiment of pure evil. The segment is a powerful indictment of the system's failure to protect defenseless children. When Logan confronts a Juvenile Services worker about not investigating the case quickly, she scrolls down a long, computerized waiting list of children at risk. "Indifference" is an aptly titled story that makes us feel anything but indifferent.

Relevant Testimony: ROBERT PALM (writer): "This wasn't loosely drawn on the [Joel] Steinberg case. It *was* the Steinberg case, much to the consternation of the lawyers at Universal....I remember being on the set at midnight one Friday and, when the actress [Marcia Jean Kurtz] who played [the counterpart of the other parent, the real-life] Hedda Nussbaum came out, I almost had a heart attack. They had cast a woman who looked exactly like her. I thought this was Joe Stern's perverse way of sticking it to the studio: 'You can put your disclaimer on the episode, but we're going to cast an actress who looks just like Hedda Nussbaum.'"

Episode 10: Prisoner of Love

Original air date: December 4, 1990
Teleplay by Robert Nathan, story by David Black and Robert Nathan, directed by Michael Fresco, cinematography by Ernest Dickerson

Additional Cast and Guest Stars: Frances Conroy (Elizabeth Hendrick), Larry Keith (Henry Rothman), Amy Aquino (Stohlmeyer), Ted Marcoux (Brian), Sidney Armus (Judge Fadenhecht), Wayne Maugans (Gary), Jay Patterson (Hoexter), Fran Brill (Sondra), Sam Schacht (Hurley)

Reviewing the Case: The police find artist Victor Moore hanging in a studio. A city councilman is charged with killing him as part of a sadomasochistic sex ritual. Thus, this episode challenges the viewer's perceptions about the kinds of people who might be attracted to "deviant" sexual practices, and what the definition of "deviant" sex should be. At the center of this dilemma is Sergeant Greevey, anxious to be taken off the case because he's a Catholic who believes in the concept of sin. Frances Conroy is enigmatic as Elizabeth Hendrick, who fuses both art and sex in the way she walks. When Stone finds her "hope chest" full of whips and chains, his voice sounds both alarmed and enticed when he wonders just what she was hoping for.

Episode 11: Out of the Half-Light
Original air date: December 11, 1990
Teleplay by Michael Duggan, directed by E. W. Swackhamer, cinematography by Constantine Makris

Additional Cast and Guest Stars: J. A. Preston (Congressman Eaton), Billie Neal (Angela Wilkes), Frankie R. Faison (Lester Crawford), Sandra Reaves-Phillips (Mrs. Crawford), Novella Nelson (Judge Crutcher), Kisha Miller (Astrea Crawford), John Fiore (Det. Anthony Profaci)

Reviewing the Case: Greevey and Logan investigate Astrea Crawford's claim that she was raped by Caucasian policemen. The black teenager's cause is touted by a publicity-hungry politician, Congressman Eaton, who pushes Stone and Robinette to prosecute so he can expose the racism of the system. Based on the Tawana Brawley case, this segment is an incendiary look at the way political agendas can circumvent the law when it comes to racial matters. Yet the plot line isn't quite as powerful as the concerns it raises, since the story is a bit strained, and the actors tend to give speeches rather than speak lines of dialogue. Nonetheless, they do give those lines some passion (J. A. Preston is particularly smooth). Richard Brooks furnishes his most dynamic performance thus far, especially when meeting with Eaton in the Chelsea District's trendy Empire Diner.

Noteworthy Discoveries: When Stone asks Robinette to decide whether he's a black man who is a lawyer or a lawyer who happens to be black, the question won't be answered until Robinette makes a guest appearance as a defense attorney in Episode 125: "Custody."

Relevant Testimony: RICHARD BROOKS (actor): "A black man who's a lawyer, or a lawyer who's a black man? I love that question. Of course, that question is probably one of the major dilemmas of being black in America, especially with Robinette being in the system and generally having to prosecute a lot of people like himself. But I've been faced with that question before, even in acting school: Was I an actor first who happened to be black, or was I a black man who happened to be an actor? I always thought being black was a given; it's not something I really have to work at. So do the job well and be a good actor."

Episode 12: Life Choice
Original air date: January 8, 1991
Teleplay by David Black and Robert Nathan, story by Dick Wolf, directed by Aaron Lipstadt, cinematography by Constantine Makris

Additional Cast and Guest Stars: Caroline Kava (Rose Schwimmer), Paul Hecht (Ballard), Clark Gregg (Patrick), Jaime Tirelli (Olivera), Bridgit Ryan (Celeste McClure), Kevin O'Rourke (Mary's Brother), Laurie Kennedy (Barbara), Sully Boyar (Arraignment Judge), Melinda Mullins (Patrol Cop)

Reviewing the Case: When an abortion clinic is bombed by a woman who is killed in the process, the evidence leads to a pro-life group led by Rose Schwimmer, a zealot who finds a partial ally in Greevey. Adam Schiff asks Stone and Robinette if they've noticed that they are three men trying to decide the right a woman has over her own body. That moment provides the ultimate irony of this very strong episode, which considers the pro-life movement critically, without demonizing its leaders or its followers. Instead, it asks the audience to think about what makes abortion such a volatile issue, while building that volatility into the drama itself. This episode refrains from a neat resolution, laying the moral choices squarely in the laps of its viewers.

Noteworthy Discoveries: As with Episode 3: "The Reaper's Helper," some advertising was pulled because of this episode's very controversial subject matter. Greevey's Catholic beliefs clash here with the more liberal views of Cragen and Logan, as they did in Episode 10: "Prisoner of Love." It is also discovered that Stone is Catholic as well.

Relevant Testimony: DAVID BLACK (writer): "I identify myself as a liberal but probably would fully characterize myself as an eighteenth-century classic enlightened individual. To me, it's better drama if you present both sides of the case equally strong; you get that collision of realities. And there was some pressure from the network to downpedal the pro-life side.... I was in the process of becoming pro-life. So I really put my heart into presenting the pro-life case. I was exploring my beliefs as I wrote it."

Episode 13: A Death in the Family
Original air date: January 15, 1991
Teleplay by Joe Viola and David Black, story by Joe Viola, directed by Gwen Arner, cinematography by Ernest Dickerson

Additional Cast and Guest Stars: Wendy Makkena (Sandoval), David Margulies (Simpson), Louis Guss (Yost), Nan-Lynn Nelson (Cassie), Jerome Preston Bates (Brutus Walker), John Fiore (Det. Anthony Profaci)

Reviewing the Case: Greevey and Logan search for the killer of a police officer. Stone and Robinette discover that the circumstances of his death might be known only to the man's partner, Sandoval. The episode examines a familiar theme: the cost of loyalty between cops when one is corrupt and the other is compelled to remain silent. It's also about the way a sudden death on the police force reminds them all how mortal they really are, as we see how different people handle that fear. Profaci wants vengeance, Logan is haunted by the sound of the zipper on the body bag, Sandoval isn't talking, and Greevey smells something fishy. While it concerns corruption, what lingers most from this story is the scent of death and the cost of never knowing when or where it will come.

Noteworthy Discoveries: Logan inadvertently learns that Greevey once lost a partner in the line of duty.

Relevant Testimony: CHRIS NOTH (actor): "The one thing a New York cop had was a certain deadness in the eyes that sometimes I tried to experience. Dealing with the kind of crime, homicide, rape—especially in the early '90s with the crack epidemic—New York was a terrible place. It just does something to you, and in a way you become detached while still watching. You see the most intensely gruesome scene and treat it as if it was just a spilled cup of milk....Ultimately, it's probably a survival technique."

Episode 14: The Violence of Summer

Original air date: February 5, 1991
Teleplay by Michael Duggan, directed by Don Scardino, cinematography by Constantine Makris

Additional Cast and Guest Stars: Megan Gallagher (Monica De Vries), Samuel L. Jackson (Louis Taggart), Randy Danson (Diana Manso), Sandy Baron (Mike Lucia), Ken Johnston (Ryan Cutrona), Philip Hoffman (Hanauer), Gil Bellows (Metzler), Al Shannon (Tim Pruiting), Mike Hodge (Judge)

Reviewing the Case: Greevey and Logan reopen an investigation into the gang rape of a TV reporter and build a stronger case against the person accused of assaulting her, after one of the suspects is threatened by the other two. The basic explanation here is the legal concept of reasonable doubt. The story line also explains how Stone can detest people's lifestyles yet still seek justice for them. Monica De Vries might be a sleazy tabloid journalist, but Stone doesn't want the young rapists to go free. What's distinctive about this segment is how Greevey and Logan demonstrate that the system can be bent without violating it. This isn't one of the great *Law & Order* offerings. One admires it more for its cleverness than its power.

Episode 14: "The Violence of Summer" (Season One), in which ADA Paul Robinette (Richard Brooks) sees a rape suspect draw a gun in court. [courtesy of Photofest/Copyright ©1991 by Universal City Studios, Inc. Courtesy of Universal Publishing Rights, a Division of Universal Studios Licensing, Inc. All rights reserved.]

Noteworthy Discoveries: This is the first *Law & Order* segment to feature the prosecutors in court during the show's first half-hour. It is also unusual in that Robinette witnesses a skirmish in the courtroom as one of the suspects grabs a gun.

Episode 15: The Torrents of Greed (Part One)

Original air date: February 12, 1991

Teleplay by Michael S. Chernuchin, story by Michael Duggan and Michael S. Chernuchin, directed by E. W. Swackhamer, cinematography by Constantine Makris

Additional Cast and Guest Stars: Bruce Altman (Harv Biegel), Christine Baranski (Mrs. Biegel), Charles Cioffi (Frank Masucci), Robert Fields (Mario Zalta), Steven Keats (George Zuckert), Stephen McHattie (Joe Pilefsky), Lee Richardson (Biegel's Attorney), Anna Katrina (Elena), James Noah (Arraignment Judge), Doris Belack (Judge Margaret Barry),

Christopher McCann (Edgar Hoover), Jacques Sandulescu (Isaac Skolnick), Luis Ramos (Valdez)

Reviewing the Case: When liquor store owner Isaac Skolnick is badly beaten, Greevey and Logan find that mobster Frank Masucci is involved. Stone pursues him with such zeal that he becomes embroiled in perjured testimony that allows Masucci to go free. With a title borrowed from a Buddhist koan ("There is no snare like folly; There is no torrent like greed"), and a plot borrowed from the career of John Gotti, this engrossing story demonstrates how Stone's single-mindedness can backfire when he becomes too ambitious. The episode also works like the lovely metaphor Stone uses to explain the conspiracy leading to the Masuccis: The crime family's chain of command is like a line of dominoes set in motion. That is exactly how this expertly told story falls into place.

Noteworthy Discoveries: This is the first and, to date, only two-part *Law & Order* episode. It's also the series' debut script of writer Michael Chernuchin, who later became a story editor, then a producer on the show. In addition, it is the second time around for the Masucci Family, the first appearance being the pilot, Episode 6: "Everybody's Favorite Bagman."

Relevant Testimony: MICHAEL CHERNUCHIN (writer): "I had a meeting with Michael Duggan who was the supervising producer, and he said he wanted to do a show about the mob and John Gotti.... Whenever I write a show, I always say: What is the show about? And that show was about greed. The mob has it for money. Stone has it for power, and he overstretched his bounds. Even at the beginning, the two uniformed cops are talking about winning the lottery. So if you go through it scene by scene, everybody is a little greedy."

Episode 16: The Torrents of Greed (Part Two)
Original air date: February 19, 1991
Teleplay by Michael S. Chernuchin, story by Michael Duggan and Michael S. Chernuchin, directed by E. W. Swackhamer, cinematography by Constantine Makris

Additional Cast and Guest Stars: Bruce Altman (Harv Biegel), Christine Baranski (Mrs. Biegel), Charles Cioffi (Frank Masucci), Robert Fields (Mario Zalta), Steven Keats (George Zuckert), Stephen McHattie (Joe Pilefsky), Lee Richardson (Biegel's Attorney), Ronald Hunter (Thompson), Philip R. Allen (Pilefsky's Attorney), Anna Katrina (Elena), David Cryer (Arraignment Judge), Sidney Armus (Judge Fishbein), Connie Masucci (Maria Cellario), Jacques Sandulescu (Skolnick)

Reviewing the Case: Ben Stone tries to salvage his prosecution of the Masucci Family by getting brother-in-law Harv Biegel to testify against the don. However, the plan backfires when Biegel is killed. The case is eventually settled out of court by Mrs. Biegel. If justice is blind and rarely fair, the twists in this story would fit that definition. Stone gets what he wants but not the way he wished it. Only death results from his pursuit of Masucci, played with great relish by Charles Cioffi. Stone's righteousness takes the form of a personal vendetta, and vendettas become self-perpetuating, on whatever side of the law they may occur. Actors Christine Baranski (Maryanne on the TV sitcom *Cybill*, 1995–98) and Bruce Altman turn in good performances while knocking over every last domino.

Relevant Testimony: MICHAEL CHERNUCHIN (writer): "Michael Duggan…called me in and said, 'Okay, great episode. We're putting you on staff and we're turning it into a two-parter.' And that's how 'Torrents 2' came along."

Episode 17: Mushrooms
Original air date: February 26, 1991
Teleplay by Robert Palm, directed by Daniel Sackheim, cinematography by Constantine Makris

Additional Cast and Guest Stars: Brad Sullivan (Joe Anson), Michael Mantell (Edward Kaye), S. Epatha Merkerson (Denise Winters), Malachi Throne (Judge Real), Tom Mardirosian (Brian Doxsee), Victor Raider-Wexler (Harold Morton), James McDaniels (Michael Ingrams), Justin Cozier (Franklin "T-Ball" Howard), Terrance Telfair (Dizz Williams), Merlin Santana (Ronell Griggs), Regina Taylor (Evelyn Griggs), Barbara Spiegel (Judge Harriet Doremus), Merwin Goldsmith (Judge Gollub), Alex Bess (Gregory Winters)

Reviewing the Case: The accidental shooting death of eleven-month-old Andrew Winters and the wounding of his older brother are tied to a fourteen-year-old killer. The latter boy was hired by a powerful drug lord to assassinate a double-crossing real estate agent. This story is compelling enough in its depiction of innocent children gunned down in American cities. However, it also makes its audience profoundly aware of how so many of us automatically associate black youths with drugs and crime. Then the segment winds down to a conclusion that transcends the urban myths of the drug world. Robert Palm's script illuminates the way the white yuppie appetite for cocaine has had a destructive impact on the black community. The end result is a powerful drama with poignant social criticism.

Noteworthy Discoveries: S. Epatha Merkerson would later join the regular cast in Season Four (1993–94) as Lt. Anita Van Buren. Also, James McDaniels, who plays drug dealer Michael Ingrams, would in a few years have a starring role as Lt. Arthur Fancy on the cop series *N.Y.P.D. Blue* (1993–).

Relevant Testimony: ROBERT PALM (writer): "This was a very emotional episode to write. My family is from back East and my wife at that time was pregnant with our first child, and we just rented a summer place. While she was eight months pregnant, I started noticing that in the papers there were numerous cases of children being hit by stray bullets in New York City. There were five in one week. It was just appalling. So the link between reading those stories and looking at my pregnant wife made it a very visceral experience."

Episode 18: The Secret Sharers
Original air date: March 12, 1991
Teleplay by Robert Nathan, directed by E. W. Swackhamer, cinematography by Constantine Makris

Additional Cast and Guest Stars: J. D. Cannon (Chet Burton), Paul Calderon (Father Abrams), Lorraine Toussaint (Shambala Green), Enrique Munoz (Nicky Guzman), Stephen Elliott (Judge Markham), Miriam Colon (Mrs. Rivers), Paula Garces (Lucy Guzman), Cordelia Gonzalez (Anita Urbano), Diane Kagan (Judge Durren), Stephen Mendillo (Harmon), Daniel Kenney (Forensics), Duke Stroud (Hurley)

Reviewing the Case: When Jose Urbano, a drug dealer, is shot four times in the crotch, Greevey and Logan suspect controlled substances are involved, until they discover that Nicky Guzman committed the crime because Urbano raped his sister Lucy. This episode ponders whether the rape of a woman gives a decent man license to kill. Stone, with his strict legal sensibilities, obviously doesn't think so. However, Chet Burton, a Texas lawyer brandishing his own six-gun style of justice, believes otherwise. Thus, the fires of vengeance are stirred up in the jury by this Lone Star cowboy. Also intriguing is the sexual component of the continued scrapping between Stone and Shambala.

Relevant Testimony: ROBERT PALM (writer): "I created the character of Shambala Green to the degree that any characters are created on *Law & Order*. It was a guest role that I wrote. Shambala comes right out of Tom Wolfe 'mau-mauing' the radical chic! I thought that Lorraine Toussaint was fabulous in the part, too."

Episode 19: The Serpent's Tooth
Original air date: March 19, 1991
Teleplay by Rene Balcer and Robert Stern, story by I. C. Rapoport and
Joshua Stern, directed by Don Scardino, cinematography by Constantine
Makris

Additional Cast and Guest Stars: Frances Sternhagen (Margaret, the
Housekeeper), Stephen Mailer (Greg Jarmon), Matt Hofherr (Nick
Jarmon), George Morfogen (Jack Epstein), Lewis Stadlen (Eli Schwab),
Olek Krupa (Sasha Osinski), Jonathan Hadary (Alex Petrovich), Duke
Stroud (Hurley), Richard M. Ticktin (Judge Rosenblum), Bernie
McInerney (Judge Callaghan), John Fiore (Det. Anthony Profaci)

Reviewing the Case: When their parents are murdered, Greg and Nick
Jarmon find themselves suspects until evidence points to their father's
business partner. For a change, this episode leads its audience along one
path and then takes a hairpin turn down another. What begins as a
drama based on the infamous real-life case of the Menendez brothers of
California very quickly (and unexpectedly) becomes a glimpse into the
Russian mob. (It's interesting to note the distinctions between Russian
gangsters and their Italian or Jewish counterparts we've come to know in
the movies.) The episode contrasts the lifestyle of the wealthy Jarmons
with the cold reality of a strictly unsentimental crime family, which has
made these brothers orphans.

Noteworthy Discoveries: Here, Rene Balcer, writer and executive producer, contributes his first script to *Law & Order*. There's more information provided here about Logan's abusive mother and angry father. The
Russian mafia will also figure in the last episode featuring Ben Stone
(Michael Moriarty), Episode 88: "Old Friends."

Relevant Testimony: ROBERT NATHAN (writer): "[Greevey and Logan]
were detectives earning $50,000 a year and the two kids were unfath-
omably wealthy. The class and political issues in our country about the ill-
paid members of the criminal justice system dealing with the vastly
wealthy criminal defendant, allows our characters to be reflections of us
on the screen. [The detectives] are looking at the way those kids live, the
same way *we* are. At its core, *Law & Order* is an examination of class,
power, money, and gender."

Episode 20: The Troubles
Original air date: March 26, 1991
Teleplay by Robert Palm, story by Dick Wolf and Robert Palm, directed
by John P. Whitesell, II, cinematography by Constantine Makris

Additional Cast and Guest Stars: Anthony Heald (Ian O'Connell), Donel Donnelly (Mallahan), Paxton Whitehead (Fenwick), Alan North (Mr. Reilly), Robert Silver (Axelrod), Bill Nelson (Shelby), Paul-Felix Montez (Montez), Betty Miller (Bridget MacDearmot), Kevin J. O'Connor (Patrick McCarter), Parvin Farhoody (Mrs. Mustafa), William Severs (Judge)

Reviewing the Case: The murder of a federal prisoner prompts Greevey and Logan to investigate the involvement of Ian O'Connell, an IRA suspect who is trying to get political asylum in the United States and stalling the extradition process that would send him back home to Ireland. The episode addresses terrorism by showing how international, federal, and local agencies can either join forces to defeat it or let the expediency of political jurisdiction give it room to flourish. Greevey goes through hell, and the longest ribbon of red tape, to get Ian O'Connell. When Stone finally brings him to trial, it takes the (far too casual) cooperation of British Intelligence to finally bring in a prosecution witness to testify. This segment has a dense plot, and almost the shape and feel of a miniature movie. When Schiff holds a press conference congratulating the Feds and the local police for their efforts, Dzundza brilliantly conveys the frustrations of that joint venture by putting an ironic expression on Greevey's face.

Noteworthy Discoveries: This story was based on the case of Joe Doherty who, in 1991, began his ninth year of incarceration in the United States. When Logan initially falls under the sway of O'Connell, it is learned that the detective has relatives in Ireland. Stone reveals that his grandmother was an Irishwoman named Fahey.

Relevant Testimony: ROBERT PALM (writer): "This story was a personal thing for me, a mea culpa for my early younger days when I wrote a pro-Sinn Fein piece for a paper in New Haven. I wanted to tell the other side of the story, but looking back I think I was a bit naive in waving the flag for the IRA. I'm not sure if I really succeeded in getting that across in this episode, but when the woman takes the stand and talks about losing her family, *that* was my mea culpa."

Episode 21: Sonata for Solo Organ
Original air date: April 2, 1991
Teleplay by Joe Morgenstern and Michael S. Chernuchin, story by Joe Morgenstern and Michael Duggan, directed by Fred Gerber, cinematography by Constantine Makris

Additional Cast and Guest Stars: Paul Roebling (Dr. Reberty), Fritz Weaver (Phillip Woodleigh), Deborah Hedwall (Elaine Hale), Dominic

Episode 21: "Sonata for Solo Organ" (Season One), with EADA Ben Stone cross-examining the accused (Fritz Weaver). *[courtesy of Photofest/Copyright ©1991 by Universal City Studios, Inc. Courtesy of Universal Publishing Rights, a Division of Universal Studios Licensing, Inc. All rights reserved.]*

Chianese (Dan Rebell), Bill Moor (William Patton), Chuck Cooper (Drew McDaniel), Lonny Price (Intern on Motorcycle), Randy Graff (Dr. Kershan), Kevin O'Morrison (Judge Boyack), Tanya Berezin (Judge Rosalyn Lenz), Fred J. Scollay (Judge Pursley), Zach Grenier (Lemish), Jennifer Van Dyck (Joanna Woodleigh), Ann Dowd (Teresa Franz)

Reviewing the Case: When the police find that the unconscious Drew McDaniel is missing a kidney, Greevey and Logan learn that it was snatched by a prominent doctor for the daughter of a wealthy philanthropist. This installment explores the issue of intent when someone is paid to commit a crime. It covers some of the same ground as Episode 1: "Prescription for Death," and has some of the same predictability of Episode 5: "Happily Ever After" (although this is a much more ambitious script). What does work is Fritz Weaver's lively villain and Chuck Cooper's McDaniel, who brings both stupefaction and regret to the part. Dominic Chianese is dignified as Woodleigh's attorney. When Weaver and Chianese sit next to each other in the courtroom, they look like candidates for Mount Rushmore.

Relevant Testimony: CHRIS NOTH (actor): "The problem with these writers is that they looked at the dialogue, at least in the first half, as just one-liners. In 'Sonata For a Solo Organ,' when the guy had his kidney removed, my last line is: "Talk about getting your pocket picked.' People don't f***ing talk that way. So it's a lot harder than you think to make those lines work. They substituted that for a moment-to-moment reality in dialogue. It drives you f***ing crazy. It makes my skin crawl."

Episode 22: The Blue Wall
Original air date: April 9, 1991
Teleplay by Robert Nathan, story by Dick Wolf and Robert Nathan, directed by Vern Gillum, cinematography by Constantine Makris

Additional Cast and Guest Stars: Robert Lansing (Officer Pete O'Farrell), John Christopher Jones (Dennis Shearer), Gerry Bamman (Kimball), David Leary (Chan), William Andrews (Al McCrory), Joey Buscalera (Dylan Price), John Newton (Judge Caffey), John Ramsey (Judge Dowling), Catherine Wolf (Judge Harris), Pirie MacDonald (Congressman Billy Wilson), Ellen Tobie (Marge Cragen), Anthony DeRiso (McCrory's Attorney)

Reviewing the Case: When charges against some white-collar criminals are dismissed in court, Cragen comes under suspicion. His mentor, Pete O'Farrell, may have been involved in laundering drug money and destroying evidence. The subject of police corruption was tackled earlier this season in Episode 8: "Poison Ivy" and Episode 13: "A Death in the Family," but this installment probes deeper into the psychological meaning of "the blue wall," a term for the invisible barrier that is *supposed* to prevent one cop from informing on another. Greevey and Logan must convince themselves that Cragen is not guilty. The scenes between Greevey and Cragen are extremely charged because they were once partners. Dann Florek gives his best performance as a man who feels completely isolated. After the trial, Greevey tries to assure Cragen that he's done the right thing, but coming clean and staying clean cannot wash away guilt in bringing down a colleague and a friend.

Noteworthy Discoveries: This is the first time that Cragen's wife, Marge, appears. As in Episode 14: "The Violence of Summer" from earlier this season, this episode begins with the DAs in the courtroom. Also noteworthy is that this installment is George Dzundza's last appearance on *Law & Order* as Sgt. Max Greevey.

Relevant Testimony: DANN FLOREK (actor): "In the first three years, I tried to get out of the series three times. . . . I kept saying, 'You promised me you were going to make me more of an equal with these guys [the detectives]. But it's clearly two guys and me, and you have me sitting in the office.' I would joke and say, 'You can probably pull the two scenes I did in the last episode and stick them in this one.' Dick kept promising and I got 'The Blue Wall.' I said, 'I'd like to do one or two of those each year and that would be fine.' That's why it was such a treat."

Season Two
September 1991–May 1992
60-minute episodes

Production Team:

Dick Wolf (Executive Producer), Joseph Stern (Co-Executive Producer), Robert Palm (Producer), Daniel Sackheim (Producer), Jeffrey Hayes (Co-Producer), Robert Nathan (Co-Producer), Michael Duggan (Supervising Producer), David Black (Supervising Producer), Arthur W. Forney (Associate Producer), Robert Nathan (Executive Story Editor), Michael S. Chernuchin (Executive Story Editor), Rene Balcer (Story Editor), Lewis H. Gould (Unit Production Manager), Richard Bianchi (Production Designer), Mike Post (Music), Lynn Kressel C.S.A. (Casting), Suzanne Ryan (Casting), Constantine Makris (Cinematographer), Phil Oetiker (Camera Operator), Christopher Misiano (Camera Operator), Drake Silliman (Editor), Michael Kewley (Editor), Billy Fox (Editor), Mark Newman (Editor), Arthur Forney (Editor), Mike Struk (Technical Advisor), Bill Fordes (Technical Advisor)

Regular Cast:

Richard Brooks (Assistant District Attorney Paul Robinette), Dann Florek (Capt. Donald Cragen), Steven Hill (District Attorney Adam Schiff), Michael Moriarty (Executive Assistant District Attorney Ben Stone), Chris Noth (Det. Mike Logan), Paul Sorvino (Det. Phil Cerreta)

Second Season Overview

At the end of its first year on the air, Law & Order was the highest-rated new drama of the 1990–91 season. The media had praised the show for its realism. Tom Shales wrote in the Washington Post that "[Law & Order] has all the ingredients associated with quality television: strong scripts, relevant themes and a cast that qualifies as first-rate-plus." John J. O'Connor lauded the cast in the New York Times, adding that "the on-location filming in New York doesn't hurt either."

But *Law & Order* still had to find its own stylistic consistency. In Season Two, that goal is achieved as a new confidence emerged. In the first season, everyone discovered who they were; by the following year, they are tapping even deeper resources.

George Dzundza left the series at the end of Season One, and film and theater actor Paul Sorvino became Mike Logan's new partner, Det. Phil Cerreta. Carolyn McCormick, as psychiatrist Dr. Elizabeth Olivet, is the first woman to work with the entirely male ensemble but it will be another year before she becomes a recurring regular on the series.

The enormously gifted cinematographer Constantine "Gus" Makris is now the full-time director of photography and his old friend Christopher Misiano has been brought in as the camera operator. Also in Season Two, a talented new director named Ed Sherin arrives on the scene and changes the course of *Law & Order* for years to come. Rene Balcer and Michael Chernuchin become story editors, while continuing to write the TV show's riveting installments.

Starting with Logan's loss of a partner, Season Two of *Law & Order* explores other areas of crime: murder among the wealthy (Episode 36: "Blood is Thicker..."), gang rape (Episode 30: "Out of Control"), sexual abuse in a Catholic shelter (Episode 39: "Sisters of Mercy"), arson and fraud (Episode 32: "Heaven"), and the death penalty (Episode 38: "Vengeance"). The show also breaks new ground in terms of social injustice and corruption (Episode 44: "The Working Stiff"), the legal dimensions of a homeless person's accommodations (Episode 26: "Asylum"), and religion versus the state (Episode 27: "God Bless the Child").

Episode Descriptions

Episode 23: Confession

Original air date: September 17, 1991
Teleplay by Michael Duggan and Robert Palm, directed by Fred Gerber

Additional Cast and Guest Stars: Vyto Ruginis (Daniel Magaden, Jr.), Daniel Von Bargen (Lambrusco), Val Avery (Daniel Magaden, Sr.), Carolyn McCormick (Dr. Elizabeth Olivet), Tanya Berezin (Judge Silverman), Sam Gray (Judge Leon), Nicolas Coster (Morgan Stern), Karen Shallo (Marie Greevey), Peter Crombie (Howie Neffer)

Reviewing the Case: Max Greevey is gunned down in front of his home the day before he's scheduled to testify in an extortion scandal. Logan coerces a confession out of Greevey's killer that threatens to jeopardize the legality of the case. This installment questions the way cops sometimes approach their suspects and the kind of confessions they elicit. Noth gives a commanding performance, in which he is transformed from a brash kid into a wizened adult. His scenes with Dr. Elizabeth Olivet have nice shadings, as his emotional defenses gradually melt away. Sorvino makes a fine first impression as Logan's new police partner, Cerreta. He provides an anchor for this stormy younger cop at sea. However, the story itself is a bit weak. Would the authorities really believe a suspect's claim of coercion, rather than the facts as told by Logan? It's a tiny flaw in a great character study that carries a poignant realization: Though a confession might bring acknowledgment of trauma, it doesn't take away the horror of the event.

Noteworthy Discoveries: Paul Sorvino makes his first appearance as Detective Cerreta. Carolyn McCormick shows up as Dr. Olivet. Also, this is the first (and last) appearance of Greevey's wife, Marie.

Relevant Testimony: CAROLYN MCCORMICK (actor): "I wanted Olivet to be a genuine listener. A lot of time on TV, actors aren't listening, they're just waiting for their turn. I wanted her to be kind of neutral, on the non-subjective side of therapy. I've never been in therapy but everyone says that [it's about] maintaining your objectivity and not feeling their pain, just observing it, thinking about it, and trying to diagnose it—that really fascinates me."

Episode 24: The Wages of Love

Original air date: September 24, 1991
Teleplay by Ed Zuckerman, story by Ed Zuckerman and Robert Nathan, directed by Ed Sherin

Additional Cast and Guest Stars: Shirley Knight (Melanie Cullen), Geoffrey Nauffts (Jamie Cullen), Joan Copeland (Judge Rebecca Stein), Ben Hammer (Judge Herman Mooney), David Lansbury (Doug Phillips), Benjamin Hendrickson (Merril), Jerry Orbach (Frank Lehrman), Christine Farrell (Arlene)

Reviewing the Case: A middle-aged man named Cullen and his young lover are found shot to death in their bed by his former wife, whom he'd abandoned after twenty-five years of marriage. From the standpoint of good drama, this episode is rather tepid. It suggests themes of class distinction similar to those of the film *A Place in the Sun* (1951), but, in this case, it's as if Shelley Winters had killed Montgomery Clift instead of the other way around. Stone has to set aside his belief that Mrs. Cullen was cold-blooded in committing this crime because the jury might sympathize with her as a victim. Shirley Knight gives a richly enigmatic performance that doesn't turn masochistic, and Jerry Orbach makes a great lawyer. The episode puts a mirror up to the simple view that only bad guys leave their wives, and then shatters it.

Noteworthy Discoveries: The story is based on the case of Betty Broderick, a California woman who killed her estranged husband and his lover. Orbach would rejoin the cast as Det. Lennie Briscoe during Season Three (1992–93). This is the first appearance of Christine Farrell as the ballistics officer Arlene. In the future, her character's name is Shrier.

Episode 25: Aria
Original air date: October 1, 1991
Teleplay by Christine Roum, story by Michael S. Chernuchin, directed by Don Scardino

Additional Cast and Guest Stars: Tony Roberts (Mr. Pollat), Marilyn Rockafellow (Elizabeth Blaine), Maura Tierney (Patty Blaine), Michael Countryman (Medical Examiner), Tovah Feldshuh (Probate Lawyer), Lisa Nicole Carson (Jasmine), Maria Pitillo (Angel), Lewis Black (Franklin, the Film Director), Dylan Haggerty (Roger Glenn), Stephen Newman (Dr. Seliger), William Severs (Judge Freitag), Catherine Wolf (Judge Hale), Frank Vincent (J. Z.)

Reviewing the Case: When a young actress is found dead of a drug overdose, Cerreta and Logan come upon an aggressive stage mother who forced her daughter into pornography. This episode lapses into the same kind of predictable theatrics that Episode 5: "Happily Ever After" did in Season One. Rather than exploring the dynamics between mother and daughter, the story line simply leaves the blame at the mother's door. Credibility is sacrificed because it's hard to understand what would drive the woman to such heartless behavior. (Could it just be her own failed ambitions? Had she hoped to star in *Deep Throat?*) "Aria" is no more than an archetype of victimization clichés.

Relevant Testimony: JOSEPH STERN (executive producer): "That's the first show we shot with [Paul] Sorvino. They had written it for Dzundza, but they didn't adapt it for Paul. So Paul spoke differently. Dick Wolf's idea was that his parents were haberdashers, so they put him in these three-piece suits. I called Dick to say, 'We've got to get rid of these three-piece suits. He looks like a banker.... And you've got to start writing differently for him because his rhythms are different. You can hear his consonants.' So, in that show, I started taking the jacket off him and put him in his vest. These are all conscious things to soften him up because he looks so formal. It took us two or three shows to straighten him out."

Episode 26: Asylum
Original air date: October 8, 1991
Teleplay by Kathy McCormick, story by Robert Palm, directed by Kristoffer Siegel-Tabori

Additional Cast and Guest Stars: Matthew Cowles (Christian "Lemonhead" Tatum), Ron McLarty (Skolar), Elizabeth Lawrence (Elsie Hatch), Lycia Naff (Mimi Sternhagen), Carolyn McCormick (Dr. Elizabeth Olivet), Wendy Radford (Alice Fahey), Michael Tolan (Norman Ackerman), Stuart Rudin (James Polesky), Irving Metzman (Judge Strozzek), Bill Alton (Judge O'Malley), Alexander Draper (Nathan Robbins)

Reviewing the Case: Logan and Cerreta arrest James Polesky, a homeless man, for a stabbing death, but the conviction is threatened by an illegal search for the weapon in his only place of residence, Central Park. This is a terrific narrative that demonstrates how Fourth Amendment rights apply even to unsavory individuals. It's also the first *Law & Order* installment to take a truly tragic situation and play it with off-the-wall humor, while exploring the law as it applies to people we often don't acknowledge as inhabiting the "normal" world.

Relevant Testimony: ROBERT PALM (writer): "I remember having long discussions with Kris Tabori [the director]. . . . I was afraid we were going to take a doctrinaire approach, and wear our liberalism on our sleeve. I didn't want the patronizing bullsh** of the 1930s hobo presented. So I told him that we all feel bad about the homeless, and yes, it's a tragic issue, but there are also dangerous people out there and the world is screwy. I wanted us to take a funhouse-mirror approach. We have to be able to laugh at how we are often living in an open-air asylum—hence the title."

Episode 27: God Bless the Child
Original air date: October 22, 1991
Teleplay by David Black and Robert Nathan, directed by E. W. Swackhamer

Additional Cast and Guest Stars: Byron Jennings (Ted Driscoll), Kaiulani Lee (Nancy Driscoll), Henderson Forsythe (Carpenter), Marian Seldes (Sharon Barlow), James Noble (Judge Kurland), Joyce Reehling (Eleanor Harding), Caroline Aaron (Susan), Biff McGuire (Reverend Morley), Susan Blommaert (Judge Steinman)

Reviewing the Case: Ted and Nancy Driscoll refuse medical help for their critically ill daughter because they believe in the healing power of prayer.

The wrenching story line opens in the emergency room, where the mother, deeply ambivalent about her decision, cries over the dying child. Logan and Cerreta are shocked by this and we're left wondering how to maintain any empathy or understanding for these parents. Like the Meryl Streep feature film *A Cry in the Dark* (1988), this episode dredges up complicated feelings about the place of spirituality in criminal procedures. In disagreeing about whether or not the parents are negligent, Cerreta reminds Logan that the Catholic Church also has its rituals. Despite all that happens, the mother remains certain that if she had been closer to God, her daughter would have lived. *Law & Order* condemns the neglect of the parents without ridiculing their faith.

Noteworthy Discoveries: We see the *voir dire* process of jury selection as prosecutors try to find a tolerant group of people, given the sensitive nature of the case.

Episode 28: Misconception
Original air date: October 29, 1991
Teleplay by Michael S. Chernuchin, story by Michael Duggan and Michael Chernuchin, directed by Daniel Sackheim

Additional Cast and Guest Stars: Molly Price (Amy Newhouse), Reed Diamond (Chris Baylor), Stanley Anderson (Jerry Manley), Gordana Rashovich (Bayliss), Nicolas Surovy (David Alcott), Yancy Butler (Beverly Kem), William Jay Marshall (Judge Burton), Zina Jasper (Judge Appel), Len Gochman (Judge Gillion), Robert Katims (Jacob Blum), Shirley Stoler (Maylen), Ronnie Farer (Mrs. Alcott)

Reviewing the Case: The mugging of Amy Newhouse, a legal secretary who is in her twenty-second week of pregnancy, leads to her lover. The two are blackmailing her boss, threatening to accuse him of murder when she loses her baby. This episode makes an engrossing murder mystery about a devious couple using the law to absolve themselves in an extortion scam. What's intriguing here is how Moriarty invests Stone with the chutzpah to convince the jury they should ignore the evidence. By law, it's not murder before the twenty-fourth week of pregnancy, so the couple's awareness of the statute is the truth that comes back to haunt them. This is one of the few times that Stone sidesteps the law in order to underscore the guilt of the people who are abusing it.

Noteworthy Discoveries: We find out that Logan was a cabdriver during his college years.

Episode 29: In Memory Of...

Original air date: November 5, 1991
Teleplay by David Black and Robert Nathan, story by David Black and Siobhan Bryne, directed by Ed Sherin

Additional Cast and Guest Stars: Mary-Joan Negro (Catherine Messimer), Michael Higgins (Thad Messimer), Rosemary Murphy (Mrs. Messimer), Tresa Hughes (Doris Keegan), Richard Hamilton (Ed Conover), Carolyn McCormick (Dr. Elizabeth Olivet), Richard Venture (Doug Greer), Mark Hammer (Judge Welch), Kevin O'Morrison (Judge Spector)

Reviewing the Case: The remains of Tommy Keegan, a boy who disappeared thirty-one years earlier, are found during the renovation of a Manhattan brownstone. This discovery revives a painful and long-suppressed memory for Catherine Messimer, who had been Tommy's friend as a child and whose father may have killed him. This segment is ambiguous in suggesting that, even though the father is guilty, there is only the testimony of a disturbed woman to attest to it. The tragic beauty of the story is that the viewer observes everything through Catherine's eyes, thus becoming aware only as she does. Ed Sherin directs the revelation scene (in which Dr. Olivet takes Catherine through her old home) with such great authority that it never seems hokey. Mary-Joan Negro is magnificent in the role of Catherine and Michael Higgins gives a persuasive performance as her father. Once Stone convinces him to agree to a plea, he confesses, but, in making it sound like something his daughter might have imagined, the man is a ghost trying to haunt her.

Episode 30: Out of Control

Original air date: November 12, 1991
Teleplay by Jack Richardson, story by David Black and Robert Nathan, directed by John P. Whitesell

Additional Cast and Guest Stars:
Noelle Parker (Andrea Fermi), Cynthia Harris (Elise Gifford), Joe Grifasi (Ezra Gould), Carolyn McCormick (Dr. Elizabeth Olivet), David Burke (Gary Burnham), Mark Kiely (Ted Campion), Danny Zorn (Joel Holder), Brian Tarantina (Corso), Isaiah Washington (Derek Hardy), Jennie Ventriss (Judge Amelia Paul), Billie Allen (Judge Gloria West)

Reviewing the Case: Although college sophomore Andrea Fermi accuses some fraternity brothers of gang rape after a Halloween party, the fact that she was drunk and doesn't remember certain details makes her a less than a solid witness. Thus, this episode becomes the third one that deals with rape or perceived rape. Others include Episode 11: "Out of the Half Light" and Episode 14: "The Violence of Summer," both from Season One (1990–91). This entry, however, concentrates more on the issue of a person's sexual history in regard to the law and the perception jurors have of promiscuity. When he finds that Andrea and her boyfriend have been dishonest about their relationship, Stone is forced to separate the young woman's behavior from that of the boys who took advantage of her. Moriarty is adept at revealing how mortified Stone feels about losing the case, as "Out of Control" conveys the sense that a rape of justice has taken place.

Noteworthy Discoveries: The case is based on an actual rape that took place at St. John's University in Collegeville, Jamaica, New York. This is the first episode that sets a scene in the holding cell and the room where mug shots are taken.

Relevant Testimony: ROBERT NATHAN (writer): "David Black knew from the beginning that there were two interesting ways to approach this—one of which is, you simply don't leave the victim clean. If you make her perfect, then you have no story and there's no ambiguity. And conversely, you don't make the defendants clearly and obviously guilty from an emotional perspective. What he did so brilliantly was [illustrate] that the guys aren't testifying to lie [about their actions], they actually think they are innocent. And so we know that they are wrong, but that's different from us believing that they are lying."

Episode 31: Renunciation
Original air date: November 19, 1991
Teleplay by Michael Chernuchin and Joe Morgenstern, directed by Gwen Arner

Additional Cast and Guest Stars: Ashley Crow (Jenna Kealey), David Seaman (Roy Pack, Jr.), Victor Arnold (David Kaufer), Dan Desmond (Roy Pack, Sr.), Cheryl Giannini (Rydell), Jean DeBaer (Constance Pack), Ben Lang (Irv Isaacson), Bernie McInerney (Judge Callahan), Matthew Lewis (Judge Link), Donald Corren (Carl Dibbs), John Ottavino (Larry Kealey)

Reviewing the Case: When Larry Kealey is killed in a hit-and-run murder while out walking his dog (named O. J.), Cerreta and Logan find that his wife, Jenna, may have conspired to commit homicide with the high school student who is her lover. The title of this episode, "Renunciation," refers to an act of violence that is commissioned and then called off. Jenna hired David Kaufer to kill her husband before terminating the contract. Can she still be guilty of the crime if it's renounced? Although it has roots in the infamous Pamela Smart case, this is one of several episodes about adolescents seduced by adults. Others include Episode 58: "Promises to Keep" in Season Three (1992–93), and Episode 92: "Family Values" from Season Five (1994–95). There is a prescient irony in the use of the name O. J. for Kealey's dog. Here, a wife conspires to kill her husband a few years before the notorious O. J. Simpson murder trial in Los Angeles.

Noteworthy Discoveries: Donald Corren makes his first appearance as the forensics specialist. Here, he is Dibbs; in Episode 32: "Heaven," he is Ezra Stine; and by Episode 36: "Blood is Thicker..." he would be renamed Medill. This switching of the name of a "recurring" character is a frequent practice on the series. Sometimes it is done as a kind of inside joke.

Relevant Testimony: MICHAEL CHERNUCHIN (writer): "What we tried to do in each episode was not avoid the law as many shows do, but use the law as part of the plot. [Because of that] people not only know there's a Constitution, they also know that there are fourteen amendments to it. Instead of avoiding a legal problem, we highlighted it. It became a hurdle our guys had to get over, or a weapon they could use, or even a shield the defense could use."

Episode 32: Heaven

Original air date: November 26, 1991
Teleplay by Nancy Ann Miller and Robert Palm, story by Robert Palm, directed by Ed Sherin

Additional Cast and Guest Stars: Jose Perez (Robert Diaz), Lisa Emery (Van Brocklen), Luis Guzman (Cesar Pescador), Victor Campos (Domingo Guerra), Robert Hogan (Patrick Monahan), Phyllis Somerville (Head Nurse), Nelson Landrieu (Jose Rivera), Tom Tammi (James Collins), Kurt Knudson (Judge Waxman), Donald Corren (Ezra Stine)

Reviewing the Case: This episode, based on the Happy Land Club fire, has the most haunting opening of any *Law & Order* story. Cerreta and Logan arrive in the aftermath of a blaze at a Latin social club called Heaven in East Harlem and see fifty-three charred bodies on the sidewalk. Their investigation leads to two men involved in the sale of illegal "green cards": Domingo Guerra, an influential member of the Latin community, and James Collins, a dishonest official at the Immigration and Naturalization Service. This plot line climbs, step by step, up the ladder of corruption that has resulted in a local holocaust. This world of illegal immigrants is not new to television drama, but the episode (much like Tony Richardson's underrated 1982 feature film, *The Border*) tackles human iniquity as an extension of our bureaucracies and the evil of those who profit from the misery of the less fortunate. It is a troubling, and brilliant, look at one of the most vile aspects of a democratic system.

Relevant Testimony: JOSEPH STERN (executive producer): "We were downtown in our courthouse and it was eleven o'clock at night, and I had this idea [for the ending] that what we would do is pan all of these faces. But we didn't have any Latino extras. So I sent the production assistants down to the street...and paid people ten or twenty bucks to come up and be extras. Two-thirds of those faces are not union extras. Ed [Sherin] and I came up with that whole go-around-the-room thing. And that woman at the end, on the last beat, crossing herself—that was a woman we took off the street."

Episode 33: His Hour Upon the Stage
Original air date: December 10, 1991
Teleplay by Robert Nathan and Giles Blunt, directed by Steve Cohen

Additional Cast and Guest Stars: Finn Carter (Leslie Hart), Frank Converse (Gary Wallace), John Cunningham (Jon Cobb), Alan Feinstein (Eliot Ketcham), Mike Starr (Pollard), Bruce MacVittie (Gabriel Hunt), Dylan Baker (Sean Hyland), Alberta Watson (Charlotte Hanley), Francine Beers (Judge Janis Silver), David Cryer (Judge Lee Rowan), Tony Darrow (Mario), John Fiore (Det. Anthony Profaci)

Reviewing the Case: Dead for five years, Broadway producer Joshua Foster's defrosted body is found in a dumpster. His former lover and his co-producer conspired to have him murdered because of a problematic drug deal. This less than thrilling episode is saved primarily by colorful acting. There seems to be an awareness that the story is obvious; so, playing on the theatrical aspect of the plot, the performers are encouraged to bow to the gallery and they do so with great aplomb. Tony Darrow and Mike Starr ham it up as mob goons. Frank Converse portrays the sneaky co-producer with sly humor. Finn Carter airs out a role that would seem custom-made for the soaps, and Francine Beers, as the arraignment judge, gets to kvetch more than these cranky *Law & Order* characters usually do. "His Hour Upon the Stage" is essentially a pleasant trifle.

Noteworthy Discoveries: This is Michael Chernuchin's first episode as executive story editor of *Law & Order*.

Episode 34: Star Struck

Original air date: January 7, 1992
Teleplay by Robert Nathan and Sally Nemeth, story by David Black and Alan Gelb, directed by Ed Sherin

Additional Cast and Guest Stars: Blanche Baker (Lucy Nevin), Stephen Joyce (Jack Gaffney), Bradley White (Jesse Unger), Jordan Charney (Dr. Mandel), Carolyn McCormick (Dr. Elizabeth Olivet), Lenka Peterson (Housekeeper), Werner Klemperer (Bill Unger), Allison Janney (Nora), Currie Graham (Mitchell Burkitt), Julie White (Sandy), John Ramsey (Judge Walter Schreiber), Kimberly Pistone (Sara Bergstrom)

Reviewing the Case: Lucy Nevin is a soap opera star who has been assaulted in Central Park. Cerreta and Logan discover that Jesse Unger, an obsessive fan, was to blame. With echoes of the John Lennon assassination, John Hinkley's attempted killing of President Ronald Reagan, and the fan obsession that led to the attempted murder of actor Teresa Saldana, this segment is a timely drama on the subject of stalking and the validity of the insanity defense. It is graced by Bradley White's chilling and ethereal performance as the obsessed fan. Stone must choreograph a tricky dance around the issues of insanity and culpability. The script sets up a no-win situation in the courts because our culture sanctions celebrity adulation. The Jesse Ungers are the dark shadows we are only now beginning to recognize.

Noteworthy Discoveries: This is the first episode with Rene Balcer as a story editor for *Law & Order*.

Episode 35: Severance

Original air date: January 14, 1992
Teleplay by Michael Chernuchin and William Fordes, story by Michael Duggan and William Fordes, directed by Jim Frawley

Additional Cast and Guest Stars: George Grizzard (Arthur Gold), Maureen Anderman (Sharon Styger), Sam Groom (Larry Teasdale), Steve Rankin (Frank Kemp), Joseph Urla (David Werner), Lisa Ryall (Bettina McManus), Ralph Bell (Judge McIntyre), J. Smith-Cameron (Mindy Moskowitz), Jay Devlin (Martine), Frank John Hughes (Rozakis), David Rosenbaum (Judge Alan Berman), John Fiore (Det. Anthony Profaci)

Reviewing the Case: Stone goes up against his old nemesis, defense attorney Arthur Gold, as he tries to prove that the mysterious murder of two men in a parking lot is connected to the disappearance of a government informant. (It turns out that she was killed by a hit man hired by the suspect against whom she was informing.) This is one of the rare *Law & Order* episodes in which Stone's emotions cloud his judgment. George Grizzard's Arthur Gold is the quintessentially *professional* lawyer, the guy who will bury his adversary in paper work, with specious motion after motion, if it will get him a conviction. And this is what offends Stone's basic belief in the law. For Gold, the law is a means to an end, that of victory in the courtroom. He knows Stone's vulnerabilities, which is why he can fool him into making a severance motion that would ultimately hurt the prosecution. Since Grizzard plays to Gold's cleverness, rather than presenting him as sleazy, he makes "Severance" seem like a peppy tennis match. We're waiting to see who will drop the ball.

Noteworthy Discoveries: Stone has broken his wrist playing tennis with Robinette. It's one of the few *Law & Order* episodes that doesn't culminate in a trial.

Relevant Testimony: MICHAEL CHERNUCHIN (writer): "Arthur Gold was my creation. A really smart defense lawyer, and a good foil. Usually they are slimy guys in two-thousand-dollar suits who'll do anything, or they are complete nebbishes. This guy was Stone's equal. We wanted somebody who could provide a challenge to Stone's righteousness."

Episode 36: Blood is Thicker...

Original air date: February 4, 1992
Teleplay by Ed Zuckerman, story by Ed Zuckerman and Robert Nathan, directed by Peter Levin

Additional Cast and Guest Stars: Nancy Marchand (Barbara Ryder), John Bedford Lloyd (Jonathan Ryder), Joel Polis (Dr. Friedman), Sam Freed (Kent Meeker), Carolyn McCormick (Dr. Elizabeth Olivet), Jude Ciccolella (Morgan), Kim Hamilton (Judge Vivian Jackson), Alan Manson (Judge Eric Bryan), John McMartin (Ryder's Attorney), Donald Corren (Medill), Nicholas Turturro (Poletti), Emma Tammi (Alison Ryder), John Fiore (Det. Anthony Profaci)

Reviewing the Case: When Lois Ryder's body is found in an alley, Cerreta and Logan suspect a serial mugging, until their investigation takes them closer to home and to the motives of her husband, Jonathan, and his mother, Barbara. Lois, who was killed by Jonathan after he learned she had had an affair with a Jewish man, was also from a lower social class, so the Ryders are upset in ways other than the obvious anti-Semitism. And now Barbara Ryder's main focus is control over the upbringing of her granddaughter. When a cover-up comes undone over a revelation about heirlooms (a few cherished brooches), and the spineless husband is convicted, the viewer watches with trepidation as Lois's daughter walks innocently into the arms of her grandmother. This installment is about how the privileged commit crimes and often get away with them, and it looks into the tensions inherent in the class system.

Noteworthy Discoveries: We find out that Profaci has a wife named Shirley. Nicholas Turturro would become a regular on *N.Y.P.D. Blue* as Det. James Martinez (1993–).

Episode 37: Trust
Original air date: February 11, 1992
Teleplay by Rene Balcer, story by Michael Duggan and Rene Balcer, directed by Daniel Sackheim

Additional Cast and Guest Stars: Tom Mason (Ian Maser), Michael Constantine (Barnett), Lizbeth MacKay (Pamela Maser), Carolyn McCormick (Dr. Elizabeth Olivet), Harley Cross (Jamie Maser), John Juback (Mr. Fenwick), Lynn Niederman Silver (Mrs. Fenwick), Christine Farrell (Shrier), Michael Harney (Detective Gullickson), Barbara Spiegel (Judge Harriet Doremus), Ben Hammer (Judge Frank Markham), Lee Shepherd (Judge Joseph Gannon)

Reviewing the Case: When young Jamie Maser kills his best friend during a game called Trust, Stone is determined to see that he doesn't get away with the murder. However, a previous shooting by Jamie is inadmissible because of a sealed record that was part of his parents' divorce settlement. This segment gets at the need to take personal responsibility for our actions. Jamie tries to hide behind the law and the medication he was taking to justify the shooting of his friend. Moriarty's smart performance allows Stone to convincingly draw this curtain aside to show that Jamie is a sexually and psychologically abused boy. This is where the episode becomes a heart-rending father-and-son story. "Trust" isn't very distinguished but its variables add up to an affecting hour-long drama.

Noteworthy Discoveries: Christine Farrell appears for the second time as the ballistics expert, here called Shrier. Previously, the character (and actor) appeared in Episode 24: "The Wages of Love," but the character's name was given as Arlene, with no last name.

Episode 38: Vengeance
Original air date: February 18, 1992
Teleplay by Michael Chernuchin and Rene Balcer, story by Peter Greenberg and Michael Chernuchin, directed by Daniel Sackheim

Additional Cast and Guest Stars: James Rebhorn (Albert Chaney), Barbara Barrie (Mrs. Bream), Allen Garfield (Carl Berg), Rutanya Alda (Sara Chaney), Jay Patterson (O'Connell), Jane Cronin (Judge McKeever), Roger Serbagi (Judge Quinn), Fred J. Scollay (Judge Barsky), Nicholas Levitin (Dr. Cohen), Melinda Mullins (Forensics Technician)

Reviewing the Case: Judy Bream's naked and tortured body is found atop an elevator. Albert Chaney, a mild-mannered accountant and ex-con, might have committed the crime. This episode depicts how the legal system can be subverted to convict unfairly. Chaney (brilliantly played by James Rebhorn) is a serial killer. However, Stone does not believe that having him tried in Connecticut (a state with the death penalty) rather than in New York ultimately serves the law. To this prosecutor with a conscience, it would merely be an act of revenge. The dramatic tension in the episode stems from the fact that, if Stone loses the trial in New York, double jeopardy prevents him from ever trying the killer again. Brooks and Moriarty bring tremendous passion into the debate their characters stage about the death penalty. Of note is the cogent cross-examination sequence with Allen Garfield and Barbara Barrie, and the profound look of horror on Rutanya Alda's face when Stone shows her photos of the girls her husband has killed. In addition, Dann Florek is very resourceful in the (daringly lengthy) interrogation of Chaney. "Vengeance" is one of those potent polemics condemning the barbarism of the death penalty while recognizing the emotions behind society's desire to have it.

Noteworthy Discoveries: This is the first time Cragen helps the two detectives interrogate a suspect.

Relevant Testimony: RENE BALCER (writer): "I liked the nine-page interrogation scene which we did before [the rival TV cop series] *Homicide* [*:Life on the Street*, 1993–] came on [television]. When you're working with the rhythm of the episode, the questions [used in the interrogation] have to have a point. It has to build into a verbal trap. So it is as difficult to do as a courtroom scene."

DANN FLOREK (actor): "In the second year, another favorite episode of mine was 'Vengeance.' That's one I fought for again and again. I said, 'Put me in the f***ing interrogation room.' And they did. I had more to do in that one than probably any episode that year."

Episode 39: Sisters of Mercy
Original air date: March 3, 1992
Teleplay by Rene Balcer, story by Robert Palm and Rene Balcer, directed by Fred Gerber

Additional Cast and Guest Stars: Kate Burton (Sister Bettina), William H. Macy (Jack Powell), Kelli Williams (Maggie), Judy Reyes (Maria), Carolyn McCormick (Dr. Elizabeth Olivet), Larry Joshua (Chris McCarter), Latanya Richardson (Anne Houston), Deborah White (Francine Hughes), Bernard Grant (Judge Irwin Reisman), Vincent Laresca (Danny)

Reviewing the Case: Sister Bettina, a nun in charge of a shelter for troubled teens, is accused of molesting an addict named Maggie. However, while investigating these charges Cerreta and Logan uncover the fact that Jack Powell, the administrator at Haven House, has a history of seducing the young women in his care. This installment takes the volatile subject of rape and attempts to redefine the meaning of the crime. Powell is a predator masquerading as a milquetoast (William H. Macy plays him to queasy perfection), and he extorts sex by taking advantage of the fear the girls have about being back on the mean streets. As vigorously dramatized by Moriarty, the brilliance of Stone's thinking here is that the psychological power Powell has regarding a teenager's fate is as potentially threatening as the physical harm of an actual rape. "Sisters of Mercy" also never lets the audience forget that society is still a long way from solving the problems that brought these kids to Jack Powell's door in the first place.

Noteworthy Discoveries: In this episode Paul Sorvino's daughter, Mira, a future Oscar winner, has a small role as Olivia, another young woman in the shelter. Although her scene was cut, she still earned a Screen Actors Guild card for her trouble. Logan's conversations with Sister Bettina reveal more about his own Catholic background, and Cerreta divulges something to Logan about his religious past when he confesses a youthful theft of unblessed sacramental wafers.

Relevant Testimony: RENE BALCER (writer): "I wrote that in the first season. Originally the character of the nun was a militant, and a nonpracticing lesbian. It had to do with a group of nuns fighting the patriarchy of the church. The Bill Macy character originally was a priest. The episode was very controversial and sent alarm bells ringing down the halls of the Catholic Church. Anyway, we didn't do it in the first season because we already had five hot-button episodes with advertiser pullouts, so we thought we'd better wait and fight the battle for lesbian nuns later."

Episode 40: Cradle to Grave
Original air date: March 31, 1992
Teleplay by Robert Nathan and Sally Nemeth, directed by James Frawley

Additional Cast and Guest Stars: Tony LoBianco (Marc Meneger), Victor Argo (Jose Tirador), Bill Cwikowski (Horvath), Karen Lynn Gorney (Iris Corman), Doris Belack (Judge Margaret Barry), Richard Bright (Albert Boxer), Edouard DeSoto (Sanchez), Rocco Sisto (Joseph Turner), Idina Harris (Jackie Ward), Brenda Denmark (Nurse Rhonda James), Leonard Thomas (Lucas, the Hospital Janitor), John Speredakos (Dr. Orton)

Reviewing the Case: A janitor finds a cardboard box containing Henry Ward, a baby who has frozen to death. Cerreta and Logan discover that the two landlords of the building, Iris Corman and Joseph Turner, have been trying to circumvent the city's rental laws and drive out tenants by keeping the heat off. What starts as another case of child abuse becomes a story about the most defenseless people in society victimized by human greed. Rocco Sisto and Karen Lynn Gorney (John Travolta's dance partner in *Saturday Night Fever*, 1977) play people with little regard for anything other than their own well-being. "Cradle to Grave" isn't a real treasure (it lacks the character complexity of, say, Episode 32: "Heaven"), but the segment offers an absorbing moral lesson: When greed is acceptable, depravity becomes its worst companion.

Noteworthy Discoveries: There's an unusual *Law & Order* plot wrinkle here. A juror is responsible for a mistrial when it's discovered that he speaks Spanish and, during deliberation, has contradicted the court-appointed translator's interpretation of a key phrase.

Relevant Testimony: ROBERT NATHAN (writer): "This episode was written during a period when the Upper West Side of Manhattan was undergoing massive renewal. . . . There were several landlords who were notorious for hiring thugs to throw little old ladies out in the street with their belongings, and then trash the building so they couldn't get back in. And the city did not have the capacity at the time to cope with how much of it was happening. You were sickened every day with wonder as to how anybody could do this."

Episode 41: The Fertile Fields
Original air date: April 7, 1992
Teleplay by Rene Balcer and Michael Chernuchin, directed by Ed Sherin

Additional Cast and Guest Stars: David Spielberg (Isaac Shore), Tom Mardirosian (Joe Tashjian), Daryl "Chill" Mitchell (Reggie Baggs), Josh Weinstein (Caleb Shore), Lenore Harris (Mrs. Shore), Jerry Stiller (Mr. Tobis), Raymond Genadry (Andonian), Leslie Hendrix (Rogers), Charles Blackwell (Judge Gillman), David Lipman (Judge Moodie)

Reviewing the Case: Police find the burned and beaten body of a Jewish man, Ezra Shore. Although two black teenagers were seen fleeing the scene, it turns out that Shore might have been involved in money laundering. This episode begins as an examination of the deteriorating relations between blacks and Jews but, while quickly exploring that terrain, it shifts gears into a story of family betrayal. This angle isn't well handled because there seem to be no larger implications, and even the shock ending feels like an afterthought. "The Fertile Fields" does have one fascinating aspect: Talmudic law, with its prohibition against incriminating your own family, is invoked so that both Isaac and the dead man Ezra's son, Caleb, receive something called "transactional immunity."

Episode 42: Intolerance
Original air date: April 14, 1992
Teleplay by Robert Nathan and Sally Nemeth, directed by Steven Robman

Additional Cast and Guest Stars: Kelly Bishop (Marian Borland), Stephen Pearlman (Leonard Willis), Pat McNamara (Mrs. Silbert), David Lipman (Judge Torledsky), Lee Wallace (Judge Simon), Allelon Ruggiero (Carl Borland), Liana Pai (Claudia Chong), Rex Robbins (Steinman), Sam Rockwell (Randy Borland), Sabrina Lloyd (Kate Silbert), Christine Farrell (Shrier), Lily Froehlich (Mrs. Chong), Stephen Xavier Lee (Tim Chong)

Reviewing the Case: Chinese teenager Tim Chong, a star physics student, is shot down in the street and killed. Cerreta and Logan investigate whether or not the crime is gang-related. They learn that Tim was actually murdered by his best friend, Carl Borland, and Carl's mother—over a science competition. This episode is rather unique (and brave) in depicting the way bigotry can adapt itself to the nuances of each minority under attack. In this case, it's an assault on the Chinese-American culture's quest for academic excellence. From a legal standpoint, the episode is also very adept at pinpointing how a search warrant might be deemed illegal after an anonymous tip leads detectives to the evidence. There is perjured testimony as well, brought forth out of remorse rather than a desire to lie, which leads Stone to ask for a mistrial. As in the best *Law & Order* episodes, nothing is resolved. While embracing the American dream, Tim Chong is murdered by an American family self-destructing from its own inability to fulfill that goal.

Noteworthy Discoveries: A similar story, based on a Texas mother who tried to have a young girl killed so her own daughter could become a cheerleader, found its way into the award-winning 1993 HBO movie *The Positively True Adventures of the Alleged Texas Cheerleader-Murdering Mom*, with Holly Hunter and Beau Bridges. This is the first time Stone must call a mistrial because a witness has perjured herself.

Episode 43: Silence

Original air date: April 28, 1992
Teleplay by Rene Balcer and Michael Chernuchin, story by Rene Balcer and Michael Chernuchin, directed by Ed Sherin

Additional Cast and Guest Stars: George Martin (Edward Vogel), James Sutorius (Colson), Reed Birney (Malcolm Barclay), Jimmy Ray Weeks (Harris), Richard Levine (Judge Strelzik), Harry Johnson (Brewer), Billie Neal (Rhoden), Joanna Merlin (Carla), Joe Aufiery (Harold Dwyer), John Seidman (Jay Lingard), Gloria Hoye (Murphy), Alba Oms (Valdez), Leslie Hendrix (Medical Examiner Rogers), Fred J. Scollay (Judge Barsky), Len Gochman (Judge Scholl)

Reviewing the Case: The death of a closeted gay city councilman, James Vogel, is found to be part of an extortion plan. His father, an influential politician, opposes prosecution of the murderer because it would reveal the truth about his son. This story concerns some of the same complex social and psychological perspectives on sexual identity explored in Episode 65: "Manhood" (Season Three, 1992–93) and Episode 111: "Pride" (Season Five, 1994–95). It grapples with the kinds of self-censorship gay people might impose on themselves because of the prejudice they're forced to confront: One character is a former ball player, who must project a heterosexual image for fear of losing his job. Vogel's father is nicely played by George Martin, who probably has his best acting moment on the stand as he reluctantly acknowledges his son's sexual preference. The greatest tension in this story comes from his silence, which is deafening.

Noteworthy Discoveries: It is discovered that Edward Vogel was instrumental in the process by which Adam Schiff became district attorney of New York City.

Episode 44: The Working Stiff

Original air date: May 12, 1992
Teleplay by Robert Palm, story by William Fordes and Robert Palm, directed by Daniel Sackheim

Additional Cast and Guest Stars: Eli Wallach (Simon Vilanis), George DiCenzo (Eddie Palmieri), William Prince (Governor Corcoran), Victor Slezak (Cousins), Mia Dillon (Dr. Bergman), Ron Parady (Chessman), Joseph Siravo (Joey Palmieri), David Rosenbaum (Judge Berman), Philip LeStrange (Corcoran's Lawyer)

Reviewing the Case: A merger-and-acquisitions shark, McFadden, is found murdered at his desk. This killing opens a can of worms involving

Simon Vilanis, an ailing union worker, and the complicity of a former governor named Corcoran in bank fraud. To complicate matters, Corcoran just happens to be one of Adam Schiff's old friends. This episode is the best story yet in the series about the corporate and blue-collar corruption of the 1980s and the consequent economic collapse in the following decade. It's also the first episode that is centered on the DA, and Steven Hill's performance shines like a gem. He has a beautifully expressive moment when Schiff discovers that Corcoran paid for the hit on McFadden: He faces the window with his shoulders hunched up around his ears, as if to block what he is hearing. Eli Wallach might seem a little too precious with his constant chatter and hacking cough, but he's also funny in an acerbic way. "The Working Stiff" is a perfect season closer, with its air of faint nostalgia. It is an elegy for another time as it re-imagines life as it was before the McFaddens of today turned the economy into a junk-bond graveyard.

Noteworthy Discoveries: This was writer Robert Palm's last script for *Law & Order*. Schiff and Corcoran cut their teeth in politics when Schiff served as the former governor's campaign manager. This is the second consecutive installment that concers Schiff's friendships.

Relevant Testimony: ROBERT PALM (writer): "[I]t was inspired by some stories my father told me.... One of his oldest clients was the vice president of this company outside of Boston that had been taken over by the British. They fired him right in front of his own people and wouldn't even let him go down on the shop floor and say goodbye after forty years [of service].... What I did in the story was create a man who was dying and had nothing to lose. It was a complicated story with some complicated issues that a lot of people internally didn't get or care about. After I left the show, I heard that Ed Sherin said that it was one of his favorite programs. Maybe it's all a question of age on this one. The older guys could relate to it."

Season Three
September 1992–May 1993
60-minute episodes

Production Team:

Dick Wolf (Executive Producer), Joseph Stern (Co-Executive Producer), Walon Green (Co-Executive Producer), Robert Nathan (Producer), Jeffrey Hayes (Producer), Michael Chernuchin (Co-Producer), Arthur Forney (Co-Producer), Lewis H. Gould (Associate Producer), Rene

Balcer (Executive Script Consultant), Lewis H. Gould (Unit Production Manager), Richard Bianchi (Production Designer), Mike Post (Music), Lynn Kressel C.S.A. (Casting), Suzanne Ryan (Casting), Constantine Makris (Cinematography), Christopher Misiano (Camera Operator), Billy Fox (Editor), Michael Kewley (Editor), Mark Newman (Editor), Mike Struk (Technical Advisor), Bill Fordes (Technical Advisor)

Regular Cast

Richard Brooks (Assistant District Attorney Paul Robinette), Dann Florek (Capt. Donald Cragen), Steven Hill (District Attorney Adam Schiff), Carolyn McCormick (Dr. Elizabeth Olivet), Michael Moriarty (Executive Assistant District Attorney Ben Stone), Chris Noth (Det. Mike Logan), Jerry Orbach (Det. Lennie Briscoe, for Episodes 53–66), Paul Sorvino (Det. Phil Cerreta, for Episodes 45–53)

Third Season Overview

At the end of Season Two, NBC chose *Law & Order* as the network's first renewed show for 1992–93. When series costar Chris Noth was asked by *USA Today* what to expect, his answer was, "We're going to get tougher." He wasn't joking. During this season, the show plunges into more contentious subjects, while revisiting certain types of crime with a new authority.

Episode 46: "Conspiracy" not only borrows from the Malcolm X assassination; it probes one of the controversies about that shooting: Did black leaders conspire to kill him? Episode 49: "Wedded Bliss" exposes the horrors of slave labor in American sweatshops (an issue that has haunted talk show host Kathie Lee Gifford in recent years). Episode 52: "Prince of Darkness" shines a light on the Colombian drug cartels, showing how ineffectual the law can be in the face of their power. Then, Episode 65: "Manhood" takes on the so-called "blue wall" again, this time as it applies to a gay police officer left to die without backup from cops in his own precinct.

Despite the creative peaks of the previous year, actor Paul Sorvino leaves the show mid-season, ostensibly to concentrate on his opera career. Like his predecessor, the character Greevey (played by George Dzundza), Sorvino's Cerreta is also the victim of a shooting but he survives and moves on with his life. Jerry Orbach, who appeared as a lawyer in Episode 24: "The Wages of Love" from Season Two, becomes Logan's new partner, Det. Lennie Briscoe.

Carolyn McCormick debuts as the first woman to join the regular cast of *Law & Order*, albeit only in a recurring manner. From this point on, Olivet is called in as a psychiatric consultant on a case-by-case basis. McCormick's character is raped by a gynecologist in one of the more harrowing installments of the season, Episode 50: "Helpless."

By now, Robert Palm has left the *Law & Order* production team and legendary screenwriter Walon Green, perhaps best known for the graphically violent western film *The Wild Bunch* (1969), comes on board. Meanwhile, Rene Balcer assumes the status of executive script consultant. *Law & Order* also moves to Wednesday evenings at 10:00 P.M. By season's end, executive producer Joseph Stern will return to his home in Los Angeles, and NBC will insist on recruiting more women characters for the program. As a result, Dann Florek and Richard Brooks will be dropped from the cast. However, even rougher times lie ahead for *Law & Order*.

Episode Descriptions

Episode 45: Skin Deep

Original air date: September 23, 1992
Teleplay by Robert Nathan and Gordon Rayfield, directed by Daniel Sackheim

Additional Cast and Guest Stars: Alberta Watson (Angela Brant), Lorraine Toussaint (Shambala Green), Murphy Guyer (Jeff Brant), Claire Danes (Tracy Brant), Donald Corren (Medill), David Baily (Alan Rohmer), Gina Torres (Laura Elkin), Yul Vazquez (Eddie Vasquez), Scotty Bloch (Judge Baum), David Rosenbaum (Judge Alan Berman)

Reviewing the Case: Julian Decker, a sleazy photographer, is found murdered. One of his models, Angela Brant, appears to be guilty. However, DNA evidence leads to her daughter, Tracy, who was having an affair with Decker. This episode dips into the turbulent waters of adolescent sexuality, illustrating how a teenager's desires can be entwined with the need to be accepted and wanted. Yet, it's not an entirely effective saga about thwarted dreams. And in "Skin Deep" justice is not alone in being blind, as the eye that beholds beauty can be just as unseeing.

Noteworthy Discoveries: During one of the entertaining debates between Shambala Green and Ben Stone, it is discovered that he has a daughter. Claire Danes, who plays Tracy Brant, went on to star in TV's *My So-Called Life* (1994–95) and such theatrical features as *Little Women* (1994) and *William Shakespeare's Romeo and Juliet* (1996), in the latter costarring with Leonardo DiCaprio.

Episode 46: Conspiracy

Original air date: September 30, 1992
Teleplay by Michael Chernuchin and Rene Balcer, directed by Ed Sherin

Additional Cast and Guest Stars: Joe Morton (Roland Books), Eric Bogosian (Gary Lowenthal), Gloria Foster (Satima Tate), Cynthia Martells (Sandra Koblin), Michael Jayce (Otis Cooke), Jeff Gendelman (Mitchell Koblin), Ben Hammer (Judge Herman Mooney), Victor Truro (Judge Spivak), Harold Miller (Marcus Tate)

Reviewing the Case: The assassination of Marcus Tate, a prestigious African-American leader, leads to the arrest of a man who believes his ex-wife has been having an affair with the victim. Stone suspects, but cannot prove, that another movement figure, Roland Books, conspired within the organization to have Tate eliminated. Filled with familiar echoes of the real-life Malcolm X murder in 1965 and ongoing rumors that Nation of Islam head Louis Farrakhan somehow had been involved, this episode peers down the hall of mirrors that surrounds most assassinations and conspiracy theories. It cleverly illustrates how political agendas of every stripe often obfuscate the pursuit of justice. Books assures Stone that a lone gunman rocks the comfort zone, while conspiracies make for good drama. However, what lingers most in this very satisfying episode is the final shot of Robinette alone in the doorway, contemplating the possible complicity of an organization devoted to establishing justice for his people.

Noteworthy Discoveries: This episode was honored with the Edgar Allen Poe Award from the esteemed Mystery Writers of America. Director Ed Sherin was nominated for an Emmy, and Constantine Makris won his first such award for cinematography. In a sequel to this installment, Episode 143: "Entrapment," Gloria Foster reprises her role as Satima Tate.

Relevant Testimony: JOSEPH STERN (executive producer): "In 'Conspiracy,' the only [*Law & Order*] script ever nominated [to this date] for an Emmy, it was Joe Morton's idea [to end it without a real resolution]. He said, 'We, as blacks, always circle the wagons. We don't give each other up.' And that was the touchstone. I went to the writers and we changed it to that whole oblique ending, where Moriarty couldn't nail him."

Episode 47: Forgiveness

Original air date: October 7, 1992
Teleplay by Ed Zuckerman, story by Ed Zuckerman and Robert Nathan, directed by Bill D'Elia

Additional Cast and Guest Stars: Laurence Luckinbill (Cy Weaver), Luis Antonio Ramos (Tommy Beltran), Luke Reilly (Father Gregory), David Leary (Curtis Milgram), Cynthia Hayden (Claudia Milgram), Francine Beers (Judge Janis Silver), William Jay Marshall (Judge Burton), Donald Corren (Medill), Clea Montville (Beth Milgram)

Reviewing the Case: Beth Milgram is found murdered the morning after her going-away party and her Latino boyfriend, Tommy Beltran, confesses to the crime. His attorney pleads his client's temporary insanity, while Stone seeks a charge of premeditated murder. This segment contemplates the notion that poverty may explain, but not excuse, our behavior. Stone tries to persuade jurors to see past their own feelings of guilt and look at the full facts of the case. As Stone reasons, when Beltran slugged Milgram with a pipe because she rejected him, it wasn't poverty committing the crime.

Relevant Testimony: ED ZUCKERMAN (writer): "['Forgiveness'] was mostly based on an outrageous story of a kid who went to Yale and killed his girlfriend and got a very light sentence because the church backed him up. Well, our intent was always that the guy was full of sh**. I was surprised a couple of years later when [some of] the L.A. writers said they didn't like 'Forgiveness.' They thought that the attempt to make that guy sympathetic was really obnoxious because he was so vile, but our intention was always that he was not worthy of sympathy or forgiveness."

Episode 48: The Corporate Veil
Original air date: October 14, 1992
Teleplay by Michael Chernuchin and Joe Morgenstern, directed by Don Scardino

Additional Cast and Guest Stars: Dennis Boutsikaris (Al Archer), Bruce Norris (Steven Cleary), Robert Milli (Roger Cleary), Carla Pinza (Mrs. Martinez), Elizabeth Hubbard (Annette Cleary), Michael Lombard (Harrison Miller), Maryann Urbano (Sharon Adler), Harriet Sansom Harris (Fran Kenny), George Murdoch (Judge Eric Bertram), Barbara Spiegel (Judge Harriet Doremus), Sully Boyar (Judge Harvey Sirken), Leslie Goldman (Judge Byman)

Reviewing the Case: Teenager Roberto Martinez dies of a heart attack when his pacemaker fails, leading the detectives to investigate Roger Cleary, president of the medical equipment company that manufactured it. The episode's title refers to the corporate veil protecting businesses from civil liability, and the story is all about the profit motive, which can affect the quality of products, even those that are supposed to save lives.

After an assured opening, however, the story bogs down with too many technical details about corroded wires and bad batteries. All this exposition leads to the familiar scenario of a father-son conflict; it isn't just the pacemakers that are dysfunctional.

Episode 49: Wedded Bliss

Original air date: October 21, 1992
Teleplay by Robert Nathan and Edward Pomerantz, directed by Vern Gillum

Additional Cast and Guest Stars: Patti D'Arbanville (Betty Drake), John Pankow (Charles Meadow), Bill Raymond (Ellis Drake), Jose Zuniga (Rudy Armandariz), Larry Keith (Francis Dunlap), Lisa Vidal (Lina Armandariz), Walter Bobbie (Fred Drake), Iraida Polanco (Katy Andon), John C. Vennema (Victor Shay), Donald Corren (Medill), Lee Shepherd (Judge Joseph Gannon), Carol Harris (Judge Adrianne Goldman)

Reviewing the Case: The discovery of a body in the Hudson River leads to the investigation of illegal sweatshops run by Ellis and Betty Drake, who make money by enslaving young immigrants. Along with Episode 32: "Heaven" and Episode 52: "Prince of Darkness," this segment is a powerhouse exposé, with a title that is perfectly fitting because it is both the name of the bridal gowns these workers (literally) give their lives to make and an ironic commentary on the Drakes' creepy marriage. The episode presents an obscene version of capitalism and a perversion of the Emma Lazarus poem at the Statue of Liberty: "Give me your tired, your poor, your huddled masses yearning to breathe free..." And we'll crush you?

Noteworthy Discoveries: It is revealed that Cerreta has a daughter named Linda. It's also the first time the show makes reference to a forensics process that allows a computer to reformat a face when only the skull remains.

Episode 50: Helpless

Original air date: November 4, 1992
Teleplay by Michael S. Chernuchin and Christine Roum, directed by James Frawley

Additional Cast and Guest Stars: Paul Hecht (Dr. Merritt), Tovah Feldshuh (Danielle Melnick), Felicity Huffman (Diane Perkins), Tracey Ellis (Nurse Gregg), Howard Witt (Judge Silver), Michele Pawk (Donna Marx), Maggie Burke (Celia Walsh), Adam LeFevre (Dr. Helman), Michael Levin (Dr. Reitman), Mark Shannon (Dr. Lewis)

Reviewing the Case: When Dr. Elizabeth Olivet is sexually assaulted by Dr. Merritt, a gynecologist, the subsequent investigation and trial uncover information that makes it difficult to convict him. Of all the fabulous episodes that *Law & Order* has done about rape, this is probably the most visceral. From the first chilling scene in Merritt's office to the anguish of Diane Perkins (Felicity Huffman) describing *her* encounter with the doctor, the story certainly lives up to its title. However, it never veers toward histrionics, as the law remains the focus, especially when Olivet fails to give police and prosecutors some key information. This astute script also draws a clear distinction between consensual sex, no matter how deviant, and rape. Carolyn McCormick is extraordinary as a professional whose good instincts fail her. Paul Hecht's remarkable performance conveys the smugness of a man who gets sexual pleasure from the fear of others. The true sting of "Helpless" is that some crimes never go away.

Noteworthy Discoveries: The indelibly etched events of this episode will come back to haunt Dr. Olivet later in Episode 53: "Point of View."

Relevant Testimony: CAROLYN MCCORMICK (actor): "I felt more sorry for the guy [Paul Hecht] playing the doctor [than for my character's plight]. He was so nervous, especially in the scene where he has to put the gloves on. He kept breaking the gloves. So we'd crack up. I was in the stirrups for four hours with little bike shorts on while he was trying to get his lines right. Every time he came over to me, he couldn't remember what he was supposed to say. He was so good in that episode but it was very hard for him to tap into whatever that doctor was about. I mean, no one really wants to go there."

Episode 51: Self Defense
Original air date: November 11, 1992
Teleplay by Rene Balcer and Hall Powell, directed by Ed Sherin

Additional Cast and Guest Stars: Adam Arkin (George Costas), Paul Butler (Judge Edmond Francis), Marissa Chibas (Christine Costas), Ron Rifkin (Alex Dracos), Frank Savino (Nick Fortas), Christine Farrell (Shrier), David Lipman (Judge Morris Torledsky), Ron Brice (Marvin Welles), Peter Yoshida (Joon Rhee), Wai Ching Ho (Mrs. Rhee)

Reviewing the Case: George Costas, a Greek immigrant and jewelry store owner, claims he was merely defending himself and his property when he shoots two black armed robbers. However, Stone goes after him for murder when the evidence indicates otherwise. This segment resembles Episode 2: "Subterranean Homeboy Blues" except that the subject of vigilante justice is seen from another perspective: an outsider who wants in.

Adam Arkin brings just the right measure of self-righteousness to this man who believes that arming himself is the American way. Although Cerreta has compassion for Costas, his sympathies are tested in the next installment, Episode 52: "Prince of Darkness," when the detective comes face to face with a man pointing a gun at *him*.

Noteworthy Discoveries: The reference to the Montreal Expos in the opening scene might be a concoction of writer Rene Balcer, who hails from Quebec. It's the first time one of the detectives (Cerreta) is called as a witness for the other side (the defense). Adam Arkin later will play Dr. Aaron Shutt on the hospital drama *Chicago Hope* (1994–).

Episode 52: Prince of Darkness
Original air date: November 18, 1992
Teleplay by Robert Nathan and William Fordes, directed by Gilbert Shilton

Additional Cast and Guest Stars: Carlos Sanz (Javier Gaitan), Rosana De Soto (Alicia Ortega), Joe Lisi (O'Donnell), Saundra Santiago (Sandra Alvaro), Mark Margolis (George Lobrano), Shawn Elliott (Buenoventura), Jaime Sanchez (Mr. Christobal), Lonny Price (Mr. Hoover), Gary Perez (Manuel Ortega), Carrell Myers (Natalie Ortega), Catherine Gardner (Felice Ortega), Bernie McInerney (Judge Michael Callaghan), Alice Spivak (Judge Esther Fein), Lizanne Mitchell (Judge Lerner), Christine Farrell (Schrier)

Reviewing the Case: When Manuel and Natalie Ortega are gunned down by Colombian hit man Javier Gaitan in retaliation for another killing, Cerreta and Logan try to nab him before he leaves New York. But Gaitan, known as "The Prince of Darkness," is hard to catch. In the process, Cerreta is seriously wounded. This episode is one of *the* bleakest offerings in the series, as it highlights the impotence of the American justice system in the face of the drug cartels. The narrative moves like one constant chase scene going in circles. Gaitan is referred to as "Elvis," a sick joke in that The King is forever sighted but never found. The shooting of Cerreta is particularly shocking, as guns are rarely fired on *Law & Order*. But it's business as usual for the cartels.

Noteworthy Discoveries: Cerreta, the second of Logan's partners to be shot, is married to Elaine. It is also learned that he is almost fifty years old.

Relevant Testimony: ROBERT NATHAN (writer): "We knew just as the episode was being written that Paul wanted to leave. So we thought we'd send him out with a real flash, where he would put himself on the line.

The story was crafted around that moment, and the scene was built on the notion that [Lobrano, the gun dealer] was as nervous as Cerreta. Cerreta is nervous because he is [faced] with an unstable character. We played against the convention of the suave undercover scene, where the bad guys are [totally] in control. And Mark Margolis plays a guy who is clearly drugged up, and he plays it with a frenetic madness in his eyes."

Episode 53: Point of View
Original air date: November 25, 1992
Teleplay by Walon Green and Rene Balcer, directed by Gilbert Moses

Additional Cast and Guest Stars: Elaine Stritch (Lanie Stieglitz), Lisa Eichhorn (Mary Kostrinski), Gary Basaraba (Kevin Reilly), Paul Sorvino (Det. Phil Cerreta), Caroline Aaron (Valerie Walker), Alan North (Jimmy Scanlon), Michael Ingram (Officer Andy Libik), Delphi Harrington (Suzanne Delaye), Maria Cellario (Elaine Cerreta), Cara Duff-MacCormick (Maggie Duff), Damon Chandler (Judge Bonner)

Reviewing the Case: Tommy Duff's murder in front of a pub launches an investigation by Logan and his new partner, Det. Lennie Briscoe. A suspect, Mary Kostrinski, may or may not have been a victim of sexual harassment. This segment would be the perfect *Rashomon* (1951 film) episode but for the fact that the real truth of the situation is finally reached. Along the way, the story line settles a number of issues. Still hoping Cerreta will return to active duty as his partner, Logan doesn't care for Briscoe. Noth is magnificent in giving his character the depth to begin letting go of the old and making room for the new. Then, the trauma of Dr. Olivet's rape (detailed in Episode 50: "Helpless") now creates a barrier to her good judgment. When Stone must discredit her testimony, McCormick gives another exquisite performance as Olivet faces the reality of her emotional state. It's a beautifully constructed episode with the always dazzling Elaine Stritch playing defense lawyer Lanie Stieglitz. "Point of View" gives us many views to ponder and certain truths that are irrefutable.

Noteworthy Discoveries: Elaine Stritch won an Emmy Award for her performance in this episode, which was also nominated for an Edgar Allen Poe Award. Paul Sorvino reappears as Cerreta, recovering in the hospital from the gunshot wounds he suffered in Episode 52: "Prince of Darkness" before retiring as Logan's partner. Also seen in the proceedings is his wife, Elaine.

Relevant Testimony: CHRIS NOTH (actor): "In 'Prince of Darkness,' after Cerreta had been shot, I was saying goodbye to Paul Sorvino. Jerry was coming on and I didn't know what was going to happen with that relationship. I was just getting used to Paul, so you use what exists. But I love Paul. Everybody knows he has a huge ego, but he was also very loving. He's got a big heart. So that scene was real in many ways."

Episode 54: Consultation
Original air date: December 9, 1992
Teleplay by Matt Kiene and Joe Reinkemeyer, directed by James Hayman

Additional Cast and Guest Stars: Roscoe Lee Browne (Sir Idris Balewa), Andrew Robinson (Phillip Marietta), Wendell Pierce (Chief Nwaka), Keith Szarabajka (Marian Sebelius), Talia Balsam (Lynette Turner), Seth Gilliam (Babatunde), Robert Katims (Jacob Bloom), Beatrice Winde (Sarah De Witt), Afemo Omilami (Michael Kano), Seth Sibanda (Fabian Ayinde), Kwaku Sintim-Misa (Joseph Amoda), David Rosenbaum (Judge Alan Berman), Charlotte Colavin (Judge Lisa Pongracic)

Reviewing the Case: An engineer and a tribal chief become the key suspects in the death of a pregnant Nigerian woman, killed by the ingested heroin she had been smuggling into the United States. This isn't one of the best episodes, despite some fine actors who aren't bad in it. The story is not farfetched; it just fails to build to any significant surprises. We know that Chief Nwaka is guilty, so why just pile up legal points without making them particularly dramatic? Like Episode 48: "The Corporate Veil," this story line becomes mired in uninteresting details.

Noteworthy discoveries: It should be noted that actor Keith Szarabajka will appear later, in Episode 149: "D-Girl," as the ex-husband of one of the newer members of the prosecuting team, Jamie Ross.

Episode 55: Extended Family
Original air date: January 6, 1993
Teleplay by Wendell Rawls and Robert Nathan, story by Wendell Rawls, directed by Charles Correll

Additional Cast and Guest Stars: Barry Primus (Gary Silver), Michael McGuire (David Preston), Anna Holbrook (Janet Silver), James Murtaugh (Dr. Jenner), Joyce Van Patten (Ramona Stark), Robert Emmet (Harold Zorn), Lisen Sundgren (Christina Jurgson), Madeline Zima (Samantha Silver), Melinda Wade (Leslie Silver), Bruce Fitzpatrick (Mark Sanders), John Ramsey (Judge Walter Schreiber), John Fiore (Det. Anthony Profaci)

Reviewing the Case: Samantha Silver is kidnapped by her natural mother, Janet Silver, but the case becomes more complicated when the woman charges her ex-husband with sexual abuse of their child. The suspense here rests solely on whether or not the father, Gary Silver, has molested his daughter. Barry Primus's wily turn as this nominally unsympathetic man keeps us guessing. This segment also suggests that psychiatrists who specialize in what is called "recovered memory" may have hidden agendas. Joyce Van Patten gives a thoughtful performance as abused-child rescuer Ramona Stark, who could easily have been painted with shades of villainy. Instead, she comes across as a woman who believes her own press clippings. The skin on the face of actress Anna Holbrook (Janet Silver) seems wrapped so tight from anger that it threatens to crack her bones. "Extended Family" gets at the brutal way divorced parents sometimes manipulate their children to punish each other.

Relevant Testimony: ROBERT NATHAN (writer): "In the middle of the story, when we are not even committed to an ending, the actor [Barry Primus] calls Joe Stern and tells him that he didn't want to play a child molester. He had a young child and he did not want even the possibility of his kid seeing him on television portraying someone [like that]. Joe then asked me if we know whether he is guilty or not.... The script wasn't done yet, so we didn't know. I told Joe to tell Barry that the easiest thing to do was to play the character as if he believes he's innocent. And if he does, at the end, no one will know if he's guilty or not. When it was first screened... we discovered that most of the women who saw it thought he was guilty, and most of the men thought he was innocent."

Episode 56: Right to Counsel
Original air date: January 13, 1993
Teleplay by Michael S. Chernuchin, directed by James Frawley

Additional Cast and Guest Stars: Darrell Larson (Kevin Doyle), Mary Mara (Sally Knight), Richard Cox (Stephen Gregg), Bill Moor (William Patton), Mady Kaplan (Carole Spiegelman), Alice Hirson (Sally Baker), Carol Rossen (Judge Gelfant), Bill Buell (Douglas Pomerantz), Donna Murphy (Karen Unger), Vince O'Brien (Judge Franks), Jay Harris (Judge Mark Burns)

Reviewing the Case: Was Barbara Spiegelman, a wealthy and elderly woman, murdered by her much younger boyfriend? Briscoe and Logan suspect as much but other evidence points to her estate lawyer, Kevin Doyle. The class system in America is once again evaluated here. Doyle comes from a low-income neighborhood and wants to join the privileged strata of society, even though he's in massive debt to the IRS. Attorney

Sally Knight is another get-rich-quick character who always secures plea bargains for her clients, whether they're guilty or not. Stephen Gregg is the sad-sack designer who was Spiegelman's lover. "Right to Counsel" is a moderately entertaining episode about desperate people who will do anything to get ahead.

Episode 57: Night and Fog
Original air date: February 3, 1993
Teleplay by Michael Chernuchin and Rene Balcer, directed by Ed Sherin

Additional Cast and Guest Stars: Eric Bogosian (Gary Lowenthal), Nehemiah Persoff (David Steinmetz), Reizl Bozyk (Mrs. Liebman), Chip Zien (David Green), Joan Copeland (Judge Rebecca Stein), Diane Venora (Mara Feder), Don T. Maseng (Rabbi Dworkin), Leslie Hendrix (Rogers), John Driver (Malcolm Haynes), Fred J. Scollay (Judge Andrew Barsky)

Reviewing the Case: David Steinmetz is an elderly Jewish man who claims he assisted the suicide of his ailing wife. Stone suspects he may have killed her to cover up his complicity in the horror of the Nazi death camps. The title of this episode, "Night and Fog," is borrowed from the 1953 documentary about Auschwitz by Alain Resnais. It is a strong episode with a passing resemblance to Costa-Gavras's film *The Music Box* (1990), in which a daughter discovers her father's true World War II identity and horrible past. However, the fascinating legal and moral issue at the heart of this story is whether Stone should prosecute Steinmetz for the murder of his wife or allow him to be extradited to face punishment for crimes against humanity. Nehemiah Persoff gives a subtle performance throughout, and Diane Venora is quite astonishing as a woman who can't put the face of a butcher on the man she knows as her father. Although the truth is liberating, it may not offer any reassurances.

Noteworthy Discoveries: It is discovered that Briscoe's father, a G.I. in World War II, was part of the first Allied regiment that went into the Buchenwald concentration camp. Not a religious man, after that fateful day he came to believe in the devil. Stone mentions his daughter reading another haunting account of that era, *The Diary of Anne Frank* (1952).

Episode 58: Promises to Keep
Original air date: February 10, 1993
Teleplay by Robert Nathan and Joshua Stern, story by William Fordes and Douglas Stark, directed by Ed Sherin

Additional Cast and Guest Stars: Lindsay Crouse (Dr. Diane Meade), Fritz Weaver (Lawrence Webber), Gail Strickland (Ellen Gorham), Jenny O'Hara (Carol Janssen), Dennis Creaghan (Leonard Gorham), Frederick Weller (Daniel Garrett), Jesse Moore (Dr. Howard Malone), Robert Serbagi (Judge Robert Quinn), John Fiore (Det. Anthony Profaci)

Reviewing the Case: Daniel Garrett murders his girlfriend, Jennifer Gorham, in Central Park. Briscoe and Logan determine that he did it as a result of psychological pressure from his psychiatrist, Dr. Diane Meade, with whom he has been having a sexual relationship. The primary issue here is how the patient-therapist relationship can be abused. Lindsay Crouse is bloodcurdling as a rational woman with insane ideas about therapy, prompting a vigorous confrontation with Dr. Olivet. The most alarming moments come not with the verdict but the sentencing, when the judge dispenses uneven justice and Meade's profession shields her from responsibility in the destruction of her patient.

Noteworthy Discoveries: For the first time, Briscoe and Logan play good cop-bad cop in the line of duty.

Episode 59: Mother Love
Original air date: February 24, 1993
Teleplay by Robert Nathan, story by Walon Green and Robert Nathan, directed by Daniel Sackheim

Additional Cast and Guest Stars: Mary Alice (Virginia Bryan), Kelly Neal (Lucian Bryan), Edie Falco (Sally Bell), Phyllis Yvonne Stickney (Janine Holleran), Nancy Ticotin (Carla Gomez), Douglas Turner Ward (Fred Bryan), Leland Gantt (Jonas Stark, a.k.a. "Skate"), Rafael Baez (Angel Suarez), Fatima Faloye (Keisha White), Brenda Thomas Denmark (Beverly Harris), David Lipman (Judge Morris Torledsky), Donald Corren (Medill), John Fiore (Det. Anthony Profaci)

Reviewing the Case: Dawn Bryan, a drug-addicted black girl, is found dead. Briscoe and Logan initially believe she was killed by her boyfriend, until the investigation leads to Dawn's own family. The episode asks whether or not sympathy should be extended to a black mother who felt compelled to end her daughter's life in what was, at least in part, a mercy killing. Robinette demands equal justice, but Stone doesn't want to indict. In a wrenching confession scene, Mary Alice puts heartbreak at the center of the moral quandary in this deeply moving drama.

Noteworthy Discoveries: The grand jury process is demonstrated when we see how an indictment for Manslaughter One is established.

Relevant Testimony: ROBERT NATHAN (writer): "Mary Alice's long speech is probably the longest uninterrupted piece of dialogue in the history of *Law & Order*. It runs just under five minutes. And on television anything over twenty seconds is considered long. But we had one of the great actresses, with over thirty years of extraordinary work behind her. You can't take your eyes off her. Film crews are used to watching actors do powerful things and they are naturally oblivious because they are checking the lighting, or looking to see if the focus is good, but even they were weeping. Everyone was transported."

Episode 60: Conduct Unbecoming
Original air date: March 10, 1993
Teleplay by Michael Chernuchin and Rene Balcer, story by Walon Green and Peter Greenberg, directed by Arthur Forney

Additional Cast and Guest Stars: Len Cariou (Capt. Allard Bunker), Boyd Gaines (Lieutenant St. Claire), George Coe (Lee Hastings), Michael Dolan (Ensign Evan Walters), Julianna Margulies (Lt. Ruth Mendoza), Dick Latessa (Vice-Admiral Cody), Richard Hamilton (Chief PO James Hagen), Victor Truro (Judge Spivack), Barbara Spiegel (Judge Harriett Doremus), Josh Pais (Keller), Michael Noth (Court Clerk)

Reviewing the Case: When Lt. Janet Hagen is found dead in a hotel room during an orgy involving other Navy personnel, Stone and the police battle the closed ranks of military jurisdiction to investigate. Captain Allard Bunker comes under scrutiny. Although the episode is a fairly basic murder mystery, it also becomes a rather absorbing study of sexual harassment. Actor Len Cariou is terrific at revealing some of the deep hatred and envy that men in authority sometimes have for women. It's particularly satisfying to hear the tone Stone uses when he addresses him as "Sir." Nonetheless, "Conduct Unbecoming" is not very memorable except for the way it topples the barrier of sexual machismo.

Noteworthy Discoveries: This episode was nominated for the Edgar Allen Poe Award. Julianna Margulies later will become Nurse Carol Hathaway on the hospital drama *ER* (1994–). Also of note, Michael Noth, who plays the court clerk, is actor Chris Noth's brother.

Episode 61: Animal Instinct
Original air date: March 17, 1993
Teleplay by Michael Chernuchin and Sibyl Gardner, directed by Ed Sherin

Additional Cast and Guest Stars: Frances Fisher (Susan Boyd), John Cunningham (Donald Walsh), Charles Brown (Mr. Riggs), Allen Arbus (Dominick Keith), Edmond Genest (Judge Feldman), George Murdock (Judge Eric Bertram), Peter Maloney (Sean Delaney), Lawrence Pressman (Wes Burke), David Schechter (Dirk Chesney), John Fiore (Det. Anthony Profaci)

Reviewing the Case: The investigation into the death of Fay Walsh, a research scientist, leads Briscoe and Logan to an animal rights group. Their suspicions change, however, when it appears that her husband may have been having an affair with Susan Boyd, an administrator at the same university whereh the Walshes worked. The public's common perception is that all stalkers are males, but this episode presents the exception to that rule. Frances Fisher gives a splendid performance as Boyd that is both erotic and twisted. She's absolutely brilliant in the final confrontation scene with John Cunningham, who has the furtive look of a man who isn't sure if his honesty can be believed. "Animal Instinct" proves to be a sharp and perceptive script that spotlights the writers' solid instincts.

Relevant Testimony: MICHAEL CHERNUCHIN (writer): "Wasn't that last scene spooky? What I love to do, when the networks do their ripped-from-the-headlines ads, is then take it somewhere else. Right out of left field. We did get a lot of mail from animal activists on this one."

Episode 62: Jurisdiction
Original air date: April 7, 1993
Teleplay by Walon Green and Rene Balcer, directed by Bruce Seth Green

Additional Cast and Guest Stars: Dan Hedaya (Det. Brian Torelli), Lorraine Toussaint (Shambala Green), Mark Blum (Assistant District Attorney Frank Lazar), Paul McCrane (James Pawl), Michael Badalucco (Davy Zifrin), Monique Cintron (Aloma), James Lewis DeLorenzo (Marty Lake), Rosemary DeAngelis (Sally Goldman), Leslie Ayvazian (Pam Korolek), David Wolos-Fonteno (Gavin McCrea), Bill Alton (Judge Bernard O'Malley), Merwin Goldsmith (Judge Feist), Nancy Franklin (Judge Walton), John Fiore (Det. Anthony Profaci)

Reviewing the Case: Davy Zifrin, a retarded man, confesses to the murder of two nurses but Stone must take jurisdiction over a witness in prison to prove that Davy is merely a patsy. The crime was planned by Brian Torelli, a detective, and Frank Lazar, the Brooklyn district attorney. They want to set up an innocent man if he fits the right profile, and Zifrin is such a person. He is eager to prove himself by claiming he committed the crimes. The chief flaw of this episode's plot structure is that it is unclear why the Brooklyn DA would protect a cop who is putting away an innocent man. Nonetheless, that great character actor Dan Hedaya plays Torelli with all the charm of Richard Nixon, and Mark Blum is a wonderfully pompous functionary. "Jurisdiction" has some messy moments, but as drama it is certainly in the right neighborhood.

Noteworthy Discoveries: Shambala Green subpoenas Stone to appear at Davy Zifrin's trial in Brooklyn. This is the first and last time Stone ever takes the witness stand in court.

Relevant Testimony: RENE BALCER (writer): "This was my second collaboration with Walon Green.... There's case after case where an innocent man goes to jail and everybody but the prosecutors are admitting that the guy is innocent—it still takes forever for a prosecutor to admit that they're wrong."

Episode 63: Virus

Original air date: April 21, 1993
Teleplay by Michael Chernuchin and Rene Balcer, directed by Steven Robman

Additional Cast and Guest Stars: Stephen Elliott (Dr. Hogan), Steven Keats (George Zuckert), Dana Elcar (Robert Cook), Joanna Merlin (Carla), Paul Calderon (Rodriguez), Stivi Paskoski (John Cook), Tanya Berezin (Judge Janine Pate), William Severs (Judge Henry Fillmore), Jim Moody (Judge Stuart), Beth Fowler (Mrs. Wrenn), Harold Perrineau, Jr. (Kenny Rinker), Patricia Kilgarriff (Nurse Berg), David Kener (Stan Lohr), Irving Metzman (Gene Magee), Leslie Hendrix (Medical Examiner Rogers), John Fiore (Det. Anthony Profaci)

Reviewing the Case: The death of several patients at a diabetes clinic leads Logan and Briscoe to John Cook, a computer hacker, and then to his father's overriding desire for vengeance. Many of Michael Chernuchin's stories for *Law & Order*, like Episode 43: "Silence" or Episode 48: "The Corporate Veil," are father-son tales. This one is no different. In this case, the father, who suffers from diabetic retinopathy, blames the Hogan-Hayes Clinic for blinding him, and the man's rage is carried out by his son. Dana Elcar (costar with Richard Dean Anderson in the TV series *MacGyver* from 1985 to 1992, and who suffered a debilitating eye condition) is marvelous in the role of Robert Cook, creating an intricate portrait of bombast and vulnerability. "Jurisdiction" is, in one sense, about a new type of criminal mentality: that of someone who hurts others through cyberspace. However, the title, and the episode, also convey something about the psychological virus that passes from one generation to the next.

Relevant Testimony: MICHAEL CHERNUCHIN (writer): "The relationship is based on a member of my family who has diabetes. Rene and I got the American Diabetic Association Award for that episode. And the award [was made up of] pictures drawn by people with juvenile diabetes. It was the most touching award that we've gotten. And it made me think that maybe we are doing some good here. We're not telling lies on the screen."

Episode 64: Securitate
Original air date: May 5, 1993
Teleplay by Matt Kiene and Joe Reinkemeyer, directed by James Hayman

Additional Cast and Guest Stars: Morgan Weisser (Leon Iliescu), Irene Bordan (Karen Iliescu), David Margulies (Tommy Zanuscu), Richard Council (Alex Iliescu), Alan King (Jonathan Shapiro), Laurie Taylor-Williams (Ronda Rubin), Sidney Armus (Judge Arnold Fishbein), Diane Kagan (Judge Kleinfeldt), Stan Lachow (Judge Renner), Richard Ziman (David Kaplan), Joe Taylor (Skank), Chris Orbach (Finkle), John Fiore (Det. Anthony Profaci)

Reviewing the Case: Leon Iliescu is a Romanian youth who tries to plead that he was suffering from cultural insanity when he murdered his cruel father, a member of the dreaded Securitate back home. Here is a different kind of father-son story. The parent is a beast and the son, through his own actions, locates the monster in himself. Leon's father, Alex, murders his own brother to prevent him from turning him in to the police for a fraudulent credit card operation he is running. However, Leon has guilt to spare in the situation, and he is a boy who seeks safety from his own murderous impulses by feigning helplessness. "Securitate" offers the ugly side of becoming your father's son.

Noteworthy Discoveries: Chris Orbach, who plays the character of Finkle here, is a cousin of co-lead Jerry Orbach.

Episode 65: Manhood
Original air date: May 12, 1993
Teleplay by Robert Nathan, story by Walon Green and Robert Nathan, directed by Ed Sherin

Additional Cast and Guest Stars: Charles Hallahan (Capt. Tom O'Hara), Adam Trese (Craig McGraw), Sam Rockwell (Officer Weddeker), Philip

Bosco (Gordon Schell), Robert Moresco (Sgt. Hank Rhodes), Ron Ryan (Sgt. Jack Harley), Rochelle Oliver (Judge Grace Larkin), Michael Egan (Judge Leonard Fein), Donald Corren (Medill), Kenneth Rock (Burnett)

Reviewing the Case: When Officer Newhouse, a gay policeman, is badly wounded in a shootout, his fellow officers abandon him to die in the belief that there is no place on the force for homosexuals. This episode begins with one of *Law & Order*'s most exceptional sequences, from the opening moment in the dispatch room, where Newhouse is heard pleading for help, until his radio silence indicates he's been shot. The psychological undercurrent of the episode is set. Ed Sherin directs the imaginative show with supreme confidence, and Michael Moriarty gives one of his most impassioned summations to the jury. When the prosecution doesn't win the case, it makes perfect sense. "Manhood" is about more than just prejudice against homosexuals on the police force; it's about the very definition of masculinity.

Noteworthy Discoveries: This installment won a GLAAD/LA Award. Robert Nathan and Walon Green received an Emmy nomination for their script.

Relevant Testimony: ROBERT NATHAN (writer): "The most telling creative experience was when Michael Moriarty received his pages of Stone's summation to the jury. He had them for a day or two, and he called me late one night and told me that it was weak. He said that it ran away from the truth of what the episode was about. And he faxed me that night a notion of what that speech should be about. It was his variation on that famous World War II speech about when they came for one group, I said nothing, and when they came for another group, I said nothing, and when they came for me, there was nobody left. Moriarty said that this should be about [telling the jury] if they don't like gay people one day, when do they start disliking black people, Catholics, Czechs, or whatever you happen to be? Michael was right. I rewrote the summation."

Episode 66: Benevolence
Original air date: May 19, 1993
Teleplay by Rene Balcer and Douglas Palau, story by Douglas Palau, directed by Ed Sherin

Additional Cast and Guest Stars: Leon Russom (Gordon Bryce), Sam Gray (Judge Stevens), Meredith Scott Lynn (Corrine Sussman), George Grizzard (Arthur Gold), Camille Jeter (Marcia Hendricks), John Cleary (Paul Crandall), Martin Priest (Jacob Brinkman), James Villemaire (Ben

Freed), Ann Sachs (Mrs. McKenna), George Bamford (Mr. McKenna), Peter Kaas (Judge Peters), John Fiore (Det. Anthony Profaci)

Reviewing the Case: A deaf student, Kathy McKenna, is found murdered in an alley and Stone suspects Gordon Bryce, the unimpaired head of the institute she attended. It turns out that he was jealous because she no longer needed his help. This is not one of the better season-enders, partly because it's an awfully simple story in a series known for its wonderful plot tangles. What makes this installment at all interesting is the way the particulars of the case have to be interpreted through the perceptions of someone who is deaf. The viewer experiences an investigation in an entirely new way, but it all boils down to an obsessed man who can't separate his job from his cause.

Noteworthy Discoveries: This is the last episode for cast regulars Cragen and Robinette.

Season Four
September 1993–May 1994
60-minute episodes

Production Team:

Dick Wolf (Executive Producer), Ed Sherin (Co-Executive Producer), Walon Green (Co-Executive Producer), Michael S. Chernuchin (Producer), Arthur Forney (Producer), Jeffrey Hayes (Producer), Rene Balcer (Co-Producer), Lewis H. Gould (Co-Producer), Robert Nathan (Supervising Producer), Jody Milano-Vanderputten (Associate Producer), Janace Tashjian (Associate Producer), Billy Fox (Associate Producer), Ed Zuckerman (Executive Story Editor), Lewis H. Gould (Unit Production Manager), Richard Bianchi (Production Designer), Mike Post (Music), Lynn Kressel C.S.A. (Casting), Suzanne Ryan (Casting), Christopher Misiano (Camera Operator), Phil Oetiker (Camera Operator), Moe Bardach (Location Manager), Michael Kewley (Editor), Billy Fox (Editor), Kevin Krasny (Editor), Laurie Grotstein (Editor), Mike Struk (Technical Advisor), Bill Fordes (Technical Advisor), Park Dietz, M.D. (Technical Advisor)

Regular Cast:

Jill Hennessy (Assistant District Attorney Claire Kincaid), Steven Hill (District Attorney Adam Schiff), Carolyn McCormick (Dr. Elizabeth Olivet), S. Epatha Merkerson (Lt. Anita Van Buren), Michael Moriarty

(Executive Assistant District Attorney Ben Stone), Chris Noth (Det. Mike Logan), Jerry Orbach (Det. Lennie Briscoe)

Fourth Season Overview

The fourth season heralds in a new era for the long-running *Law & Order*. Joseph Stern leaves the New York-based show to return home to Los Angeles, a journey that is soon also to be taken by actors Richard Brooks and Dann Florek, who are summarily replaced. One of the show's best directors, Ed Sherin, steps in as executive producer. He institutes some welcome changes on the program, such as roundtable discussions between the actors and the writers, and develops a "tutorial" system that allows crew members to move into different positions on the show (for example, cinematographer Constantine Makris begins directing, and camera operator Christopher Misiano periodically becomes director of photography). However, the most profound change is the addition of S. Epatha Merkerson, as Lieutenant Van Buren, and Jill Hennessy, as Assistant District Attorney Claire Kincaid. Merkerson had appeared once before in the riveting Episode 17: "Mushrooms." With NBC introducing what is arguably a feminist perspective on a predominantly male program, the chemistry of the show shifts significantly. The two detectives now have a lady commander in the precinct, and Ben Stone has a female deputy.

There is no episode story line to explain what has happened to Cragen and Robinette, but Dann Florek comes back to *Law & Order* this year to direct two segments, Episode 76: "The Pursuit of Happiness" and Episode 82: "Big Bang." (Florek also will direct and make a guest appearance in Episode 108: "Bad Faith" in the next season, and Robinette (Richard Brooks) will show up as a defense attorney for Episode 125: "Custody" in Season Six.) Finally, Michael Moriarty stages a dramatic departure at the end of this season, claiming that his days are numbered on the show thanks to the public stand he has taken against Attorney General Janet Reno's plans for strenuous television censorship.

This is both the biggest year for changes and *Law & Order*'s most popular season thus far, with an average 11.3 rating and a 19 share. This means the ratings have grown by eight percent in a twelve-month period. As a possible indication of the popularity of the new cast members, women in the audience accounted for a ratings increase of five percent; male viewers go up by three percent. The series celebrates by kicking off the new season with Episode 67: "Sweeps," about a talk show host who orchestrates a murder on his live show to boost ratings.

Episode Descriptions

Episode 67: Sweeps

Original air date: September 15, 1993
Teleplay by Craig McNeer and Robert Nathan, directed by James Frawley, cinematography by Constantine Makris

Additional Cast and Guest Stars: Robert Klein (Rick Mason), David Krumholtz (Scott Fisher), Alexandra Gersten (Sarah Fisher), Steve Ryan (Ross Fisher), Stewart Steinberg (Dr. Joseph Vinton), Jim Beaudin (Tommy Turner), Jim Boyd (Howard Turner), David Little (Bob Hudson), Margaret Gibson (Deborah Corrio), Melissa Leo (Alice Sutton)

Reviewing the Case: Talk show host Rick Mason, who stages the on-air murder of a therapist convicted for child molestation, is out for higher ratings during "sweeps" week. The opening scene, shot on video to depict a live television show, is the most audacious teaser that *Law & Order* has ever offered viewers. The rest of the episode doesn't quite live up to that moment, but it does have comic Robert Klein in fine dramatic form. He's especially good when needling Stone with a comparison of television entertainment to a prosecutor grandstanding in the courtroom. However, the story is really only a simple cautionary tale with an unintentional irony: Later this season, Michael Moriarty enters his own personal war against the country's attorney general over—what else?—the censorship of television violence.

Noteworthy Discoveries: This episode anticipates the shooting aftermath of a controversial Jenny Jones TV talk show, in which a gay man reveals his secret crush on a straight neighbor. This is the first time we meet Lt. Anita Van Buren, who has transferred from the narcotics division. Claire Kincaid replaces Robinette in the DA's office.

Relevant Testimony: ROBERT NATHAN (writer): "We wanted to shake up the audience with that opening [the video shot]. The idea came from an old friend of mine, a writer named Craig McNeer. Craig came to me with the thought of opening the show with a talk show in progress. Right after the opening title, you see someone [camera operator Christopher Misiano] blowing on a camera lens, and the lens is on its side. It throws you. Am I watching *Law & Order*? Or am I watching some other show? It was new and interesting. [Director Jim] Frawley did that opening in almost one continuous shot."

Episode 68: Volunteers

Original air date: September 29, 1993
Teleplay by Rene Balcer, directed by James Quinn, cinematography by Constantine Makris

Additional Cast and Guest Stars: Nicolas Coster (Reid Mullen), Kent Broadhurst (Dr. Creighton), Stephen Mendillo (Prosky), Marion Killinger (Roland Kirk), Joan Copeland (Judge Rebecca Stein), Denis O'Hare (Harold Morrissey), Stuart Burney (Creighton's Attorney), Sully Boyar (Judge Fabrikant)

Reviewing the Case: Police want to know who has left Roland Kirk, a homeless man, severely beaten in an alley. His attacker is Harold Morrissey, a block association member who claims Kirk was a threat to everyone in the neighborhood. This thought-provoking drama seeks to shed light on the inability of government bureaucracies to cope with homelessness and the anger of citizens who feel threatened by the problem. Kirk has fallen through the cracks because drug treatment programs won't take addicts who are mentally ill, and psychiatric hospitals refuse to treat addicts. In this episode, the system seems crazier than the troubled street people who are denied treatment. "Volunteers" doesn't provide any facile answers to the problem, but does suggest that if we lose our capacity to be humane we forfeit the right to judge the untenable world of Roland Kirk.

Relevant Testimony: RENE BALCER (writer): "The first draft of this one had the homeless guy dead, and we suddenly realized that the story is lacking something if that guy isn't around. You don't see what everyone in the neighborhood was pissed off about. So, in the second draft, we kept him alive and he became the whole back half of the story."

Episode 69: Discord

Original air date: October 6, 1993
Teleplay by Michael Chernuchin, directed by Ed Sherin, cinematography by Christopher Misiano

Additional Cast and Guest Stars: Cynthia Harris (Adele Diamond), Lucy Deakins (Julia Wood), Sebastian Roche (Clarence Carmichael, a.k.a. "C-Square"), Avi Hoffman (Teddy Wayne), Tanya Berezin (Judge Silverman), Alex Wipf (Michael Wood), Karen Byers (Sheila Pierson), Diane Dilascio (Sharon Carmichael), Fred Scollay (Judge Barsky), Kurt Knudson (Judge Waxman)

Reviewing the Case: A rock'n'roll star named C-Square is charged with raping Julia Wood, a nineteen-year-old college student, even though she voluntarily came to his hotel room. While drawing ideas from the Mike Tyson case, this episode also offers a variation on the theme explored in Episode 30: "Out of Control," in which the credibility of a rape victim is scrutinized. Placing the story in a heavy metal context is unusual (Sebastian Roche seems ideally cast as the debauched musician) and the detectives engage in some funny generational repartee while discussing the validity of rock music. S. Epatha Merkerson has a riveting scene with guest actress Lucy Deakins as the lieutenant questions the victim about the particulars of the rape. Cynthia Harris plays the feminist lawyer defending C-Square with a nice touch of ambiguity. While "Discord" sometimes hits too many familiar chord progressions, the tune ain't all that bad.

Noteworthy Discoveries: Stone almost fires Kincaid when she fails to give him information about Julia's discussions with an entertainment lawyer. We find out that Logan's cousin once played bass in a band. It is Christopher Misiano's first episode as director of cinematography.

Relevant Testimony: MICHAEL CHERNUCHIN (writer): "I wrote C-Square's [heavy metal] song originally as a rap song because it was supposed to be a rap star [who was the rapist]. With what's happened subsequently with rap music—and "Cop Killer" [by Ice-T, later to star in Dick Wolf's TV series *Players*]—it might have worked better. But my proudest moment is that I wrote a song."

Episode 70: Profile

Original air date: October 13, 1993
Teleplay by Gordon Rayfield and Ed Zuckerman, story by Ed Zuckerman, directed by E. W. Swackhamer, cinematography by Constantine Makris

Additional Cast and Guest Stars: James Earl Jones (Horace McCoy), William Carden (Arthur Tunney), Joe Seneca (Henry Jackson), Cecilia Hart (Mary Bradley), Bruce Katzman (Allen Bradley), Brian Davies (Reingold Bishop), Frances Chaney (Amelia Whitney), Lenore Harris (Marya Levinson), Christine Farrell (Shrier), Lynn Cohen (Judge Elizabeth Mizener), Charlotte Colavin (Judge Lisa Pongracic)

Reviewing the Case: Arthur Tunney, a white racist and serial killer who shoots blacks, hires noted black attorney Horace McCoy to defend him at trial. This episode is a suspenseful story about tracking down a deranged murderer, but it is also an examination of the way race relations have changed over the years. Schiff is quick to point out to Stone and Kincaid that people now say about blacks what they were ashamed to think ten years ago. When a character then says that the Upper West Side used to be "a nice neighborhood," that observation reverberates. "Profile" depicts a world where people are gunned down because of the color of their skin. There are some unbearably tense scenes between Van Buren and Tunney (nicely played by William Carden). James Earl Jones lends his famously bombastic voice to McCoy, a role that fits him perfectly. If the hate rhetoric weren't so awful, it would almost be fun to watch the defense attorney reign in his anger at Tunney's white-supremacist gibberish.

Noteworthy Discoveries: It is revealed that the Upper West Side is Briscoe's old neighborhood. Logan goes undercover as a homeless man.

Episode 71: Black Tie
Original air date: October 20, 1993
Teleplay by Walon Green and Michael Chernuchin, directed by Arthur Forney, cinematography by Constantine Makris

Additional Cast and Guest Stars: Caroline Lagerfelt (Danielle Keyes), Jeffrey DeMunn (Norman Rothenberg), Viveca Lindfors (Helga Holtz), John McMartin (Private Investigator), Beverly Johnson (Marcela Di Portago), Heidi Leick (Cathy Rodgers), Robert Cicchini (Gerald Aubrie), Malcolm Gets (Lance Keys), Richard Bright (Mr. Quinn), Michael Hayward-Jones (Butler), Lewis Arlt (Garrett Darby), Leslie Hendrix (Medical Examiner Rogers), Ben Hammer (Judge Herman Mooney), John Fiore (Det. Anthony Profaci)

Reviewing the Case: The wealthy Jonathan Keyes is found dead of what is assumed to be natural causes but the evidence points to foul play, and his wife, Danielle. This is a familiar but not altogether bad episode about how the wealthy can afford the type of lawyer that almost guarantees acquittal by virtue of knowing the fine points of the law. Norman Rothenberg, like Arthur Gold, is an attorney who is only concerned with points of law, never justice. The key to Stone's dedication to fairness comes in the final scene, when Kincaid asks him if there is any point at which the outcome of this case will stop bothering him. Naturally, he cannot say there is. Here, the facts and the law are not enough to outweigh the money.

Noteworthy Discoveries: Van Buren and Logan battle about his discomfort with a woman being in charge, after he questions a decision she has made in an investigation.

Relevant Testimony: S. EPATHA MERKERSON (actor): "[When Logan and Van Buren have a dispute] we actually filmed a little bit more because he was very suspicious of that character [Van Buren] when I came in [to the show], and he really didn't like it. Chris and I wanted to explore that. We started to, when something happened in the filming of the shows and they were taken out of sequence. So we had to remove some of the stuff that we had done. It was really kind of disappointing because, if we had started with that through-line, we could have carried it to another place."

Episode 72: Pride and Joy
Original air date: October 27, 1993
Teleplay by Ed Pomerantz and Robert Nathan, directed by Gilbert Shilton, cinematography by Constantine Makris

Additional Cast and Guest Stars: Pamela Payton-Wright (Katherine MacKinnon), Gabriel Olds (Sean MacKinnon), Lauren Ambrose (Maureen MacKinnon), Johnny Giacalone (Mitchell Lewis), Paul Collins (Roger Easton), Patrick Collins (Ned Hughes), Sam Gray (Judge Manuel Leon), Vince O'Brien (Judge Franks), Heather Willihnganz (Sandy Resnick), Lauren Klein (Dr. Grace Henderson), Donald Corren (Medill)

Reviewing the Case: Sean MacKinnon is a seventeen-year-old boy who becomes the chief suspect in the murder of his father, a crime that then raises questions about a possible history of physical abuse against the parent. This installment certainly provides a twist to the common perception that it is parents who batter their children. The issue of class also emerges. Sean's rage comes from shame about his father's status as superintendent of an apartment building. Like Kevin Doyle in Episode 56: "Right To Counsel," Sean aspires to a higher social standing. The episode peers into the mirror of self-delusion, where murderous impulses erupt when we are reminded of what we don't want to see.

Episode 73: Apocrypha
Original air date: November 3, 1993
Teleplay by Michael Chernuchin, directed by Gabrielle Beaumont, cinematography by Constantine Makris

Additional Cast and Guest Stars: Sam Robards (Daniel Hendricks), Lawrence Pressman (Nicholas Burke), Bibi Besch (Margaret Berman), Cheryl Giannini (Louise Fryman), Ted Sorel (Stuart Melnick), Raymond Genadry (Assad Asalam), Deena Martin (Barbara Munn), Joyce Ebert (Maria Hendricks), Rhea Silver-Smith (Joanne Rudolph), Maggie Burke (Judge Link), Stan Lachow (Judge Renner), Cheryl Adam (Wendy Berman), John Fiore (Det. Anthony Profaci)

Reviewing the Case: Stone and Kincaid try to prove that a young woman believed to have planted a bomb in a Wall Street parking garage may have been brainwashed by cult leader Daniel Hendricks. This episode echoes the bombing of the World Trade Center and the assault on Branch Davidians at Waco, Texas, but is long before the Heaven's Gate madness. Logan and Briscoe automatically suspect it is a case of politically-motivated Middle East terrorism. Nobody even considers the homegrown variety. In this install-ment, cult members look like average Americans. Sam Robards, playing the Grand Wazoo himself, has the beatific look of a saint. When one of them, Barbara Munn, develops a brief rapport with Logan while discussing their Catholic school experiences, it puts a human face on religious fanaticism. After subtly peering into Logan's soul, "Apocrypha" delivers a stunning, wordless *coup de grâce*. This mass suicide prompts Logan to kneel over Munn's body, crossing himself in a conclusion that is both exquisitely sim-ple and remarkably complex.

Noteworthy Discoveries: Logan mentions that his mother used to beat him with her right hand while holding a rosary in her left.

Relevant Testimony: MICHAEL CHERNUCHIN (writer): "Sam Robards was great in it. And Chris [Noth] at the end with the 'Hail Mary' was amaz-ing. We got a lot of mail on that one too. When Chris mentioned being beaten up by nuns, that caused some trouble. The inspiration for that show was the title of a poem called 'Avenue Bearing the Initial of Christ Into the New World.' I just loved that title."

Episode 74: American Dream

Original air date: November 10, 1993
Teleplay by Sibyl Gardner, directed by Constantine Makris, cinematogra-phy by Christopher Misiano

Additional Cast and Guest Stars: Zeljko Ivanek (Phillip Swann), Scott Sowers (Billy Doyle), Mark Tymchyshyn (Chip Rafferty), Guy Davis (Russell Bobbitt), Sophie Hayden (Beverly Dorfman), Stephen Payne (George Mazlansky), Bernie McInerney (Judge Michael Callaghan), Norma Fire (Appellate Judge Jensen), Tanny McDonald (Appellate Judge Fraser), George Bartenieff (Appellate Judge MacNamara), Chester A. Sims (Appellate Judge Humphrey), John Fiore (Det. Anthony Profaci)

Reviewing the Case: A skeleton unearthed at a building site resurrects one of Stone's old cases, bringing him face to face with Phillip Swann, the tenacious Wall Street hustler who has been behind bars for murder. Over the years, respectable attorneys like Arthur Gold and Shambala

Green have taken turns as Stone's nemesis. Yet, their machinations seem paltry compared to the evil brilliance of Swann, probably the best yuppie villain ever in a show that loves to create such characters. Zeljko Ivanek gives a sly, thrilling performance in this role. What makes this episode so fascinating is how Swann uses the law (learned while doing time) to undo all of Stone's work in putting him away in the first place. "American Dream" makes it clear that Swann was a successful criminal mastermind because he could seduce willing participants. The frightening thing is that there are still victims waiting to be seduced.

Noteworthy Discoveries: This is Constantine Makris's first episode as director on *Law & Order*. It's also the first time Stone is featured pretty much from beginning to end. It is made clear that Stone is divorced, and that he was appointed Executive Assistant District Attorney after Swann's previous conviction. Kincaid emerges from Stone's shadow to help him with his civil court deposition.

Relevant Testimony: CONSTANTINE MAKRIS (director): "Michael [Moriarty] was very mad at me in one scene because I moved the camera. He thought it would take away from the acting: 'Why are you doing a camera scene when it should be an acting scene?' I told him I wasn't doing anything very tricky; it was just to create a little more tension in what was already a very tense scene between two people. He was infuriated."

Episode 75: Born Bad

Original air date: November 17, 1993
Teleplay by Michael Chernuchin and Sally Nemeth, directed by Fred Gerber, cinematography by Constantine Makris

Additional Cast and Guest Stars: Maria Tucci (Helen Brolin), Wil Horneff (Chris Pollit), Helen Gallagher (Florence Bishop), Barbara Eda-Young (Judge Martha Kershan), Melissa Fraser Brown (Tracy Pollit), Lily Knight (Tori Lasky), Robert C. Wheeler (Zack Mohr), James Madio (Andy Costello), Vivienne Benesch (Delia), Michael Cullen (Father Malone), Kitty Chen (Medical Examiner Chong)

Reviewing the Case: Chris Pollit is a teenager charged with murder as an adult offender but his lawyer, Helen Brolin, claims that he's violent because of a genetic predisposition. This powerful story traces the nature of violence and also looks at the helplessness a lawyer feels when defending a boy whose parents have no use for him (Pollit's father is in Attica and his mother doesn't care). Eventually Brolin, unable to transfer the case to family court, attempts to confuse a jury with a chromosome theory that suggests Chris's violent outbursts are hereditary. The episode juxtaposes the system's dilemma when faced with a Chris Pollit and the despair of Pollit himself. He believes he'll kill again. The tragedy of "Born Bad" is that Chris would rather do time than get help.

Noteworthy Discoveries: For the first time, Stone is seen drinking a beer.

Episode 76: The Pursuit of Happiness
Original air date: December 1, 1993
Teleplay by Morgan Gendel and Robert Nathan, directed by Dann Florek, cinematography by Constantine Makris

Additional Cast and Guest Stars:: Natalia Negoda (Irina Cooper), Bruce Altman (Tom Morrison), Jesse Corti (Alex Nunez), Bill Marcus (Phil Guardino), Peter Van Wagner (Stan Feldman), Faith Prince (Ms. Ferrell), Jack Davidson (George Berman), Marya Kazakova (Eva Berman), Yo Han Lim (Richard Kim), Peter Jay Fernandez (Dr. Isaac Kerwin), Donald Corren (Medill), David Lipman (Judge Morris Torledsky), Roger Serbagi (Judge Quinn)

Reviewing the Case: Irina Cooper, a mail-order bride from Russia, is suspected of murdering her rich husband, who was threatening to divorce her just weeks before she could qualify to remain in America. This is a simple murder story with not much mystery, but Dann Florek (returning to the show for the first time since his dismissal at the end of last season) has directed it with care. In one fascinating sequence, a defense lawyer argues that a Korean man who witnessed the murder can't properly identify non-Asians, a premise that Stone disputes as a precedent for interracial homicide. Beyond that, and despite its title, "The Pursuit of Happiness" doesn't pursue much else.

Episode 77: Golden Years
Original air date: January 5, 1994
Teleplay by Doug Palau and Ed Zuckerman, story by Doug Palau, directed by Helaine Head, cinematography by Christopher Misiano

Additional Cast and Guest Stars: Tovah Feldshuh (Danielle Melnick), Julie Dretzin (Laura Bauer), Frederica Meister (Eileen Bauer), Jan Miner (Mrs. Hotch), Denise Hernandez (Maria Gonzales), Doris Belack (Judge Margaret Barry), Miguel Sierra (Felix Ortega), William Meisle (Dr. Matthewson), Michael St. Gerard (Kent Halliwell), Elaine Eldredge (Mildred Bauer)

Reviewing the Case: When Mildred Bauer's elderly and emaciated body is found in her apartment after an apparent break-in, police discover that her granddaughter, Laura Bauer, actually starved the woman to death.

Although a fairly absorbing story, this episode includes a very tricky case. Laura confesses, indicating that she merely assisted in the suicide of a grandmother in great pain. What the viewer has to settle for in this installment is the gentle sparring between Michael Moriarty and actress Jan Miner, who plays Mildred's friend. Otherwise this story fades from memory pretty quickly.

Noteworthy Discoveries: This is the second time we see the *voir dire* process of jury selection. The other segment was Episode 27: "God Bless the Child," in which lawyers attempted to find a jury sensitive to religious views.

Episode 78: Snatched

Original air date: January 12, 1994
Teleplay by Walon Green and Rene Balcer, directed by Constantine Makris, cinematography by Christopher Misiano

Additional Cast and Guest Stars: Theodore Bikel (Solomon Bregman), Vyto Ruginis (Shepherd Watson), Reg Rogers (Jason Bregman), Leo Burmester (Lester Hastings), George Guidall (Marvin Cattleman), Vince Pacimeo (Jimmy Ameche), Bernadette Penotti (Helena Navarro), John Newton (Judge Caffey), Jack Ryland (Judge Derrick), John Fiore (Det. Anthony Profaci)

Reviewing the Case: Sol Bregman, a millionaire friend of District Attorney Schiff, becomes a willing victim of deception after his son Jason's kidnapping, as the police suspect that the young man set the whole thing up to extort money from his father. The episode is a beautifully detailed portrait of a parent's masochistic dedication to a child who loves the advantages of wealth, but maintains contempt for the person who provides it. Theodore Bikel brings a quiet desperation to the role of the older Bregman, who seems nourished by his efforts to save the arrogant Jason. Like Episode 44: "The Working Stiff," Adam Schiff has to face the ending of a friendship when Sol refuses to cooperate with the DA. The best moment in "Snatched" is the look on Schiff's face when he has to arrest Sol Bregman for hindering prosecution.

Noteworthy Discoveries: Adam Schiff was at Sol Bregman's wedding and later at his wife's funeral. They've known each other for thirty years.

Episode 79: Breeder

Original air date: January 12, 1994
Teleplay by Michael Chernuchin and Rene Balcer, directed by Arthur Forney, cinematography by Constantine Makris

Additional Cast and Guest Stars: Angie Phillips (Debra Elkin), Deidre O'Connell (Jane Schuman), Ann Dowd (Dorothy Baxter), Ellen Parker (Gwen Savitt), Stephen James (Les Savitt), Michael Mantell (Morris Hoffman), Judson Mills (Stephen Shaw)

Reviewing the Case: Debra Elkin claims that she passed out in a taxi and awoke to find her newborn baby missing. However, during their investigation, Briscoe and Logan uncover a scam involving private adoptions. This story line bears a strong resemblance to both Episode 28: "Misconception," in which a couple with a child tries to use the law for their own avaricious purposes, and Episode 103: "Seed," which concerns the desperation of parents who want kids. Unlike those installments, this episode also looks at the "haunted womb syndrome" that sometimes afflicts women who have miscarried. Ann Dowd's portrayal of Dorothy Baxter suggests a nervous vulnerability, and Debra Elkin uses the law as a sword instead of a shield in order to manipulate needy people.

Noteworthy Discoveries: Logan tells Briscoe about a former girlfriend who decided to have an abortion.

Episode 80: Censure
Original air date: February 2, 1994
Teleplay by William Fordes, directed by Ed Sherin, cinematography by Constantine Makris

Additional Cast and Guest Stars: David Groh (Judge Joel Thayer), George Grizzard (Arthur Gold), Jane Kaczmarek (Janet Rudman) Roberta Wallach (Michelle Selig), Kip Niven (Dan Rudman), John Ramsey (Judge Walter Schreiber), Baxter Harris (Art Diamond), Isabel Segovia (Olivia), Mike Cicchetti (John Blanchard), Lee Bryant (Melissa Thayer), Leslie Denniston (Sara Felder), Janna Silver-Smith (Laura Rudman), Christopher Misiano (Billy Spiros, the Video Technician)

Reviewing the Case: A phone call threatening Janet Rudman's young daughter winds up as a case involving Judge Joel Thayer, who once had an affair with the woman, and, coincidentally, years before with Claire Kincaid. Jill Hennessy gives her first dynamic performance, as the novice ADA comes into her own during the biggest crisis of her career. Claire is censured from practicing law because her former relationship with the judge taints the investigation. David Groh hits just the right note to convey Thayer's obsessive personality. Kincaid had already stepped out of the shadow in Episode 74: "American Dream" and, here, she's caught in the full glare of the headlights.

Noteworthy Discoveries: Thayer gave Kincaid a glowing recommendation for her job in the DA's office because she had been his law clerk, her first job out of law school. Camera operator Christopher Misiano makes his acting debut as the videotape technician, Billy Spiros.

Episode 81: Kids

Original air date: February 9, 1994
Teleplay by Michael Harbert and Robert Nathan, directed by Don Scardino, cinematography by Constantine Makris

Additional Cast and Guest Stars: Robert Hogan (Ted Parker), Eric Alperin (Kevin Parker), Philip Bosco (Gordon Schell), Danny Gerard (Billy Wojack), Tresa Hughes (Adele Sugarman), Marilyn Cooper (Ida Abel), Elizabeth Parrish (Judge Sally Norton), Blanca Camacho (Mila Ramirez), Anthony Ruiz (Mr. Ramirez), Guillermo Diaz (Juan Domingo), Jose Soto (Ricky Morales), Bob Kaliban (Judge Bernard Kelman), Christine Farrell (Shrier), John Fiore (Det. Anthony Profaci)

Reviewing the Case: The shooting death of fourteen-year-old Angel Ramirez involves the son of a former police detective, Ted Parker, who happens to be Briscoe's old friend. This is the first (but not the last) time Briscoe will be forced to make certain ethical choices based on someone from his past stepping back into his life. This is a decent enough episode about how kids no longer settle differences with their mouths, or even their fists; now they use artillery. Yet, the acting isn't of the usual caliber seen on *Law & Order*. Eric Alperin has some weak scenes (especially an embarrassing one outside the courtroom, when confronted by the Ramirez family). The irony of this episode is that Ted Parker behaves in much the same violent manner as his son. The ending opens up the possibility for a sequel, but is anyone staying up nights waiting for it?

Noteworthy Discoveries: For the first time, Briscoe mentions having two daughters.

Episode 82: Big Bang

Original air date: March 2, 1994
Teleplay by Ed Zuckerman, directed by Dann Florek, cinematography by Constantine Makris

Additional Cast and Guest Stars: Randell Mell (Max Weiss), Jennifer Van Dyck (Shelley Conners), Bill Moor (William Patton), Harris Yulin (Prof. Edward Manning), Vince Viverito (Frank Rossi), Suzanne Toren (Anna

Rossi), Karen Sillas (Cynthia Thomas), Jeff Gendelman (Barry Ramsey), Ellen Lancaster (Alice Weiss), Steve Boles (Prof. Samuel Kessler), Rochelle Oliver (Judge Grace Larkin)

Reviewing the Case: Prof. Edward Manning, a physicist, becomes the chief target of an investigation when his estranged wife is the victim of a letter bomb. But a rival scientist, Max Weiss, harbors a grudge against Manning for stealing his theory about proton decay. The real surprise here is how a story of two physics professors and their decaying protons could be made so dramatically interesting. Ed Zuckerman's script, Dann Florek's crisp direction, and Randell Mell's mesmerizing performance as Max contribute to an episode with forebodings of the Unabomber (Mell, with his salt-and-pepper beard, even resembles Ted Kaczynski). "Big Bang" is about one man who loves his work too much, another who has no professional respect for it, and the woman who became a casualty of both.

Episode 83: Mayhem

Original air date: March 9, 1994
Teleplay by Michael Chernuchin and Rene Balcer, story by Michael Chernuchin and Walon Green, directed by James Quinn, cinematography by Constantine Makris

Additional Cast and Guest Stars: Tom Riis Farrell (Scott Hexter), Katherine Narducci (Louise D'Angelo), Joyce Reehling (Mildred Kaskel), Jack Hallett (Leonard Bauer), Alice Drummond (Zelda), Shae D'Lyn (Dory), Peggy Cowles (Mrs. Hexter), Robin Tunney (Jill Templeton), Charles Blackwell (Judge Gillman), George Bartenieff (Jerome), Jaime Tirelli (Santana), Saul Stein (Bruno D'Angelo), Jason Duchin (Julian Marks), Siu Wah Lau (David Lee), Hyunsoo Lee (Mrs. Lee), John Fiore (Det. Anthony Profaci), Michael Noth (Court Clerk)

Reviewing the Case: In a twenty-four-hour period, Briscoe and Logan are burdened with a heavy caseload that includes five unrelated murders that, in the end, result in the death of one innocent man. This episode is something of a departure from the usual *Law & Order* format, as the show isn't evenly divided between the cops and the DAs, and the customary 'boink-boink' sound between scenes is replaced by a ticking watch. The detectives are involved in more homicides than they normally would see in a week (the episode could be subtitled "Son of Sam Meets Lorena Bobbitt"). In addition, Ben Stone only appears briefly, in the last third of the story (see chapter 19 and its Michael Moriarty section for the full story behind this episode). Despite its frantic pace, the story has an emotional anchor provided by Tom Riis Farrell as the terrified Scott Hexter. Much like Henry Fonda in Alfred Hitchcock's film *The Wrong Man* (1957), he has a plethora of oddball coincidences linking him to the anonymous criminal the police are chasing. However, Hexter is indeed hexed on a day from hell that continues long into the night.

Noteworthy Discoveries: This is the episode that Michael Moriarty claims was written to exclude him because of his opposition to Attorney General Janet Reno's stand on television violence. Chris Noth's brother, Michael, again plays a court clerk.

Episode 84: Wager

Original air date: March 30, 1994
Teleplay by Kevin Arkadie and Harvey Solomon, story by Michael Chernuchin and Harvey Solomon, directed by Ed Sherin, cinematography by Constantine Makris

Additional Cast and Guest Stars: Malik Yoba (Pat Williams), Karen Williams (Mrs. Williams), Ray Aranha (Henry "Papa Doc" Doinel), Richard Libertini (Papa Doc's Attorney), Steve Harris (Joey Lang), Keith Hernandez (Drew Harding), Zakes Mokae (Pat Williams's Attorney), Robert Poletick (Sandler), Joseph R. Sicari (Coach Bud Genero), Larry Attile (Mr. Stefansky), Francine Beers (Judge Silver), Ben Hammer (Judge Herman Mooney), Myra Lucretia Taylor (Jocelyn Weston), Donald Corren (Medill)

Reviewing the Case: Briscoe and Logan bet that the killing of a star athlete's father, Bennie Williams, is linked to gambling debts and threats to the family. Loosely based on the murder of the father of basketball great Michael Jordan, this episode deals with a son who has been cheated in terms of both love and money. Pat Williams's success as a baseball player did not feed his father's pride, only his gambling habits. Malik Yoba's performance cleverly hides the disappointment and rage under the professional demeanor. In addition, Steve Harris, as a bookie's strong-arm man, has an exciting scene with Stone in a holding cell. "Wager" is crisp, clean, and well acted, but when it's over, it's over.

Noteworthy Discoveries: Logan reveals that he once played on the police baseball team, and also tells Briscoe that his mother had cirrhosis of the liver. Briscoe is seen showing off his pool-hall skills. Malik Yoba is the star of *New York Undercover* (1994–), another Dick Wolf series on the Fox network. Steve Harris will later become a cast member on NBC's lawyer series *The Practice* (1997–).

Episode 85: Sanctuary

Original air date: April 13, 1994
Teleplay by Michael Chernuchin and William Fordes, directed by Arthur
Forney, cinematography by Constantine Makris

Additional Cast and Guest Stars: Michael Constantine (Joshua Berger),
Tony Todd (Reverend Ott), Beatrice Winde (Corina Roberts), Kevin
Thigpen (Isaac Roberts), Lorraine Toussaint (Shambala Green), Sean
Nelson (Damon Fox), Omar Sharif Scroogins (Luther Heywood),
Sharon Washington (Mrs. Fox), John Steven Jones (Bobby Griffen),
Nicholas J. Giangiulio (John DeSantis), Arthur French (Dr. Myron
Jensen), Vince O'Brien (Judge Phillip Franks), Susan Blommaert (Judge
Rebecca Steinman), John Fiore (Det. Anthony Profaci)

Reviewing the Case: A black minister, Reverend Ott, fans the flames of
racial intolerance after a hit-and-run in Harlem claims the life of an adolescent boy but the Jewish driver is not indicted. In the subsequent riot, an
Italian man is mistaken for a Jew and killed by Isaac Roberts, a black
youth. Defense attorney Shambala Green tries to free Roberts on the
grounds of insanity brought on by mob frenzy. This is arguably the best and
most provocative episode that
Law & Order has ever done on
race relations, even, perhaps,
the best ever done on television.
The story line draws on numerous real-life sources: the riots in
Brooklyn's Crown Heights, the
L.A. aftermath of the Rodney
King verdict, and even Tom
Wolfe's incendiary novel, *Bon-
fire of the Vanities* (1987). (Tony
Todd's Reverend Ott is a clever
variation on the New York
activist minister Al Sharpton.)
The episode ventures much fur-
ther into the now-fractured
bond that once existed between
African-Americans and Jews in
America. The script is laced with
compassionate anger. As Ben
Stone and Shambala Green,
Moriarty and Toussaint have
their finest moment during a

*Lorraine Toussaint, in a recurring role as
defense attorney Shambala Green,
nemesis of EADA Ben Stone (Michael
Moriarty) in such powerful episodes as
Episode 85: "Sanctuary" (Season Four).*
[courtesy of Sanders Management]

sizzling debate about racism—one of the bravest on television—when their legal masks disappear and two deeply-committed individuals are revealed. The irony of "Sanctuary" is that it does not leave its audience any place in which to take refuge.

Relevant Testimony: MICHAEL CHERNUCHIN (writer): "This was listed in *TV Guide* as one of the hundred best [television] episodes of all time. And that sushi scene between Shambala Green and Stone was my single favorite scene in the six years that I was there. . . . Shambala tells him that 'hanging a picture of Bobby Kennedy on your wall just doesn't cut it anymore'—that is a great moment. We picked up the race issue where other shows stopped. I think we delved a little deeper in that episode than others dare to do."

Episode 86: Nurture
Original air date: May 4, 1994
Teleplay by Paris Qualles and Ed Zuckerman, directed by Jace Alexander, cinematography by Constantine Makris

Additional Cast and Guest Stars: Lisa Eichhorn (Arnette Fenady), Christine Baranski (Rose Segal), Stephi Lineburg (Wendy Sylvester), Zelda Harris (Janel Decker), Camryn Manheim (Beatrice Hines), Ann McDonough (Peggy Sylvester), Bruce MacVittie (Brian Sprague), Michael Medeiros (Detective Harding), Jesse Moore (Daniel Freeman), Jeff Weiss (Judge Romney), Scotty Bloch (Judge Naomi Baum), Mark Hammer (Judge Randall Welch), John Fiore (Det. Anthony Profaci)

Reviewing the Case: A young girl disappears from her abusive foster home and the police find her being hidden in a basement enclave by a loving but disturbed woman who insists she acted for the child's own good. This smart drama asks where the law should stand when a neglected kid seems to be better off with a gentle adult who is slightly crazy. Lisa Eichhorn gives Faraday a quiet, mournful quality that is haunting. When she talks with Olivet about her sorrowful past, one can finally identify the otherworldly glint in her eyes. "Nurture" is about a woman who imagines herself the savior of lost children, when in truth she is forever mourning the child she lost.

Noteworthy Discoveries: This is the first *Law & Order* installment to stage a competency hearing for the defendant.

Relevant Testimony: LEWIS H. GOULD (producer/unit production manager): "We were in a van scouting [locations] and we got a call from Ed [Sherin] that the network had pulled the script. They didn't want us to do it at all because originally it had to do with the kidnapping and sexual abuse of a young girl. Of course our reaction was, 'Gee, why didn't they tell us a little sooner?' Here we are, five days into prepping the thing. So we had a brainstorm to make the perpetrator a woman who was kidnapping the girl to protect her and to get her away from an abusive home. They ended up keeping every location that we had.... We were able to start right on time and it turned out to be a pretty good show."

Episode 87: Doubles

Original air date: May 18, 1994
Teleplay by Michael Chernuchin and Rene Balcer, directed by Ed Sherin, cinematography by Constantine Makris

Additional Cast and Guest Stars: John Heard (Mitch Burke), Stacey Mosely (Korey Burke), Allison Dunbar (Allison Hall), Ron Orbach (Max Hellman), Holt McCallany (Mark Henner), Leslie Lyles (Ms. Perry), Byron Jennings (Ross Fineman), Tanya Berezin (Judge Roselyn Lenz), Kevin Hagen (O'Hearn), John Ottavino (Allan Lovitz), Thom Sesma (Tom Boden), Kit Flanagan (Allison's Attorney), David Rosenbaum (Judge Alan Berman), John Fiore (Det. Anthony Profaci)

Reviewing the Case: Just before a tournament, an assailant breaks the wrist of tennis star Korey Burke. Her rival competitor, Allison Hall, is among the suspects. This episode is obviously a hybrid of the Tonya Harding–Nancy Kerrigan skating rivalry and the stabbing of tennis pro Monica Seles. However, it's also a much better version of Episode 25: "Aria," in which a parent pushes a child to be a success with no consideration for the harm being caused. Nevertheless, this installment doesn't indulge in victimization clichés. John Heard plays Allison's father as a proud coach who lives only for his team of one, which is exactly his problem. "Doubles" does provide a nice twist at the end that adds another layer of meaning to the title.

Noteworthy Discoveries: Kincaid mentions that, as a track star in high school, she got pep talks from her father. Ron Orbach, who plays Max Hellman, is Jerry Orbach's cousin. John Heard, to be seen in the comedy films *Home Alone* (1990) and *Home Alone 2* (1992), would costar with JoBeth Williams in the TV series *The Client* (1996–97), based on John Grisham's novel (1992) and the award-winning film (1994).

Episode 88: Old Friends

Original air date: May 25, 1994
Teleplay by Robert Nathan and Joshua Stern, directed by James Quinn, cinematography by Constantine Makris

Additional Cast and Guest Stars: Allison Janney (Anne Madsen), Victor Slezak (Steve Green), Doris Belack (Judge Margaret Barry), Bob Dishy (Lawrence Weaver), Deborah Genninger (Joan Renkmeyer), Brian Tarantina (Rudy), Don Creech (Nicholai Rostov), Michael Harney (Aaron Packard), David Lipman (Judge Morris Torledsky), Leslie Hendrix (Medical Examiner Rogers), John Fiore (Det. Anthony Profaci)

Reviewing the Case: A pedestrian is hit by a truck and the investigation leads to the victim's link with a baby-food company where a new partner has ties to the Russian mob. Ben Stone's career has been built on principles, and righteous justice is all that really matters to him. However, all that backfires when his witness is killed, which prompts Stone to resign. It is a nostalgic series' farewell to both a riveting character and to actor Michael Moriarty, who gave the character such absolute and true conviction during his tenure on *Law & Order*. "Old Friends" is a compelling drama about the horrible consequences that can stem from telling the truth. Allison Janney, whose Anne Madsen is always in the wrong place at the wrong time, gives a heartbreaking performance as a decent person caught in an inexorable trap of constant misfortune. Victor Slezak transforms himself in such a subtle way that his mobster persona sneaks up on the viewer. Writer Robert Nathan delivers a mesmerizing swan song with this episode. He and Moriarty could not have left a more satisfying and lasting tribute to their work together on *Law & Order*.

Noteworthy Discoveries: As he tells Kincaid what happened to Anne Madsen, Stone sips a drink, the other "bookend" to his alcohol references in Episode 1: "Prescription for Death."

Relevant Testimony: ROBERT NATHAN (writer): "In essence, we took a theme that had been developed over eighty-seven episodes. For four years, Stone had dealt with the moral quandary of the power of his job. District attorneys can compel testimony in a dozen ways from defendants and witnesses. And it's a power that must be wielded very carefully. To make Stone's moral downfall, we found a better way to illustrate that he lost sight of the things that matter. What he did to that witness, he had done to many witnesses. He had threatened them many different ways, and was forced to ask himself whether or not it was the right thing to do. And as long as it was legal, it was. This time, dealing with organized crime—the Russian mob—he went too far. And the protection was insufficient. He's forced to look in the mirror and say that he was in the wrong business."

Season Five
September 1994–May 1995
60-minute episodes

Production Team:

Dick Wolf (Executive Producer), Ed Sherin (Executive Producer), Michael Chernuchin (Co-Executive Producer), Lewis H. Gould (Producer), Rene Balcer (Producer), Arthur Forney (Producer), Jeffrey Hayes (Producer), Ed Zuckerman (Co-Producer), Jody Milano-Vanderputten (Associate Producer), Billy Fox (Associate Producer), Morgan Gendel (Executive Story Editor), Lewis H. Gould (Unit Production Manager), Richard Bianchi (Production Designer), Mike Post (Music), Lynn Kressel C.S.A. (Casting), Suzanne Ryan (Casting), Christopher Misiano (Camera Operator), Richard Dobbs (Camera Operator), Moe Bardach (Location Manager), Billy Fox (Editor), Leslie Troy Gaulin (Editor), Michael Kewley (Editor), Neil Felder (Editor), Monty DeGraff (Editor), Mike Struk (Technical Advisor), Bill Fordes (Technical Advisor), Park Dietz, M.D. (Technical Advisor)

Regular Cast:

Jill Hennessy (Assistant District Attorney Claire Kincaid), Steven Hill (District Attorney Adam Schiff), Carolyn McCormick (Dr. Elizabeth Olivet), S. Epatha Merkerson (Lt. Anita Van Buren), Chris Noth (Det. Mike Logan), Jerry Orbach (Det. Lennie Briscoe), Sam Waterston (Executive Assistant District Attorney Jack McCoy)

Fifth Season Overview

Many fans wondered whether or not *Law & Order* could survive the departure of series costar Michael Moriarty after Season Four. By the end of Season Five, they would wonder whether or not the program could survive the departure of Chris Noth, the last original cast member dating back to the pilot. *Law & Order* had just had its most successful season by averaging an 11.4 rating and a nineteen share, up twelve percent in ratings and one share point. However, when Sam Waterston, a veteran stage and screen actor, joins the cast this season as Stone's successor, Jack McCoy, his presence is much more explosive, igniting the character of Claire Kincaid. Co-executive producer and writer Michael Chernuchin describes the difference between Stone and McCoy: "Stone was this moral being, and Jack wants to win and put the bad guys away. Stone was the Boy Scout and McCoy is Palladin with his guns strapped."

Viewers now begin to see a different chemistry between the series' characters, but not one that takes away from what made the show so solid. For one thing, the issues remain gripping: breast cancer (Episode 89: "Second Opinion"), radical fugitives (Episode 93: "White Rabbit"), an Anita Hill-like case (Episode 96: "Virtue"), black fury (Episode 101: "Rage"), and homophobia (Episode 111: "Pride"). There is even a brief crossover to another NBC network drama, *Homicide: Life on the Street*. In the segment on that series called "Law & Disorder" (February 24, 1995), Logan delivers a serial killer (filmmaker John Waters in a funny cameo) by train to Baltimore, where he argues with Det. Frank Pembleton (Andre Braugher) about the difference between their respective cities. In Season Six, there will be a complete crossover (Episode 124: "Charm City") with *Homicide: Life on the Street* that starts a tradition.

Despite a year of terrific shows in Season Four, such as Episode 74: "American Dream," Episode 85: "Sanctuary," and Episode 88: "Old Friends," now in Season Five, *Law & Order* is even more consistent in terms of excellence. The personal lives of several characters entwine with the crime stories: Van Buren shoots a young black child in Episode 94: "Competence," McCoy comes face to face with an old friend who has sold out to the mob in Episode 98: "House Counsel," and Logan relives the nightmare of a sexually-abusive priest in Episode 108: "Bad Faith." In many ways, Season Five is truly the beginning of executive producer Ed Sherin's era on *Law & Order*. With this season the program is moving away from the urban grit of the early years to explore the inner dimensions of the individual police and prosecutors who protect those New York streets.

Episode Descriptions

Episode 89: Second Opinion

Original air date: September 21, 1994
Teleplay by Michael Chernuchin and Jeremy Littman, directed by Ed Sherin, cinematography by Constantine Makris

Additional Cast and Guest Stars: Tony Roberts (Nicholas Bennett), Jan Maxwell (Dr. Nancy Haas), Elizabeth Ashley (Gwen Young), Mitchell Greenberg (Dr. Albert Friedland), Linda Pierce (Abagail Hurst), Michael Crider (Dr. Salinas), Polly Adams (Dr. Roberta Gellman), Leslie Hendrix (Medical Examiner Rogers), Victor Truro (Judge Douglas Spivak), Ron Frazier (Judge Aldo Iannello)

Reviewing the Case: When cancer patient Ann Bennett dies in the emergency room, her body emits the toxic fumes of cyanide. McCoy prosecutes her physician, Dr. Nancy Haas, for murder. This episode is a very smart and timely story about breast cancer. Haas offers women a risky choice that many of them are willing to undertake because the traditional medical establishment has few viable alternatives for treating the deadly disease. Sam Waterston, in his first *Law & Order* episode as Assistant District Attorney Jack McCoy, shows a cunning hustler's approach to the law. McCoy and Kincaid set off sparks the first time they meet, as the room, literally, bristles with sexual tension. "Second Opinion" is also sharp because it presents a woman, rather than a man, as the physician who dispenses false hope.

Relevant Testimony: JILL HENNESSY (actor): "Sam is such a brilliant sparring partner. He's so much fun. You throw this guy the ball; he grabs it and throws it right back. I had a little more of a joker character to work with. He was a little sly, with a different kind of sexual undertone [than Moriarty]."

Episode 90: Coma

Original air date: September 28, 1994
Teleplay by Ed Zuckerman, directed by Jace Alexander, cinematography by Constantine Makris

Additional Cast and Guest Stars: Larry Miller (Michael Dobson), Debra Monk (Kathleen O'Brien), John Cunningham (Max Weston), Brittany Slattery (Jessica Dobson), Erik Jensen (Joey), Phil Parolisi (Robin Winner), David Rosenbaum (Judge Alan Berman), Kurt Knudson (Judge Ari Waxman), Kitty Chen (Judge Elizabeth Yee), Sidney Armus (Judge Walther), Donald Corren (Medill), John Fiore (Det. Anthony Profaci)

Reviewing the Case: Comedy club owner Michael Dobson comes under suspicion for the shooting of his wife, who is now in a coma and unable to identify her assailant. This episode ranks as one of the most piquant murder mysteries *Law & Order* has ever devised because, despite Larry Miller's inventive interpretation of a conniving, slimy Michael Dobson, it is impossible to pin down the man's crime. Just when the case seems provable, Ed Zuckerman's script throws another curve. When the bullet is removed from Sandra Dobson's head, under pressure from McCoy, she dies, and the police determine that it doesn't match her husband's gun. McCoy's desire for victory is sometimes as strong as his pursuit of justice. In the tradition of the best whodunits, "Coma" confirms our worst fears about Dobson, without resolving any of our doubts.

Noteworthy Discoveries: McCoy mentions to Logan that his father was a cop for thirty-one years.

Episode 91: Blue Bamboo
Original air date: October 5, 1994
Teleplay by Rene Balcer and Morgan Gendel, story by Rene Balcer and Hall Powell, directed by Don Scardino, cinematography by Christopher Misiano

Additional Cast and Guest Stars: Laura Linney (Martha Bowen), Ron Orbach (Max Hellman), Joyce Reehling (Mildred Kaskel), Aida Turturro (Nancy Valentine), Glenn Kubota (Nakahara), Tom Shillue (Danny Zabel), Melissa Justin (Diane Elcott), Katrina Lantz (Suzy Kemecki), Shawn Elliott (Judge Joseph Rivera), John Fiore (Det. Anthony Profaci)

Reviewing the Case: The killing of Mr. Hayashi, a Japanese nightclub owner visiting New York, leads to the arrest of singer Martha Bowen, who once worked for the deceased. Her lawyer, Mildred Kaskel, uses the "battered-woman" defense in this case, and the story line deftly explores both racial and sexual fears. Martha Bowen was severely mistreated by Hayashi, but she also became a victimizer when she shot him to death. The contrasting responses between the men and the women on this issue are filled with great dramatic tension. McCoy is convinced that Bowen is hiding behind the "battered-woman" defense. Kincaid doesn't want to discard Bowen's claims of abuse, but as she discovers how manipulative the defendant truly is, her feminist sensibilities are offended. Mildred Kaskel is a women's rights lawyer, who debuted briefly in Episode 83: "Mayhem." She presents Bowen's defense by attacking the Japanese patriarchal culture, speaking directly to the latent racism in the jury. The contention in "Blue Bamboo" is that the Land of the Rising Sun doesn't want to arm-wrestle America; it wants to emulate America. So when the jurors exonerate Bowen, they are sending a message: Japanese men might be grabbing our companies, but they're not going to get our women.

Noteworthy Revelations: This is the first time that Kincaid cross-examines a suspect. Writer Rene Balcer is married to a Japanese woman, Lynne Hayashi. Ron Orbach, who plays Max Hellman, is Jerry Orbach's cousin.

Episode 92: Family Values
Original air date: October 12, 1994
Teleplay by Rene Balcer and William Fordes, directed by Constantine Makris, cinematography by Christopher Misiano

Additional Cast and Guest Stars: Stephen Shellen (Steve Martell), Sarah Paulson (Maggie Conner), Will Lyman (Victor Conner), Anna Holbrook (Christine Whitburn), Mary Beth Peil (Dr. Emma Hiltz), Robert Ari (Richard Kahn), E. Katherine Kerr (Sally Markham), Victor Raider-Wexler (Jules Wheeler), Cynthia Hayden (Miss Vincent), Tracy Lee Bell (Liza), Larry Sherman (Judge Colin Fraser), Joel Michael Simon (Judge James Palnick), Josh Pais (Medical Examiner Borack)

Reviewing the Case: Once the detectives determine that a wealthy woman did not commit suicide, her second husband, Steve Martell, and his stepdaughter, Maggie, appear to be responsible for the murder. This first-rate episode offers yet another example of how adults can manipulate a fragile child's desire to be wanted. Although it bears some similarity to Episode 45: "Skin Deep," this installment examines more thoroughly what Freud called "the family romance." Steve Martell has initiated a near-incestuous affair with the young woman, although his real passion is being part of an affluent household. Waterston is masterful when McCoy cleverly flaunts Martell's damning testimony implicating Maggie, in hopes that she will no longer protect him. "Family Values" is a compact, dramatic dissertation on a family with no values whatsoever.

Noteworthy Discoveries: This episode was nominated for the prestigious Edgar Allen Poe Award.

Episode 93: White Rabbit
Original air date: October 19, 1994
Teleplay by Ed Zuckerman and Morgan Gendel, directed by Steve Robman, cinematography by Constantine Makris

Additional Cast and Guest Stars: Mary-Joan Negro (Susan Forrest), Peter Friedman (Billy Goodwin), Peggy Roeder (Margaret Pauley), Marilyn Chris (Mary Perella), William Kunstler (as himself), Dick Anthony Williams (Sam Burdett), Norman Snow (Stuart Levitin), Don Billett (FBI Agent Tilly), Jonathan Teague (Henry), Tom Cappadona (Eddie Maybrook), Stan Lachow (Arraignment Judge), Roger Serbagi (Judge Quinn)

Reviewing the Case: A routine investigation into the theft of a safety deposit box uncovers evidence that leads Briscoe and Logan back through time to a 1960s idealist, living under an assumed name since a 1971 burglary that left a policeman dead. This episode is quite possibly popular culture's most trenchant look at the ragged legacy of the counterculture rebellion and its self-styled revolutionaries. Loosely based on the case of Katherine Ann Power, who turned herself in after going

Sam Waterston as EADA Jack McCoy (right), chatting with guest star William Kunstler between the shooting of courtroom scenes for Episode 93: "White Rabbit" (Season Five). [courtesy of Jessica Burstein]

underground for more than twenty years, the plot line probes the potential double-life of a radical on the run. The incomparable Mary-Joan Negro gives a vivid portrayal of the fictitious former activist, Susan Forrest, now a Republican with a family-values agenda. At the same time, this story stirs the generational differences that plague *Law & Order*'s regular characters. Briscoe is called a "pig" when he arrests students at sit-ins, Logan has fun with hippie chicks who believe in free love, and McCoy feels a kinship with the anti-war movement. On the other hand, Kincaid, too young to share such memories, sees the case as no different than any other. The presence of William Kunstler, playing himself, evokes the *Zeitgeist* of that turbulent period.

Noteworthy Discoveries: Schiff reveals that he and Kunstler were on the same side of the courtroom in the 1960s, defending protesters.

Relevant Testimony: ED ZUCKERMAN (writer): "I remember we kept going back and forth on what attitudes Waterston and Hennessy would have. Initially, it was Kincaid who was the sympathetic one and McCoy took the f***-you attitude. But Dick [Wolf] told us to flip the roles, just for the hell of it, and see if it makes it more interesting and less obvious. And I think it did work. ['White Rabbit'] was the perfect *Law & Order*. Everyone's right and everyone's wrong."

Episode 94: Competence

Original air date: November 2, 1994
Teleplay by Michael Chernuchin and Mark Perry, directed by Fred Gerber, cinematography by Constantine Makris

Additional Cast and Guest Stars: Omar Sharif Scroogins (Zack Rowland), Samuel E. Wright (Jerome Osborne), Lisa Louise Langford (Marjorie Gordon), Jacklyn Brooke Sanford (Gwen Sheffield), Jerry Grayson (Jeffrey Crockett), Sharon Martin (Linda Byrd), Jude Ciccolella (Capt. Dennis Burnett), Rochelle Oliver (Judge Grace Larkin)

Reviewing the Case: Lieutenant Van Buren is the victim of an attempted holdup by two teens. She kills James Gordon and finds herself under investigation for shooting the retarded and unarmed black child in the back. This tragic event puts Van Buren's professional capabilities under a magnifying glass. This episode piles on the agony of having a black kid's life ended by a black woman who is herself a mother. Merkerson gives a magnificent performance with the kind of character shadings she revealed in Episode 17: "Mushrooms." There is, in fact, almost a sad refrain extending from that episode to this one, evident during a scene when she visits Gordon's mother. A forceful legal argument erupts between Kincaid and McCoy about ignoring Gordon's motive for the robbery, which was a plan to buy a bracelet for his girlfriend. Such omissions often backfire for McCoy, in this instance coming back to haunt him indirectly in Episode 123: "Trophy."

Noteworthy Discoveries: Logan, who questioned Van Buren's authority in Episode 71: "Black Tie," now rallies to her defense against the police department's Internal Affairs division. McCoy drinks his first scotch on the show.

Episode 95: Precious

Original air date: November 9, 1994
Teleplay by Rene Balcer and I. C. Rapoport, directed by Constantine Makris, cinematography by Christopher Misiano

Additional Cast and Guest Stars: Kevin O'Rourke (Marty Willach), Julie Boyd (Eileen Willach), Maria Tucci (Helen Brolin), Joel Leffert (Robert

Cole), Brooks Rogers (Dr. Henry Royce), Nada Rowand (Dr. Margaret Slavin), Becky Borezon (Theresa Tritch), Sam Gray (Judge Manuel Leon)

Reviewing the Case: After questioning the Willachs about their missing baby, Briscoe and Logan discover that the infant has been murdered. They suspect the mother is guilty. This episode is an unsettling dramatization of Munchausen-By-Proxy Syndrome, named after a German baron who once extorted money from people by playing upon their sympathies. People with this form of mental illness tend to inflict harm on children in order to bring attention to themselves. Eileen Willach takes it to the extreme, and actress Julie Boyd is absolutely meticulous in creating the pathetic, creepy sight of a woman without a child left to harm. Actor Kevin O'Rourke reaches for a quality that is both inscrutable and dim in playing Marty, her acquiescent husband, as a willfully blind participant. When Briscoe coaxes a confession from him in a stark and emotionally devastating scene, it's like watching veils being slowly pulled away. When Eileen discovers she's pregnant again, Marty's horror equals that of the program's audience.

Noteworthy Discoveries: For the first time, McCoy is removed from a case; he won't accept a plea bargain without the stipulation of sterilization for Eileen.

Relevant Testimony: RENE BALCER (writer): "What was interesting was [having] this decision by Jack McCoy to ask that the woman get sterilized. Sam's politics are quite liberal, so he had a problem with that scene. . . . At one of our read-throughs, Sam said that he didn't want to advocate this position. I started having to convince him why he should, and why it's not so unusual for the government to interfere in one's physical body. They can prevent you from injecting drugs into your own body; they can take your body, put it in a uniform, and send it in harm's way. As I'm presenting these arguments to him, and he's seeing my point, then I realized that I should just put this argument in a scene with McCoy, Kincaid, and Schiff. So we ended up with this great scene with the three of them hashing out enforced sterilization."

Episode 96: Virtue

Original air date: November 23, 1994
Teleplay by Mark Perry and Jeremy Littman, directed by Martha Mitchell, cinematography by Constantine Makris

Additional Cast and Guest Stars: Regina Taylor (Sarah Maslin), Anthony Heald (Councilman Spencer Talbert), Joanna Merlin (Diedre Powell),

Christopher Cousins (Todd Locke), Anne Lange (Evelyn Talbert), Sharon Cornell (Jocelyn Adams), Catherine Boyd (Dr. Sandra Means), David Lipman (Judge Morris Torledsky), John Ramsey (Judge Walter Shreiber)

Reviewing the Case: McCoy uses a charge of "larceny by extortion" against a liberal councilman, Spencer Talbert, whose former colleague, Sarah Maslin, claims he demanded sex in exchange for a partnership at his law firm. This episode is an intricate, fluidly-written piece about the legal implications of harassment in the workplace. Although it resembles the Anita Hill case, the story is also very different, in that Anita Hill was not attacked or even directly propositioned by Clarence Thomas. Sarah Maslin, on the other hand, certainly has been coerced and the action does jeopardize her career. Regina Taylor gives a dignified performance, especially when she testifies about the humiliation of having to spread her legs in order to further her career. It's also the writer's smart idea to depict Councilman Talbert as a liberal politician who hides contemptible attitudes about women. Anthony Heald drapes the character with a self-serving and smugly detestable persona. There's a nice moment after the trial, when McCoy and Maslin exchange smiles that spell relief and reassurance. Sarah Maslin gets her virtue back.

Relevant Testimony: MARTHA MITCHELL (director): "I remember talking to [producer] Michael Chernuchin about a scene in a restaurant between Kincaid and Regina Taylor, and it was a very important scene for me. It was a scene between two women and I wanted it right. Most TV shows would show them eating salad. I wanted them to have steak or chicken."

Episode 97: Scoundrels

Original air date: November 30, 1994
Teleplay by Ed Zuckerman and Charles Mann, directed by Marc Laub, cinematography by Constantine Makris

Additional Cast and Guest Stars: Michael Zaslow (Willard Tappan), Jonathan Hogan (John Curren), Jane Hoffman (Jane Curren), Edie Falco (Sally Bell), Larry Pine (Edward St. John), Lisa Emery (Alice Huntley), Ross Bickell (Jeffrey Wiggins), James Saito (Tanaka), Yusef Bulos (Frank Rosebrock), Dan Grimaldi (Carl Piselli), Ben Hammer (Judge Herman Mooney), Merwin Goldsmith (Judge Ian Feist)

Reviewing the Case: When lawyer Arthur Kopinsky is murdered, the police eye Willard Tappan, the swindler who conned a woman out of her family fortune, and the woman's once-wealthy son, John Curren. This segment takes its cues from Charles Keating, the California savings-and-loan rogue banker, and covers some of the same territory that Episode 44: "The Working Stiff" did. The subtext is once again the corporate corruption of the 1980s and the rubble it left behind. No fresh turf is overturned here, but Michael Zaslow gives a colorful performance as Tappan, whose face lights up whenever a nasty thought crosses his insidious little mind. Kopinsky, Tappan, and Curren have been embroiled in a messy game of greed leading to violence, and McCoy turns the survivors against each other in court. When McCoy echoes one of Tappan's sentiments, the four-o'clock shadow in his voice is exceedingly wry.

Noteworthy Discoveries: It is discovered that defense attorney Sally Bell was once McCoy's assistant and that she had had an affair with him.

Episode 98: House Counsel
Original air date: January 4, 1995
Teleplay by Michael Chernuchin and Barry Schkolnick, directed by James Quinn, cinematography by Constantine Makris

Additional Cast and Guest Stars: Ron Leibman (Paul Kopell), Jessica Walter (Anna Kopell), Vincent Pastore (John Furini), Fil Formicola (Vincent Dosso), Leslie Ayvazian (Priscilla Lempert), Anthony Fusco (John Murphy), Michael Willis (John Monahan), Fred Scollay (Judge Andrew Barsky), Mark Hammer (Judge Randall Welch), DeAnn Hears (Judge Marie Gance), Claiborne Cary (Judge Carol Bonelli), John Fiore (Det. Anthony Profaci)

Reviewing the Case: The killing of David Lempert, who had served as a juror in a mob trial, leads to a battle of wills between McCoy and Paul Kopell, the suspect's attorney. One of the great aspects of Jack McCoy's feisty character is that he's always caught between the calculations of his actions and the consequences of where his decisions may lead him. In short, this is a man frequently bitten on the rear end. When he goes up against his friend and colleague Paul Kopell, a keen competitor who may even be a shrewder lawyer than McCoy, it becomes a war in which justice is as inconsequential as the prize in a Cracker Jack box. Kincaid rightly sees their battle as just so much macho posing, and the episode demonstrates that McCoy is in deeper than even he suspects. Ron Leibman is terrific in the flamboyant role of the shrewd lawyer, and it's easy to see how these two could be both pals and rivals. In "House Counsel" McCoy's unbridled desire to win gets the best of him. When he triumphs over his friend of twenty-five years, there's no cause for celebration.

Episode 99: Guardian

Original air date: January 11, 1995

Teleplay by Rene Balcer and William Fordes, story by Rene Balcer and Brad Markowitz, directed by Christopher Misiano, cinematography by Constantine Makris

Additional Cast and Guest Stars: Jon Cypher (Jerome Kamen), Joan MacIntosh (Mrs. Blanchard), Dallas Roberts (Matthew Blanchard), Gerry Bamman (Dean Pollard), Holter Graham (Erik Hansen), Saoul Mamby (Enrico Sariego), Jermaine Chambers (Pappi), Phil Nee (Henry Woo), Kira Arne (Teena Varga), Leslie Hendrix (Medical Examiner Rogers), Francine Beers (Judge Janis Silver), Jose Serano (Judge Luis Rodriguez)

Reviewing the Case: A dead junkie, Katie Blanchard, comes from a wealthy family. Briscoe and Logan want to find out who left her to die in the yard of a day-care center. Jerome Kamen, the family lawyer, emerges as the likely suspect. Possibly the weakest episode of the year, "Guardian" suffers from the same mediocrity as Episode 66: "Benevolence" does. Kamen is the family's business adviser who's been like a father to the kids, while busily embezzling money from their trust funds. This story concerns a thief who takes refuge in a posture of self-sacrifice, but he's clearly a pickpocket.

Noteworthy Discoveries: Christopher Misiano, who has been a camera operator for *Law & Order*, directs his first episode.

Episode 100: Progeny

Original air date: January 25, 1995

Teleplay by Ed Zuckerman and Morgan Gendel, story by Morgan Gendel and Mark Perry, directed by Don Scardino, cinematography by Constantine Makris

Additional Cast and Guest Stars: Edward Herrmann (Drew Seeley), James Rebhorn (Charles Garnett), Thomas Schall (Randall Jenkins), Anne Bobby (Nancy Gunther), Jack Gilpin (Simon Reed), Tim Donoghue (Mark Bryant), Cynthia Vance (Joanna Jenkins), Ruth Williamson (Dr. Rachel Moran), Leslie Hendrix (Medical Examiner Rogers), John Carter (Judge Harlan Newfield), Ted Kazanoff (Judge Daniel Scarletti), Judy Franks (Judge Jean Bryant)

Reviewing the Case: The investigation into the killing of Eileen Reed, an abortion clinic doctor, points to an activist group led by former priest Drew Seeley, who exhorted opponent Randall Jenkins to pull the trigger.

This episode jumps headlong into the intense debate about America's pro-choice laws and the arguments used to defend abortion. Edward Herrmann is the ideal choice to play Seeley, who compares himself to John Brown, the nineteenth-century abolitionist hanged for his militant opposition to legalized slavery. One of McCoy's best scenes—in which Waterston employs fire to counter Herrmann's brimstone—is when he asks the Bible-thumping Seeley why he *doesn't* keep slaves, a common enough practice in the scriptures. The segment paints a complicated portrait of a man who knows in his soul that murder is a sin.

Edward Herrmann, who conveyed the complexity of pro-life activist Drew Seeley, on trial for masterminding an abortion clinic bombing in Episode 100: "Progeny" (Season Five). [courtesy of Photofest]

Noteworthy Discoveries: This is the second episode that features Kincaid questioning and cross-examining witnesses (the first was Episode 91: "Blue Bamboo"). At the same time it is discovered that she attended Harvard Law School.

Relevant Testimony: ED SHERIN (executive producer): "We had to dodge a lot of bullets from NBC on [the abortion issue]. We had to make [Seeley] a defrocked priest, and skirt a lot of things. But we did it and I think we did it very well. And bringing the Eichmann defense to bear [when Jenkins claims he was only following orders] was kind of remarkable. We labored on that around the table."

Episode 101: Rage

Original air date: February 1, 1995
Teleplay by Michael Chernuchin, directed by Arthur Forney, cinematography by Constantine Makris

Additional Cast and Guest Stars: Courtney B. Vance (Bud Greer), Richard Libertini (David Solomon), Wendell Pierce (Jerome Bryant), Olivia Birkelund (Joan Stillman), Chuck Patterson (Jack Greer), Armand

Schultz (Dr. Kenneth Price), Jessica Walling (Krista Holbrook), Leslie Hendrix (Medical Examiner Rogers), Bernie McInerney (Judge Michael Callahan)

Reviewing the Case: Bud Greer, a Wall Street broker accused of murdering his mentor, Wallace Holbrook, uses the defense of "black rage" in court. This episode links up with Episode 46: "Conspiracy" and Episode 85: "Sanctuary" to form an agonizing trilogy about the state of race relations in America today. Bud Greer is an angry, arrogant, and deceptive man whose illegal trading scam has been exposed, thereby sealing Holbrook's fate. However, that's only part of it, as the story also addresses the pervasiveness of racism, which provides Greer with a convincing defense strategy: Bigots at the firm avoided and humiliated him. Actor Courtney B. Vance makes a vivid and lasting impression as a man who is utterly self-assured in his hatred for white society, while at the same time condemning black society for holding him back from the dominant power structure that he longs to join. The shocking but subtle conclusion becomes a disquieting lament for Bud Greer.

Relevant Testimony: MICHAEL CHERNUCHIN (writer): "It's funny. When I was writing the show I had no idea of how I was going to end it. Then I was visiting my aunt at 76th and 5th, and I went to get a cab. When it avoided a black man to get to me, I found the ending for the show. I realized that I'm not just telling stories, it's real life. 'Rage' tells you that racism isn't going away and [Bud Greer] is the ultimate result of it."

Episode 102: Performance
Original air date: February 8, 1995
Teleplay by Ed Zuckerman and Jeremy Littman, story by Rene Balcer and Jeremy Littman, directed by Martha Mitchell, cinematography by Constantine Makris

Additional Cast and Guest Stars: Monica Keene (Corey Russell), Maryann Urbano (Mrs. Russell), Richard Venture (David Stein), Peter Facinelli (Shane Sutter), John MacKay (John Sutter), Shane McDermott (Kyle Winters), Polly Adams (Mrs. Sutter), Lily Warren (Valerie Wright), Dash Mihok (Ethan Quinn), John P. Connolly (Nick), David Lipman (Judge Morris Torledsky)

Reviewing the Case: Briscoe and Logan set out to identify the apparently dead victim in a snuff film, but find Corey Russell alive and actually the victim of a sexual-conquest club at her prestigious high school. This story is greatly influenced by real-life incidents, including the Spur Posse in California. Mostly, however, it resembles Episode 30: "Out of Control," in which a young woman with a questionable reputation is raped and the prosecutors have trouble convicting the perpetrators. In this episode, Peter Facinelli is superb as the snide narcissist who leads a teenage gang called the Mack Rangers. Monica Keene also does compelling work as Corey, especially in a scene with Lieutenant Van Buren, when the girl's guard finally comes down like a sudden cloudburst. The legal strategies employed by McCoy are fascinating (he has to establish a criminal conspiracy). When the detectives first see the "snuff" videotape, Briscoe wonders whatever happened to games like Spin the Bottle.

Relevant Testimony: MARTHA MITCHELL (director): "I really enjoyed this episode because it gave me a chance to work with a lot of young actors. We did get into some problems with NBC Standards and Practices because we couldn't use many of the shots in the 'porno' film I shot for the opening. But it was a dynamite script. Some people thought that I went too far in letting Van Buren interrogate the young girl, but I felt that it was just right."

Episode 103: Seed

Original air date: February 15, 1995
Teleplay by Michael Chernuchin and Janis Diamond, directed by Don Scardino, cinematography by Constantine Makris

Additional Cast and Guest Stars: David Margulies (Dr. Jordan Gilbert), Mark Blum (David Aronson), Kristin Griffith (Clara Brock), Ivar Brogger (Nathan Brock), Donna Mitchell (Susan Parker), Jordan Clarke (Brandon Parker), Zach Grenier (Jim Warren), Joan Copeland (Judge Rebecca Stein), Ron Frazier (Judge Aldo Iannello), Judy Frank (Judge Jean Bryant), Stephen McKinley Henderson (Judge Kraemer), Alyson Reed (Medical Examiner Heather Coyle)

Reviewing the Case: A routine investigation into a woman's death leads Briscoe and Logan to Jordan Gilbert, an unethical fertility doctor who uses his own sperm to produce offspring for his patients but hides under the umbrella of confidentiality. With the current controversy about human cloning, this episode about a physician trying to start his own race doesn't seem all that far-fetched. Moreover, the story boasts its own seed in a real-life case of medical mischief. It begins with a simple premise but becomes more labyrinthian at each turn, and more horrifying. David Margulies makes a wonderfully imperious Gilbert, a man who compares himself to God and thinks that he's a savior to all women. Apparently, to many women desperate for children, he seems just that, which is why McCoy and Kincaid can't prosecute him. "Seed" is the darker side of planned parenthood.

Noteworthy Discoveries: In the Arts & Entertainment network's syndicated rerun, a scene has been cut from this episode that features Briscoe and Logan expressing disgust about a lesbian couple. After the initial NBC broadcast, gay rights groups protested the fictional homophobia, which might have convinced A&E to engage in some pre-censorship of the rerun.

Episode 104: Wannabe

Original air date: March 15, 1995
Teleplay by Rene Balcer and I. C. Rapoport, directed by Lewis H. Gould, cinematography by Christopher Misiano

Additional Cast and Guest Stars: Graham Sack (Colin Harrigan), Bruce Kirkpatrick (Tom Harrigan), Marian Quinn (Mrs. Harrigan), Boyd Gaines (Nathan Barclay), Matthew Thomas Carey (Stewart Barclay), Leslie Denniston (Sally Prescott), Gary Thorup (Vaughn Prescott), John Vennema (Dr. Penton), Christine Farrell (Shrier), Doris Belack (Judge Markham)

Reviewing the Case: The death of William Prescott, board member of an exclusive private school, leads to a blue-collar worker, Colin Harrigan. His son, Tom, had been expelled because he was considered socially unacceptable. Class conflicts figure prominently in this episode, which also travels the well-worn path of a troubled father-son relationship. While the story line doesn't really tackle anything new, at least it handles the familiar with some degree of flair. The gun that killed Prescott was originally brandished by Stewart Barclay, the son of the snooty chairman of the board, as a way to impress Tom. Ultimately, the working-class kid demonstrates a sort of stubborn nobility in taking the rap for a wealthy brat who will never have to go to jail. Justice?

Episode 105: Act of God

Original air date: March 22, 1995
Teleplay by Ed Zuckerman and Walter Dallenbach, directed by Constantine Makris, cinematography by Christopher Misiano

Additional Cast and Guest Stars: Robert John Burke (Buzz Palley), Melinda Mullins (Chris Chappel), Skipp Sudduth (Hank Chappel), Stephen Singer (David Pence), Randy Danson (Delores Hartman), Steve Harris (Calvin Tiller), Ileen Getz (Arlene Krasner), Lynn Cohen (Judge Mizener), John Newton (Judge Caffey)

Reviewing the Case: When a bomb at a building site accidentally kills a twelve-year-old boy, McCoy and Kincaid mistakenly convict Hank Chappel. In fact, Buzz Palley, a contractor having an affair with Chappel's wife, is responsible. The DA's office can err but this is probably the biggest blooper since Davy Zifrin was put away in Episode 62: "Jurisdiction." This present installment plays with the idea that not everything is what it appears to be. The prosecutors have ample evidence against the innocent guy, yet nothing that can nail the person who actually did it. Hank Chappel has the obvious motive: His wife has been sleeping with Palley. When the poor slob is finally released from jail, Schiff tells McCoy and Kincaid they're lucky there is no death penalty. However, by the time this episode aired, Governor George Pataki had passed legislation making capital punishment once again legal in New York State.

Episode 106: Privileged
Original air date: April 5, 1995
Teleplay by Jeremy Littman and Suzanne O'Malley, directed by Vincent Misiano, cinematography by Constantine Makris

Additional Cast and Guest Stars: Eddie Malaverca (Steven Bartlett), Katherine Borowitz (Margaret Larson), Fran Brill (Anne Bartlett), David Leary (James Bartlett), Alison Sheehy (Elizabeth Lerner), Richard Thomson (Dr. Alan Eidler), Allan Miller (Judge Margolis)

Reviewing the Case: A double murder, a bitter alcoholic, and a drunken stupor are all elements of the case against Steven Bartlett, who breaks into his old house and kills a couple he believes to be his father and abusive mother. This is a fairly provocative episode, in which McCoy has to split hairs in order to convict. The young man's attorneys claim self-defense as the justification, so McCoy must dismiss the murder charge regarding the female victim (she would have represented the abusive mother in Steven's booze-addled imagination). In the end, however, McCoy's craftiness is what separates him from the pure devotion to the law that confounded Ben Stone. Actor Eddie Malaverca, who has the forlorn quality of a Johnny Depp, proves more than adept at conveying this boy's misery. Fran Brill has a chilling moment on the stand recalling her character's years of mistreating the tormented boy. "Privileged" is a disturbing account of a victim who could find no true way home.

Noteworthy Discoveries: This script is based on a real case in Westchester, New York, where an Indian couple was killed by a stranger with a learning disability.

Episode 107: Cruel and Unusual
Original air date: April 19, 1995
Teleplay by Rene Balcer and Michael Chernuchin, directed by Matthew Penn, cinematography by Constantine Makris

Additional Cast and Guest Stars: Lawrence Pressman (Dr. Alan Colter), Jeffrey DeMunn (Norman Rothenberg), Sheila Tousey (Mrs. Vilardi), Edoardo Ballerini (David Balardi), Steven Burns (Kevin Jeffries), Daniel Ziskie (George Jeffries), Bruce MacVittie (Josh Bilken), Leslie Hendrix (Rogers), Shawn Elliott (Judge Rivera), John Fiore (Det. Anthony Profaci)

Reviewing the Case: The death of Kevin Jeffries, an autistic youth in police custody, reveals a number of unusual and possibly illegal therapies being used on kids at the Behavioral Control Clinic. Nonetheless, parents are reluctant to pursue prosecution. Because of the barbaric manner in which Dr. Alan Colter administers electroshock and sensory-deprivation helmets, he makes too easy a villain. Yet, the episode also looks at the helplessness of families with children whose capacity for humor and intellectual curiosity is frozen within them. After the prosecution wins the case, forcing Colter to forfeit his license and close the clinic, one mother asks McCoy if he's willing to take care of her unruly son. "Cruel and Unusual" makes for vivid drama because there is no clear target for blame.

Noteworthy Discoveries: When Logan is temporarily removed from the investigation, Detective Profaci becomes Briscoe's partner, but only briefly. The director, Matthew Penn, had a brief acting role in Episode 4: "Kiss the Girls and Make Them Die" as Alex Brody, the husband of a woman who was sexually assaulted.

Episode 108: Bad Faith
Original air date: April 26, 1995
Teleplay by Rene Balcer, directed by Dann Florek, cinematography by Constantine Makris

Additional Cast and Guest Stars: Bill Raymond (Joseph Krolinsky), Kit Flanagen (Joan Zinns), June Ballinger (Mrs. Krolinsky), Jan Leslie Harding (Judy Morino), Scott Sowers (Stewart Waller), Dann Florek (Donald Cragen), Christine Farrell (Shrier), Bill Marcus (Judge Novak)

Reviewing the Case: Bill Morino, a police officer who was Logan's childhood friend, is found dead of a presumed suicide in Riverside Park. Things get much more complicated when detective work traces the dead man's connection back to Joseph Krolinsky, a former neighborhood priest with a history of pedophilia. Although the drama is not as wrenching as the film *The Boys of St. Vincent* (1994), this episode does give the ever-inventive Chris Noth an opportunity to share yet another aspect of Logan's torn personality. Bill Raymond gives the unconscionable clergyman layers of banal malevolence (even more so than he did while playing the worm of a husband in Episode 49: "Wedded Bliss"). As a man once molested by Krolinsky, Scott Sowers interprets a lost soul whose face is a road map of pain. However, this is really Noth's hour to shine, and it adds immeasurably to the proceedings that director Dann Florek comes back as Cragen to be with Logan at his time of crisis. Their scene together, when Logan anticipates his testimony would tarnish the dead cop's reputation, is a small gem. The final shot, with the camera peering at Logan through the bars of a holding cell, says it all. Krolinsky may be incarcerated, but Logan is forever isolated by his memories.

Noteworthy Discoveries: Dann Florek also directed Episode 76: "The Pursuit of Happiness" and Episode 82: "Big Bang."

Relevant Testimony: DANN FLOREK (director/actor): "I came back and directed 'Bad Faith' [Episode 108], and one of the things I wanted them to do was put me in it. I said, 'If Noth is in trouble, who does he come to? I'm the guy.' I insisted on the scene in the bar. It was not unlike [what happened to me] in 'The Blue Wall' [Episode 22]. I say [in effect], 'Are you going to say what you know?' He asks, 'What's the big deal?' I say, 'Well, you might as well take that badge and throw it in the garbage. It doesn't f***ing matter anymore. You can't cross that line.'"

Episode 109: Purple Heart
Original air date: May 3, 1995
Teleplay by Morgan Gendel and William Fordes, directed by Arthur Forney, cinematography by Constantine Makris

Additional Cast and Guest Stars: Lisa Gay Hamilton (Denise Johnson), Michael Beach (Brian Elliott), Mike Starr (Steven Breck), Frank Pellegrino (Contini), Ed Wheeler (Duane Johnson), Stu "Large" Riley (Bagley), Dominic Chianese (Judge Kaylin)

Reviewing the Case: The death of Danny Johnson, a former Gulf War veteran who drove a cab, ensnares the police in a web of possible suspects, including a loan shark named Steve Breck, a plumber who is now missing, and Johnson's wife, Denise. The story line borrows some ideas from the 1991 Detroit murder of Anthony Riggs, whose wife had arranged to have him eliminated when he came home from the Persian Gulf. In this simpler story, Johnson has spent all their money, which makes it more difficult for his spouse to make a better life for herself. The fatal flaw of "Purple Heart" is that the show's audience is supposed to believe that she could see no alternative to murder. (The Riggs case was far more interesting because they were both trying to escape the poverty of the inner city. He took a legitimate route in joining the army, while she just decided to kill him and get out.) Nonetheless, there are entertaining performances by Mike Starr as the put-upon loan shark and Michael Beach as a very suave defense attorney.

Episode 110: Switch
Original air date: May 17, 1995
Teleplay by Jeremy Littman and Sibyl Gardner, directed by Christopher Misiano, cinematography by John Thomas

Additional Cast and Guest Stars: Francie Swift (Megan Nelson), Roberta Wallach (Michele Sclig), Bob Dishy (Lawrence Weaver), Sam Groom (Frank Nelson), Tom Ligon (Scott Hampton), Gerry Becker (Neal Latham), Lynne Thigpen (Judge Boucher), Bob Kaliban (Judge Kelman)

Reviewing the Case: When a psychiatrist, Dr. Lillian Hampton, is murdered, the two most likely suspects are a patient suffering from multiple-personality disorder and her obstructive father. The plot has more twists than the New York pretzels so beloved by Briscoe and Logan, but also is a satisfying (and unusual) examination of a father-daughter relationship, complicated by the fact that she is more than one person. Actress Francie Swift keeps up with her character's fast-changing identities, providing a phenomenal turn at the conclusion. However, that's also part of the problem with this kind of story: The ending is easily deduced by process of elimination.

Episode 111: Pride
Original air date: May 24, 1995
Teleplay by Ed Zuckerman and Gene Ritchings, directed by Ed Sherin, cinematography by Christopher Misiano

Additional Cast and Guest Stars: Daniel Hugh-Kelly (Kevin Crossly), Peter Gerety (Charles Powell), Mitchell Lichtenstein (Joe Gibb), Robert Joy (Leo Burnett), Hallie Foote (Marjorie Durban), Kelle Karr (Mrs. Crossly), Nance Williamson (Judge Lessing), Robert Hirschfeld (Judge McNamara)

Reviewing the Case: The investigation into the murder of gay councilman Richard Durban reveals a possible political assassination by Kevin Crossly, an opponent who may harbor a hate-crime agenda. Although Chris Noth doesn't get the glorious send-off that Michael Moriarty, Paul Sorvino, or George Dzundza received when they each left the ranks of *Law & Order*, this episode is still an intelligent and tough-minded contemplation of the issues that surrounded the real-life San Francisco killing of Harvey Milk. Instead of playing favorites, "Pride" shows how the gay rights controversy can sometimes test the cause of justice. Daniel Hugh-Kelly is rewardingly cast as the politician whose homophobia is as much a strategy as a reality (and it's a nice touch that he's an ex-cop since that fact hits some very deep nerves in Logan). Crossly cares more for power than bigotry, but he knows that bigotry can light a fuse under the gay activists, which would hide his true motives. It seems like an after-thought when Logan slugs him at the end, despite the mutual feelings about homosexuality he shares with Crossly.

Noteworthy Discoveries: Logan is transferred to Staten Island to walk a beat for three years.

Relevant Testimony: GENE RITCHINGS (writer): "The network was not real favorable toward it being a story about two gay men. At one point, while I was in California, they literally proposed that we change the characters to women. We made the argument that gay women, in some sense, do not represent the same kind of threat on a social and political level that gay men do. Lesbians, as politically committed as they are, somehow do not represent the same threat to the power structure as men do.... [As for Logan], he seems to undergo a believable character change in the end because he clearly finds either side odious."

Season Six
September, 1995–May, 1996
60-minute episodes

Production Team:

Dick Wolf (Executive Producer), Ed Sherin (Executive Producer), Michael Chernuchin (Co-Executive Producer), Lewis H. Gould (Producer), Ed Zuckerman (Producer), Jeffrey Hayes (Producer), Billy Fox (Co-Producer), Rene Balcer (Supervising Producer), Arthur Forney (Supervising Producer), Barry Schkolnick (Executive Story Editor), Lewis H. Gould (Unit Production Manager), Richard Bianchi (Production Designer), Mike Post (Music), Lynn Kressel C.S.A. (Casting), Suzanne Ryan (Casting), Christopher Misiano (Camera Operator), Richard Dobbs (Camera Operator), Moe Bardach (Location Manager), Billy Fox (Editor), Leslie Troy Gaulin (Editor), Michael Kewley (Editor), Neil Felder (Editor), Monty DeGraff (Editor), Mike Struk (Technical Advisor), Bill Fordes (Technical Advisor), Park Dietz, M.D. (Technical Advisor)

Regular Cast

Benjamin Bratt (Det. Reynaldo Curtis), Jill Hennessy (Assistant District Attorney Claire Kincaid), Steven Hill (District Attorney Adam Schiff), Carolyn McCormick (Dr. Elizabeth Olivet), S. Epatha Merkerson (Lt. Anita Van Buren), Jerry Orbach (Det. Lennie Briscoe), Sam Waterston (Executive Assistant District Attorney Jack McCoy)

Season Six Overview

When Chris Noth was dismissed last season, series creator Dick Wolf said that he wanted to see more differences between the two lead precinct detectives. Apparently, the writers believed the lines of dialogue between Briscoe and Logan were too interchangeable and wanted to have the kind of edginess that existed when Greevey and Logan had been paired in Season One. The idea was to bring on a cop younger than Logan, one who was also more straight-laced, more adept with the new technology (cell phones, computers), and Hispanic. Benjamin Bratt, who had worked with Dick Wolf on the TV series *Nasty Boys* (1990), would now join *Law & Order* as Det. Reynaldo Curtis. In the beginning, Curtis serves, literally, as the straight man for Briscoe, who quips that he has clothing older than his new partner. While Logan has many facets to his personality, Curtis seems, at first, to be one-dimensional. A Bob Dole conservative, he's happily married, with a loving wife and young daughters.

There is one main issue embroidered into the texture of Season Six: legalization of the death penalty in New York, which had been alluded to last season in Episode 105: "Act of God." This year, that topic is featured prominently in Episode 114: "Savages" (a white-collar criminal becomes the test case) and, in the messy cliffhanger, Episode 134: "Aftershock," when the police and prosecutors watch a man being executed.

In this TV year, more of the characters' personal lives come to the forefront. For example, in Episode 123: "Trophy," McCoy is confronted with a case that had been tainted by his former assistant (and lover) years earlier. Schiff is haunted by an old case in Episode 121: "Remand," when a convicted rapist successfully prosecuted years earlier now demands a new trial. In Episode 115: "Jeopardy," Schiff collides with an old friend, a judge accused of taking a bribe. (Does Schiff have any acquaintances not sooner or later implicated in crimes?) Kincaid has serious doubts about continuing in the district attorney's office, a consequence of her legal decisions regarding a schizophrenic lawyer who slaughtered three people in Episode 132: "Pro Se." However, all of these lingering threads cannot compare to the season finale, Episode 134: "Aftershock," an installment bursting at the seams with backstory.

This final episode of the season is also the final curtain call for Claire Kincaid, as Jill Hennessy fosters another *Law & Order* cast change. By this time, Kincaid has finally stepped out from the shadows of the many male prosecutors to fill a role that Ben Stone once had, that of embodying the conscience of the show. Her intelligence and vulnerability are in sharp contrast to McCoy's gun-slinging style, creating a delicate balance that is also charged with drama and sexuality. One doesn't need proof that these two are sleeping together; it is built into their repartee. Her final season proves to be her finest. She goes up against McCoy's former lover in court (Episode 123: "Trophy"), argues passionately with Schiff (Episode 132: "Pro Se"), crosses swords with her predecessor, Robinette (Episode 125: "Custody"), and then dies tragically (Episode 134: "Aftershock"). Somehow, for both actress and character, it all ends too soon.

This is also the season that allows *Law & Order* to merge with *Homicide: Life on the Street* in a two-part February 1996 broadcast (the first part is the *Law & Order* segment; the second is an episode of *Homicide*). On paper, it must have seemed an inspired idea, given that both of these high quality TV crime series cater to an intelligent audience. However, they don't really mesh very well (*Law & Order* is usually plot-driven, whereas *Homicide: Life on the Street* emphasizes character angst), a fact which hardly fails to stop these NBC shows from trying it once again in Season Eight.

Since this is the year for stirring up backstories, it's appropriate to see Paul Robinette return in Episode 125: "Custody." Now a civil rights defense attorney, he has clipped his memorable flattop hairstyle, taken up a fight against his former office, and finally has his day in court addressing a jury. In Season Six, just about everyone gets a reckoning.

Episode Descriptions

Episode 112: Bitter Fruit
Original air date: September 20, 1995
Teleplay by Rene Balcer and Jeremy Littman, directed by Constantine Makris, cinematography by Christopher Misiano

Additional Cast and Guest Stars: Ellen Greene (Karen Gaines), Tom Tammi (Lester Gaines), Marilyn Chris (Mrs. Capetti), John Ventimiglia (Nick Capetti), Richard Venture (Doug Greer), Leslie Hendrix (Rogers),

John Newton (Judge Caffey), Larry Sherman (Judge Fraser), Tanya Berezin (Judge Pate)

Reviewing the Case: Briscoe and his new partner, Reynaldo Curtis, try to determine if the death of a young girl was set in motion by her combative parents. This segment (like Episode 55: "Extended Family") tracks the ugly business of custody suits with bickering spouses who use their child as a pawn. In this case, the youngster is kidnapped and killed in a plan that goes awry. The plot takes many surprising turns (one of which involves a shooting), but remains in the service of revealing the characters' hidden motives. Actress Ellen Greene goes for either incredible sangfroid or massive denial in her portrayal of Karen Gaines, who originally appears to be a grieving mother with a justifiable ax to grind once the killer is found. However, that's only part of the story. "Bitter Fruit" is about a well-intentioned recipe for disaster.

Noteworthy Discoveries: Briscoe tries to initiate Curtis into the world-weary task of being a detective and kids him about his age.

Episode 113: Rebels
Original air date: September 27, 1995
Teleplay by Ed Zuckerman and Suzanne O'Malley, story by Suzanne O'Malley, directed by Ed Sherin, cinematography by Constantine Makris

Additional Cast and Guest Stars: Elizabeth Rodriguez (Caridad), Robert Knepper (Igor), Tim Wheeler (Stillman), Sam Schacht (Louis Bell), Tim Ransom (Green), Gary Klar ("Mountain"), James Murtaugh (Dr. Farnsworth), Donald Corren (Medill), Madeline Lee (Judge Conners)

Reviewing the Case: Tommy Bell, a college student drinking at a rough bar frequented by motorcycle gangs, might have been killed over a leather jacket. This installment is not a very gratifying murder story because it points to the improbable conclusion that Tommy's jilted girlfriend would set him up to be hurt and that he would wear a jacket with biker colors guaranteeing his demise. The episode keeps our attention with characters like Gary Klar's "Mountain," a good-natured Godzilla who throws a few curves at Curtis. Jerry Orbach also has some very funny bits that pep up the show, not to mention some tense moments of trying to calm Curtis when his ethnic heritage is insulted by these latter-day wild ones. "Rebels" does a nice job of contrasting Curtis's straight-laced bravado with the uncouth behavior of the motorcycle goons.

Noteworthy Discoveries: Kincaid has a friend who drives a Yamaha motorcycle.

Episode 114: Savages

Original air date: October 18, 1995
Teleplay by Morgan Gendel, Barry Schkolnick, and Michael Chernuchin, directed by Jace Alexander, cinematography by Constantine Makris

Additional Cast and Guest Stars: Victor Garber (Paul Sandig), Maria Tucci (Helen Brolin), Gareth Williams (Ted Quinlan), Barbara Garrick (Mrs. Sandig), Marianne Hagen (Marcie Donner), David Rosenbaum (Judge Berman), Lynne Thigpen (Judge Boucher)

Reviewing the Case: Despite protestations from Kincaid, McCoy pushes for the death penalty when an undercover detective is killed by Paul Sandig, a wealthy white lawyer. In this story line capital punishment is tackled, and in the end—pardon the pun—the prosecutors take no prisoners. Everybody's expectations (about who will be the most likely candidate for lethal injection) are challenged. Sam Waterston is sensational as McCoy fervently articulates his view that the death penalty reassures the public that the system has some control over crime. Without that satisfaction, there might be more vigilante justice. Kincaid, always there to provide the element of compassion, believes that it all amounts to political propaganda at a time when homicide is at a record low.

Relevant Testimony: MICHAEL CHERNUCHIN (writer): "I have very few strong political beliefs, but you can probably tell from that show that I'm against the death penalty. But I had to work with Sam to get a real justification for revenge, and why we needed the death penalty. We can't let the people carry it out themselves, so the state has to sanction it. The perfect show is when you have everybody with a different opinion about the death penalty. And every character had a different take on it. I felt satisfied writing that show because I had to articulate a reason for the death penalty. It *is* about revenge."

Episode 115: Jeopardy

Original air date: November 1, 1995
Teleplay by Rene Balcer and Jeremy Littman, directed by Christopher Misiano, cinematography by Constantine Makris

Additional Cast and Guest Stars: Sada Thompson (Elaine Nicodos), Peter Frechette (Peter Nicodos), Jeffrey DeMunn (Norman Rothenberg), Louis Zorich (Judge Hynes), Tom Spackman (Jules Kaiser), Zak Oarth (Tony Ricardi), Shawn Elliott (Judge Rivera), DeAnn Mears (Judge Reswick)

Reviewing the Case: Three murders at the office of a small magazine unravel a bitter family feud. The mother in question would do anything to protect the business and her remaining son, including bribery of the judge. It's a classic story of sibling rivalry between wealthy brothers that ends in tragedy, but the case also turns into a tale of legal corruption. Once again, Schiff witnesses an old friend succumbing to temptation. Judge Hynes has gone through a messy and expensive divorce, so he accepts money to throw a trial. The title refers to the double-jeopardy statute, under which a suspect cannot be tried twice for the same crime. This almost happens when Peter Nicodos is freed in the tainted trial, but "Jeopardy" is also about the hazards of selling out.

Louis Zorich, who plays corrupt Judge Hynes in Episode 115: "Jeopardy" (Season Six) and Paul Buchman's befuddled father on Mad About You *(NBC, 1991–). [courtesy of Photofest]*

Relevant Testimony: RENE BALCER (writer): "All of Schiff's friends turn bad. The ones that turn good we don't write about. I love writing for Steven Hill more than anyone else. He is one of the few actors who will call and tell the writers to give him fewer lines. And then when you give him the lines, he'll say give him fewer words. Then you give him the words and he'll say give me fewer syllables."

Episode 116: Hot Pursuit

Original air date: November 8, 1995
Teleplay by Ed Zuckerman and Morgan Gendel, directed by Lewis H. Gould, cinematography by Constantine Makris

Additional Cast and Guest Stars: Amanda Peet (Leslie Harlan), Tovah Feldshuh (Danielle Melnick), Anne Twomey (Ms. Harper), Rusty DeWees (Leon Trapp), Lee Shepherd (Mr. Harlan), Daniel Kash (Sam Franks), Ben Hammer (Judge Mooney), John Fiore (Det. Anthony Profaci)

Reviewing the Case: When the detectives solve a series of murders committed by a holdup team, it is unclear if Leslie Harlan, a young woman kidnapped by the group, was a willing participant. With a few obvious parallels to the Patty Hearst case, this episode also lives up to its title, as the first half is one long, breathless chase. Lewis Gould directs the story superbly, even if the script remains less harrowing than the more eccentric Symbionese Liberation Army saga. Actress Amanda Peet has an exhilarating presence as the protagonist, but we are left with the same questions that the Hearst trial failed to answer satisfactorily: Was she really brainwashed? This drama chooses to see Harlan as complicit in the crimes. "Hot Pursuit" entertains but does not provide much food for thought.

Episode 117: Paranoia

Original air date: November 15, 1995
Teleplay by Michael Chernuchin, directed by Fred Gerber, cinematography by Constantine Makris

Additional Cast and Guest Stars: Sharon Martin (Megan Maslin), Sandy Duncan (Michelle Kates), Glenn Fitzgerald (Merrill Grupp), Peter Sarsgaard (Josh Strand), Emmanuel Xuereb (Amos Brady), Marisa Redanty (Cheryl Diggs), Pat Moya (Deborah Curtis), Herb Downer (Judge Birch), Rochelle Oliver (Judge Larkin)

Reviewing the Case: Briscoe and Curtis try to solve a college student's murder after a graphic description of the crime appears on the Internet. McCoy goes up against Michelle Kates, a lawyer and former lover, who is reluctant to reveal elements of her client's past. This segment begins with the bloodiest scene ever to open a *Law & Order* episode, when Megan Maslin walks into the dormitory and finds her roommate stabbed to death on the bed. It is also one of those situations that fools the audience about the identity of the perpetrator. In this case, the red herring is Merrill Grupp, a computer geek with a head full of lust. (Bratt interrogates poor Grupp until his bladder starts talking.) The high-strung quality that actress Sharon Martin gives Maslin lends much credence to the character's paranoid state. The ensuing legal battle between McCoy and Michelle Kates, played by Sandy Duncan, has all the verve of a whirling dervish.

Noteworthy Discoveries: This was supposed to be the episode that introduces Det. Reynaldo Curtis to viewers, but the order of shows was changed before the season began. Here, his wife and kids are part of the story line.

Episode 118: Humiliation

Original air date: November 22, 1995
Teleplay by Michael Chernuchin and Barry Schkolnick, directed by Matthew Penn, cinematography by Constantine Makris

Additional Cast and Guest Stars: Jonathan Walker (Dr. Mark Danforth), Clare Wren (Julia Danforth), Bob Dishy (Lawrence Weaver), Brian Smiar (Gil McCracken), Rose Arrendondo (Nina), Novella Nelson (Mary Washington), Leslie Barrett (Judge Bonelli)

Reviewing the Case: A prostitute's murder implicates Dr. Mark Danforth, a plastic surgeon who was probably one of her clients. In actuality, the physician's wife may have set him up for the crime. Even though movie star Hugh Grant's real-life encounter with a hooker in Los Angeles came later in time, this episode certainly seems precognizant of that event. The story unfolds cleanly and simply; it seems totally likely that the doctor did the deed. However, it takes Kincaid's intuition, and some sloppy testimony from Julia Danforth, to open up other possibilities. There are also some other suspicious characters, such as a rather scary deli owner (played by Brian Smiar) who seems to be looking for a head to crack. The key to this crime is understanding what the vows of marriage mean to a woman scorned. As the phrase goes, hell hath no fury, and all that.

Noteworthy Discoveries: Apparently, Curtis has been married for six years. A Ben & Jerry's ice-cream truck goes by behind the *other* Ben and Jerry. This is the first homicide case that Kincaid tries on her own in court.

Episode 119: Angel
Original air date: November 29, 1995
Teleplay by Michael Chernuchin and Janis Diamond, directed by Arthur Forney, cinematography by Constantine Makris

Additional Cast and Guest Stars: Elizabeth Hanley Rice (Leah Coleman), Fisher Stevens (Ross Fineman), Michael Willis (Father Carner), Michael Dolan (Keith Coleman), Nelson Vasquez (Ricardo Hernandez), Joan Copeland (Judge Stein), John Fiore (Det. Anthony Profaci)

Reviewing the Case: Leah Coleman is a mother who murders her baby (after initially claiming she was kidnapped) and the woman's unusual defense is that God wanted her to do it. This outstanding episode comes to grips with the moral issues raised by the infamous real-life Susan Smith case. How can a rational defense be established for the type of crime that outrages the public? The realization of what the mother has done builds slowly, so it becomes clear to the viewer at about the same time that the detectives catch on. There's a beautifully structured scene of Curtis leading Leah through the events that preceded the disappearance of her baby, and it's one of Benjamin Bratt's finest moments. "Angel" then takes a macabre turn, when Ross Fineman (in a comical performance by

Fisher Stevens) appears as a green defense lawyer McCoy thinks he can intimidate. Leah even implicates her priest (actor Michael Willis, whose look of horror is unforgettable) by testifying that he told her Susan Smith's children are in heaven, a better place than the hell we all live through. At the end, there isn't any real understanding of such an atrocity, which is why stories like this continue to haunt the imagination.

Noteworthy Discoveries: Curtis mentions that one of his daughters is a second-grader named Lydia.

Relevant Testimony: BENJAMIN BRATT (actor) [on Curtis's interrogation]: "While trying to extract information from [Leah Coleman], he walks that fine line of staying true to the church and true to the rules of investigation. And yet, he is somewhat manipulating her by playing with her beliefs and religion. So, there's a subtle little dance there. That's what makes for interesting drama—when you present a character like Rey Curtis who is morally upstanding, who is very self-righteous, and then put him in a situation where he might have to go against his own nature a little bit to get to the end that he desires."

Episode 120: Blood Libel

Original air date: January 3, 1996
Teleplay by I. C. Rapoport, story by Rene Balcer and I. C. Rapoport, directed by Constantine Makris, cinematography by Christopher Misiano

Additional Cast and Guest Stars: Chris Cooper (Roy Payne), Jack Vinson (Matt Hastings), Jeanne Ruskin (Alice Marsdale), Lee Wilkof (Dr. Alvin Sabloff), Mark Zeisler (Richard Kovacs), Leslie Hibbard (Loren Nadel), Zach Grenier (Barry Aronson), Mike Mearian (Judge Busey)

Reviewing the Case: An anti-Semitic message turns up in a high school yearbook, offering a clue to the murder of art teacher Sarah Aronson. It also leads to a case that pits Jack McCoy against Roy Payne, a Ku Klux Klan lawyer who insists the killing was part of a Jewish conspiracy. Using literary precedents, suspect Matt Hastings reasons that if Ernest Hemingway and Ezra Pound could get away with making fun of Jews, why can't he justify his hateful humor at the expense of an entire race of people? However, this teenager's so-called fun masks a darker motive for homicide. In an adroit performance that couples Southern gentility with the scruples of a snake, Chris Cooper instills Roy Payne with supreme confidence that he can find at least one juror to believe in his twisted legal theory.

Noteworthy Discoveries: It is revealed that Briscoe's father was Jewish, but his mother raised him with her Catholic religious beliefs.

Episode 121: Remand
Original air date: January 10, 1996
Teleplay by Rene Balcer and Elaine Loeser, directed by Jace Alexander, cinematography by Constantine Makris

Additional Cast and Guest Stars: Anita Gillette (Cookie Costello), Edouard DeSoto (Sal Munoz), Talia Balsam (Teri Marks), Leonardo Cimino (Mr. Costello), Arthur Nascarella (Bobby Farina), Marina Durell (Olivia Valerio), Abe Vigoda (Det. Landis), Tony Lip (Eddie Murrows), Karen Shallo (Linda Santoro), Vince O'Brien (Judge Franks), Tom Stechschulte (Judge Rockwell)

Reviewing the Case: Cookie Costello, the victim in a thirty-year-old rape and stabbing attack, is fearful about the possibility of a new trial for assailant Sal Munoz. This episode imagines what would happen if the man who killed the real-life Kitty Genovese (whose murder was observed by several apathetic neighbors in New York back in the '60s) found a way to be declared innocent decades later. The case really irritates Schiff because he helped put Munoz behind bars, but now new testimony, dead witnesses, and reformed laws have helped free a very dangerous man. Anita Gillette is proficient at playing a woman whose nightmare cannot be put behind her. Above all, actor Edouard DeSoto's Sal Munoz is capable of invading anyone's nightmares. This grim fate for Cookie Costello keeps even Adam Schiff in its grip.

Episode 122: Corpus Delicti
Original air date: January 17, 1996
Teleplay by Ed Zuckerman and Barry Schkolnick, directed by Christopher Misiano, cinematography by Constantine Makris

Additional Cast and Stars: Frank Converse (Lyle Christopher), Byron Jennings (Richard Brandson), Joe Grifasi (James Linde), Dan Moran (Tibor Nichols), Lisby Larson (Susan Merriman), Maureen Moore (Judith Grayson), Delphi Harrington (Gretchen Fairchild), David Lipman (Judge Torledsky), William Severs (Judge Fillmore)

Reviewing the Case: The death of a show horse leads to a trial involving insurance fraud, a sting operation, and a wealthy woman's disappearance. This story may begin with an animal carcass, but it evolves into a tricky murder case that turns up no human body at all. Lyle Christopher has a way with horses headed for the glue factory, and with wealthy ladies as well. One of them, his fiancée, Ruth Thomas, disappears. Actor Frank Converse has that perfectly impenetrable, rugged face that helps shield his character from inquiries, while also displaying a suspicious demeanor that can radiate more heat than the sun. So it is fascinating to watch Waterston's slow burn here, since McCoy can't convict Christopher in any of his pending lawsuits until he finds a body. However, the prosecutor, who loves to walk the tightrope between what's ethical and what isn't, forces a mistrial in order to buy some time.

Episode 123: Trophy

Original air date: January 31, 1996
Teleplay by Jeremy Littman, story by Jeremy Littman and Ed Zuckerman, directed by Martha Mitchell, cinematography by Constantine Makris

Additional Cast and Guest Stars: Laila Robins (Diana Hawthorne), David Garrison (Gerald Fox), Isaiah Whitlock, Jr. (Simon Brooks), Heath Lamberts (Dr. Rigg), Jerome Preston (Ernie Bigelow), Wesley Rice (Andrew Dillard), Stephanie Berry (Estelle Walters), John Ramsey (Judge Schreiber)

Reviewing the Case: The search for what appears to be a copycat serial killer results in complications for McCoy, who tried the first case five years earlier with his former assistant—also his lover at that time. Simon Brooks, who compulsively kills young black children, is contrasted with Andrew Dillard, mistakenly sent to prison for the crime five years ago. A bad situation gets much worse when McCoy realizes that Diana Hawthorne, one of many assistants he has wooed, buried evidence to secure his promotion to district attorney. All of McCoy's chickens come home to roost, as his questionable tactics, his bravado, and his past liaisons conspire to put his career in jeopardy. However, this episode really belongs to the actresses Laila Robins and Jill Hennessy. It's as much about two woman revealing what they know about each other as McCoy's lovers and colleagues, as it is about revealing evidence at a trial. Robins is sensational as the ambitious lawyer who surprises even herself when she realizes that she's done something heinous, and for utterly sentimental reasons. As an examination of sexual politics in the workplace, "Trophy" certainly takes the prize.

Noteworthy Discoveries: This is the first *Law & Order* episode that really hints at a Kincaid-McCoy love affair and the second one that allows Kincaid to prosecute a case. (The first one is Episode 119: "Angel.")

Relevant Testimony: MARTHA MITCHELL (director): "This is the episode that I'm most proud of. It was another episode with a really good scene between two women—that scene between Jill and Laila Robins. There was some debate about Laila going to court over this, and I agree that it's debatable, but dramatically it worked. Also, I wanted to slow down that scene with Sam and Laila when they meet up at the end. Some people wanted her to be more emotional and sobbing, but I wanted her to have integrity. It turned out just right."

Episode 124: Charm City

Original air date: February 7, 1996
NOTE: This episode is the first of a joint two-part production with NBC-TV's *Homicide: Life on the Street* (1993–).
Teleplay by Michael Chernuchin and Jorge Zamacona, directed by Ed Sherin, cinematography by Christopher Misiano

Additional Cast and Guest Stars: Kevin Geer (Brian Egan), Ray Anthony Thomas (Jerome Bell), Leo Burmester (Mr. LeClair), Kyle Secor (Det. Tim Bayliss), Richard Belzer (Det. John Munch), Andre Braugher (Det. Frank Pembleton), Philip Geoffrey Hough (Kenny Egan), Catrina Ganey (Mrs. Chapman), Ted Kazanoff (Judge Scarletti), W. T. Martin (Judge Naughton)

Reviewing the Case: Subway terrorism designed to kill blacks brings two Baltimore detectives to New York in an effort to solve a five-year-old Maryland crime that left similar clues. For the fans of both *Law & Order* and *Homicide: Life on the Street*, there was a great deal of anticipation for what they felt ought to be a fabulous oncamera collaboration. This episode begins well enough as a crowd of people, all gasping for air, stumble out of a subway station, and, moments later, bodies line the street in a scene reminiscent of Episode 32: "Heaven." Thereafter, the segment tries too hard to mesh the different styles of the two NBC shows, getting away from the plot at hand (a clever variation on the chemical gas attack by a group of religious fanatics in Japan). *The Homicide* installment, Episode 46: "For God and Country," aired on February 9, 1996, pretty much abandons the story and concentrates on gossipy details, such as the news that Briscoe once slept with Detective Munch's ex-wife. There are some legal conundrums worth remembering: After catching the man responsible, Kincaid succeeds in getting the suspect extradited to New York for trial. Baltimore detective Frank Pembleton conducts such an aggressive interrogation, he violates the killer's constitutional rights. An all-white jury at the trial suggests the Rodney King case. "Charm City" sets up some fiery, dramatic possibilities, but unfortunately the *Homicide: Life on the Street* half of the two-parter cranks out mostly a lot of smoke.

Noteworthy Discoveries: Along with the gossip previously mentioned, it is discovered that Briscoe has been in the homicide field for fifteen years.

Relevant Testimony: MIKE STRUK (technical advisor): "In the first [full] *Homicide* crossover, the Baltimore cops come up to the detective squad in the *Law & Order* segment and [our detectives] outright treat them like sh**heels. I said, 'Look, you can't do this. They've got a joint cause here—to get the bad guys. If you leave the script the way it is, I'm gonna have to hide under the bed. I'm gonna get killed.' They were just outright rude to them."

Episode 125: Custody

Original air date: February 21, 1996
Teleplay by Morgan Gendel, story by Morgan Gendel and Rene Balcer, directed by Constantine Makris, cinematography by Christopher Misiano

Additional Cast and Guest Stars: Amber Kain (Jenny Mays), Lee Brock (Donna Corbin), Richard Brooks (Paul Robinette), Scott Lawrence (Michael Walters), Afemo Omilami (Henry Patterson), Michael Patterson (Alan Corbin), Ray Girardin (Sal Martel), Stacy Highsmith (Darla Walters), Andre De Shields (Dr. Elvin Simmonds), Harold Miller (Judge Metcalfe), Charlotte Colavin (Judge Pongracie)

Reviewing the Case: No longer an assistant district attorney, Paul Robinette returns to oppose his former colleagues in a case involving the murder of a social worker. At the root of the crime is a young black woman and ex-crack addict, Jenny Mays, who has kidnapped her biological son from the white couple with whom he was placed. Five years ago, Ben Stone asked Robinette whether he was a lawyer who was a black man, or a black man who was a lawyer. Here, Robinette establishes that he's the latter. Richard Brooks has shed his flattop for the most invigorating performance he's ever given on the program. In a story that resembles the film *Losing Isaiah* (1995) (starring Jessica Lange and Halle Berry), Robinette mounts a provocative defense, telling the jury that trans-racial adoption spells cultural genocide for black people. The episode is engrossing on its own, but there's something quite satisfying about Robinette, reborn in the role of a civil rights attorney, arguing a case in front of a jury. He more or less outwits the prosecutors and, in the process, comes to terms with himself.

Relevant Testimony: RICHARD BROOKS (actor): "It wouldn't have been interesting if Robinette hadn't changed and turned into an equal force to the Ben Stone character. It was a little bit of revenge for being unceremoniously released from the show—let's go for broke on this and take off the gloves. It felt amazingly easy to finally take a case [to court]. I was really amazed by how easy it was to stand up there in the courtroom. It surprised me. I know it surprised Sam Waterston. Except for Orbach, I didn't really know anybody. Poor Sam was all of a sudden put in the ring with me and had all this fury and passion of five years of sitting there, wanting to do this. All of a sudden, here was my shot."

Episode 126: Encore

Original air date: February 28, 1996
Teleplay by Ed Zuckerman and Jeremy Littman, directed by Matthew Penn, cinematography by Constantine Makris

Additional Cast and Guest Stars: Larry Miller (Michael Dobson), Cecilia Hart (Marcia Stamell), Deborah Lee Johnson (Margaret Nash), Rafeal Baez (Luis Cruz), Jean Claude LaMarre (Murphy), Tony Darrow (Giabone), Elaine Tse (Joyce Lee), Donald Corren (Medill), Greg S. Ryan (Judge Kaiser), Kurt Knudson (Judge Waxman), John Fiore (Det. Anthony Profaci)

Reviewing the Case: A jogger killed in Central Park turns out to be the second wife of Michael Dobson, the former comedy club owner acquitted of murdering his first wife in Episode 90: "Coma." Schiff wonders why this guy hasn't thought to find a divorce lawyer. Once again, Larry Miller generates a grubby humor and bristling amorality for his character in an ingenious chapter that does not simply repeat the best aspects of the former episode. More surprises are built into the new story. In this case, prosecutors know that Dobson has told many lies, including those about business ties to a mobster named Giabone (the entrancing Tony Darrow), but there is still insufficient evidence that he had a hand in killing his second wife. This episode wages a battle of nerves until a crack develops in Dobson's supposedly air-tight defense. Although most sequels never measure up to the original story, "Encore" finds a way to surpass its predecessor.

Episode 127: Savior

Original air date: March 13, 1996
Teleplay by Michael Chernuchin and Barry Schkolnick, directed by David Platt, cinematography by Constantine Makris

Additional Cast and Guest Stars: Brooke Smith (Margot Bell), Timothy Landfield (Ronald Weber), Ellen Pompeo (Jenna Weber), Linda Edmond (Laura Cochran), Shawn Hatosy (Chester Manning), Nancy

McDoniel (Sheila Gordon), Albert Makhtsier (Sergei Yentakov), Geoffrey Wade (Mitchell Weisbrod), Richmond Hoxie (Dr. Lloyd Lipman), Linda Atkinson (Judge Gaines)

Reviewing the Case: A down-and-out ad executive, Ronald Weber, becomes the prime suspect when his wife and son are killed and his daughter wounded. He claims that he was out drinking at the time. It looks like a simple case about the kind of person psychologists call a "family annihilator" but, like the best episodes of *Law & Order*, a corkscrew of doubt is waiting on the other side of certainty. Weber might be the most likely candidate, but soon attention is focused on the surviving daughter, who may have had her own reasons for carrying out the crime. Timothy Landfield gives a brooding performance as a man unable to face the demands of being the breadwinner, and Brooke Smith is a welcome addition as the defense attorney who is also Kincaid's good friend. Carolyn McCormick (Dr. Olivet) has a tingling moment of doubt when she realizes that maybe Weber isn't guilty. If "Savior" doesn't linger in the memory (the plot turns are a little too pat), it's still an enticing drama about a family whose house was not home, sweet home.

Noteworthy Discoveries: In this episode, a thought is planted in the viewer's mind about Kincaid getting out of the profession.

Relevant Testimony: DAVID PLATT (director): "After years on the set [as the sound mixer], you say to yourself, 'I could do that.' Till you're in the hot seat, where you're the sun in the middle of a universe, you really don't know what it's like. 'Savior' was my first episode. I went into it very cocky. It was sobering. I couldn't have gotten through it without the help and support of people here. On another set, a bunch of strangers would have watched me die. Ed [Sherin] still had faith that I had the tools to do it. It was definitely an intense learning experience. [Remember] the old Nietzsche saying, 'What doesn't kill you makes you stronger'? Well, I got a little stronger."

Episode 128: Deceit

Original air date: March 27, 1996
Teleplay by Rene Balcer and Eddie Feldman, directed by Vincent Misiano, cinematography by Constantine Makris

Additional Cast and Guest Stars: Peter Riegert (Jerold Dixon), Mary Beth Hurt (Sela Dixon), Robert Sella (Tony Conneca), Tom O'Rourke (Peter Behrens), Jace Alexander (Larry Philbert), Liana Pai (Dena Kobata), Emilio Del Puzo (Judge Sierra), Bernard Grant (Judge Reisman)

Reviewing the Case: Lawyer Elliot Wells, who has been killed, was supposedly fired from his firm because he was gay. In truth, he was having a homosexual relationship with a senior partner who wanted to stay in the closet. This episode bears some resemblance to Episode 43: "Silence," in which a secret life has tragic implications. In both cases, what is at stake is a family's identity, which leads to murder. Peter Riegert is a consummate actor whose character seems uncomfortable in his own body (as if his desires act independently from his will). Mary Beth Hurt matches him as a woman who holds herself tight, in denial of what she knows are the facts about her husband. Robert Sella gives the story its only lighter quality, as a queen always caught in the glare of his own spotlight. "Deceit" suggests that sometimes under the smokescreen of homophobia lies a latent homosexual waiting to come out.

Noteworthy Discoveries: It is revealed that Curtis was propositioned by his former female boss, which is why he had transferred to his present position in this precinct.

Episode 129: Atonement
Original air date: April 10, 1996
Teleplay by Morgan Gendel, story by Ed Zuckerman and Morgan Gendel, directed by Martha Mitchell, cinematography by Constantine Makris

Additional Cast and Guest Stars: Michael Imperioli (Johnny Stivers), Joanna Merlin (Diedre Powell), Josh Hopkins (Ken Soames), Mark Zimmerman (Fredrick Scannel), Hal Robinson (Mr. Lasko), Patti Allison (Mrs. Lasko), Karen Williams (Monica Wickes), Caprice Benedetti (Amber), Philip Coccioletti (Rick Kasteler), Angelina Fiordellisi (Zoe Stivers), Leslie Hendrix (Rogers), William Severs (Judge Fillmore)

Reviewing the Case: When police find the body of a missing model named Sharon Lasko, it is apparent that Johnny Stivers, an obsessed limo driver, may be responsible for her death. This installment will likely bring back memories of Episode 34: "Star Struck," but it won't replace them. Whereas the earlier offering was a thorough examination of celebrity obsession and how it translated into a legal defense of insanity, this segment dodges the darker material beneath the surface. The story concerns a hapless, lovesick guy who kills because a drug dealer made him do it. Michael Imperioli is nicely cast as Stivers, but the part doesn't allow him much of an opportunity to vent his desire for revenge against Sharon because she was likely to reject him. "Atonement" doesn't atone for quite enough.

Episode 130: Slave

Original air date April 21, 1996
Teleplay by Rene Balcer and Elaine Loeser, directed by Jace Alexander, cinematography by Constantine Makris

Additional Cast and Guest Stars: Karen Young (Cassie Rickman), Patrick Breen (Andrew Gellis), Welker White (Ms. Rubinoff), Adam B. Zolitin (Lonnie Rickman), Agustin Fernandez (Ross Morales), Ron Cephas Jones (Frank Doyle), Kim Staunton (Luanne Doyle), Tom Signorelli (James Merrick), Christine Farrell (Shrier), David Rosenbaum (Judge Berman), Stephen Berger (Judge Ingles), Lucy Martin (Judge Brent), John Fiore (Det. Anthony Profaci)

Reviewing the Case: A woman is shot while sleeping and the investigation leads Briscoe and Curtis to Lonnie Rickman, a boy whose crack-addicted mother has entrusted him to a dealer's care. The depravity depicted here might have made even crusading Victorian novelist Charles Dickens cringe. The story is similar to Episode 75: "Born Bad" and features another young man whose hopes have been demolished. However, this segment grows even bleaker than that previous one as the picture of a mother who sells her own child to pay for a drug habit becomes clear. Karen Young brings a sluggish intensity to the role, while slyly revealing how much anger is buried in her indifference to Lonnie's welfare. Adam Zolitin's performance as this lost boy is a study in pure terror. Ross Morales plays this child's monstrosity of a father, a lowlife named Agustin Fernandez. McCoy's long, wistful look, as Lonnie is led out of the courtroom, reminds *Law & Order* viewers that "Slave" is a picture of family life that Norman Rockwell could not have imagined and, certainly, never painted.

Noteworthy Discoveries: It is revealed that both Van Buren and Briscoe like reading poetry by Langston Hughes. In Briscoe's case, this cultural enlightenment stems from his beatnik days, when he wanted to impress Jewish girls from the upscale neighborhood of Riverdale, north of Manhattan.

Relevant Testimony: RENE BALCER (writer): "This is a favorite. It's my version of [François Truffaut's 1959 film] *The 400 Blows*. I had a lot of fun writing a sassy mother with her wise-ass kid. We've always had pretty good luck with kids. And the kid in this episode was very good. If you read the character on the page, this [actor] wouldn't be the kid that you would imagine."

Episode 131: Girlfriends

Original air date: May 1, 1996
Teleplay by Ed Zuckerman and Suzanne O'Malley, story by Ed
Zuckerman and Jeremy Littman, directed by Christopher Misiano, cine-
matography by Richard Dobbs

Additional Cast and Guest Stars: Cara Buono (Shelly Taggert), James
Naughton (Barry Taggert), David Little (Mitch Weiss), Joelle Carter
(Donna), Clarissa Thurston (Lisa), Peter Van Wagner (Jonathan
Freeman), Dana Ivey (Ms. Shore), Leslie Hendrix (Rogers), Doris Belack
(Judge Barry), Fred Scollay (Judge Barsky)

Reviewing the Case: When a student is murdered the detectives look for
a campus rapist, but the medical examiner's report puts them onto the
path of prostitution. Shelly Taggert, a college-aged madam, manages to
pin the blame on her father. This story could be a variation on songwriter
Willie Dixon's line about men not knowing "what the little girls understand" because Shelly Taggert certainly knows things that her father will
never comprehend, which seals his fate. Even with its slightly queasy
undertones of incest, the episode feels a little thin on character development. James Naughton is splendid as the father whose quiet presence
transmits shame and guilt because he profits from his daughter's illicit
business. Cara Buono certainly plays up the vixen side of Shelly Taggert.
Yet neither character reveals more, and "Girlfriends" doesn't tell us anything new about the transgressions between fathers and daughters.

Episode 132: Pro Se

Original air date: May 8, 1996
Teleplay by Rene Balcer and I. C. Rapoport, directed by Lewis H. Gould,
cinematography by Constantine Makris

Additional Cast and Guest Stars: Denis O'Hare (James Smith), Maryann
Plunkett (Joanne Ellis), Ann Dowd (Patricia Smith), David Aaron Baker
(Mr. Lowe), Robert Emmet (Frank Ellis), Nicole Leach (Liana Rogers),
Merwin Goldsmith (Judge Feist), Shawn Elliot (Judge Rivera)

Reviewing the Case: An investigation of a multiple murder in a clothing
store leads to the arrest of James Smith, a lawyer who decides to defend
himself even though he is schizophrenic. Smith changes identities like
someone shedding a coat, and that is the key to this episode. How does
a man defend himself when he doesn't feel connected to the self he's
defending? Denis O'Hare is completely convincing in this challenging-
role because he doesn't turn the performance into a stunt. Instead, this
stupendous actor transforms himself from a crazed apparition of

Rasputin into a calm, respectable attorney—all the while making clear that the same man is ticking away in both personalities. Yet, O'Hare isn't the whole show. Ann Dowd's Patricia Smith shows a sad dignity when she testifies that her brother is mentally ill, and Maryann Plunkett offers a touching performance as the seriously wounded Joanne Ellis. In the end, James Smith loses his case but comprehends the tragic truth of his limitations.

Relevant Testimony: RENE BALCER (writer): "I read a story in the *New York Times* about a Harvard Law School graduate who was schizophrenic and couldn't get a job, even though he was medicated. I thought, 'Well, what if this homeless guy [that the news story inspired me to create] eventually ended up murdering five people in one rampage. When we first meet him he's got long, scraggly hair and stinks to high heaven. And then when we see him in court he's got his hair cut, he's back on his medication, and he's representing himself. So that was not really a news story.' I have a cousin who was schizophrenic and committed suicide, so part of that went into [the story] too."

Episode 133: Homesick
Original air date: May 15, 1996
Teleplay by Barry Schkolnick, story by Barry Schkolnick and Elaine Loeser, directed by Matthew Penn, cinematography by Constantine Makris

Additional Cast and Guest Stars: Patti LuPone (Ruth Miller), Annika Peterson (Lila Crenshaw), Dennis Parlato (Warren Karmel), Charlie Hofheimer (Ben Karmel), Leslie Ayvazian (Eileen Karmel), Kim Raver (Wendy Karmel), Leslie Hendrix (Rogers), Rosemary DeAngelis (Judge Krieger)

Reviewing the Case: After the Karmels' infant is found dead in his crib, British au pair Lila Crenshaw is suspected of poisoning the child. Although based on other nanny murder cases up to that time, the episode certainly prefigures the shocking 1997 trial of British nanny Louise Woodward in Cambridge, Massachusetts. This television drama, however, has a very different outcome, as it plays on yuppie guilt, with parents so devoted to their careers that they turn over the complete care of their child to a stranger. Lila is a young woman caught in a family war between the father and his son from a previous marriage. Her only crime is lack of proper compassion for the child who was an inconvenience for everyone concerned. Annika Peterson resembles a young Glenda Jackson and makes Lila a rather unsympathetic teenager. Kim Raver's Wendy Karmel, the negligent mother, shows some cracks in her corporate armor when cross-examined on the stand. Patti LuPone, as the defense attorney, is a treat, especially when McCoy opens the gate for her to nail the true killer.

Episode 134: Aftershock

Original air date: May 22, 1996
Teleplay by Janis Diamond, story by Michael Chernuchin and Janis Diamond, directed by Martha Mitchell, cinematography by Constantine Makris and Christopher Misiano

Additional Cast and Guest Stars: Len Cariou (Prof. Mac Geller), Jennifer Garner (Jamie), Jennifer Bill (Cathy Briscoe), Jerry Grayson (Mike), Tom Riis Farrell (Bud), Billy Otis (Manny Ross), Charles Dumas (Don Van Buren), Mickey Scott (Chris Bauer), John Fiore (Det. Anthony Profaci)

Reviewing the Case: Briscoe, Curtis, McCoy, and Kincaid are together in witnessing the execution of a criminal and then react in individual ways, all indirectly leading to tragedy. This episode is a big departure—and a big mistake—for a program that has always tried to stick closely to the crimes. In an attempt to provide a more personal story, as well as deal (once again) with the impact of the death penalty, the segment goes painfully wrong because it begins to resemble most other television shows. It substitutes melodrama for the emotional strains on characters grappling with the issues of their demanding jobs. Do we really need to see Briscoe struggling with guilt about his neglected daughter? Does Curtis really need to commit adultery? Or do we even need Olivet giving McCoy therapy during lunch? Luckily, the actors don't embarrass themselves (Waterston and Orbach are quite good), and the execution is imaginatively depicted. As for Jill Hennessy, after Kincaid has a telling scene with her stepfather (Len Cariou) and another with Van Buren, her fate is heartbreaking. "Aftershock" is too conventional for all the effort, talent, and brains that went into it.

Noteworthy Discoveries: Claire Kincaid was initially supposed to survive the car crash but when Jill Hennessy decided not to return for a subsequent guest spot, the character was pronounced dead. This is the first time that the show dispensed with black cards, as the printed oncamera graphics about location and date are called, which also means there is no "boink-boink" sound between scenes.

Relevant Testimony: JILL HENNESSY (actor): "The car crash? That was Dick Wolf's idea. It was brutal. I'd been trying not to feel too much. So I'd invited my brother down, and we were standing on a sidewalk in the

West Village, waiting for this little car with two dummies in it to be completely destroyed by a Dodge Ram truck. We were laughing, and when they yelled 'Action!' I saw this truck destroy the car with two effigies in it that I had just been riding in with Jerry [Orbach]. I just burst into tears. I just lost it. My last day they were shooting a gas-chamber scene. They rolled out this big banner saying 'We'll miss you.'"

SAM WATERSTON (actor): "McCoy was crazy about Claire and he thought he was yards ahead of her as a lawyer. But she was pretty regularly demonstrating he wasn't all that many yards ahead. There was a definite tutorial relationship with Kincaid. But I thought that if Jill had continued to stay on the show, the only place to go was to a relationship of complete equality. Claire had graduated to a kind of independence right when I came on the show and then the writers, at first reluctantly and then enthusiastically, embraced the idea that she was an equal. Which was something that she, Jill, very much wanted all along."

Season Seven
September 1996–May 1997
60-minute episodes

Production Team:

Dick Wolf (Executive Producer), Ed Sherin (Executive Producer), Rene Balcer (Executive Producer), Ed Zuckerman (Co-Executive Producer), Lewis H. Gould (Producer), Billy Fox (Producer), Jeffrey Hayes (Producer), Jeremy Littman (Co-Producer), Gardner Stern (Supervising Producer), Barry Schkolnick (Executive Story Editor), Lewis H. Gould (Unit Production Manager), Richard Bianchi (Production Designer), Mike Post (Music), Lynn Kressel C.S.A. (Casting), Suzanne Ryan (Casting), Christopher Misiano (Camera Operator), Richard Dobbs (Camera Operator), Moe Bardach (Location Manager), Billy Fox (Editor), Michael Kewley (Editor), Neil Felder (Editor), Monty DeGraff (Editor), David Siegel (Editor), Mike Struk (Technical Advisor), Bill Fordes (Technical Advisor), Park Dietz, M.D. (Technical Advisor)

Regular Cast:

Benjamin Bratt (Det. Reynaldo Curtis), Steven Hill (District Attorney Adam Schiff), Carey Lowell (Assistant District Attorney Jamie Ross), Carolyn McCormick (Dr. Elizabeth Olivet), S. Epatha Merkerson (Lt. Anita Van Buren), Jerry Orbach (Det. Lennie Briscoe), Sam Waterston (Executive Assistant District Attorney Jack McCoy)

Seventh Season Overview

At the end of Season Six, we were left with a number of unresolved *Law & Order* plot points. With Kincaid dead, McCoy grieving, Briscoe off the wagon, and Curtis deeply remorseful about his affair, it appeared that Van Buren and Schiff were the only characters able to sleep with a clear conscience. In the real world, Dick Wolf's sleep was assured when NBC announced that *Law & Order* would be picked up for an additional season (through the end of May 1997). Consequently, it became the longest-running dramatic series on television despite the annual revolving door for cast members.

As the season opens with Episode 135: "Causa Mortis," the show receives its best-ever premiere rating of 7.9 percent with adults in the eighteen to forty-nine age range, and a twenty-two share. The show also attracts an average audience of 15.7 million viewers weekly. This success follows a year in which *Law & Order* had its highest-rated season finale (Episode 134: "Aftershock") and demographic increases that hadn't been achieved by a sixth-year drama since CBS-TV's *Dallas* in 1983–84.

To replace departing Jill Hennessy, *Law & Order*'s producers turn to comely screen actress Carey Lowell (*License to Kill* of 1989, *Fierce Creatures* of 1996), who plays McCoy's new assistant Jamie Ross, a single mother and former defense attorney. In that Lowell lacks Hennessy's vulnerability, she and Waterston are two sides of the same tough cookie.

Rather than continuing where Episode 134: "Aftershock" left off, the writers instead weave the personal revelations of the characters into the fabric of each new story. Season Seven presents McCoy looking more haggard and lonely. Curtis tells Briscoe about his affair, and Van Buren suggests that Curtis encourage Lennie to stick with Alcoholics Anonymous.

Dramatically speaking, Season Seven is a mixed bag. The best moments include a judge who sexually harasses Ross (Episode 136: "I.D."), a daughter of Holocaust survivors who crosses paths with a criminal rare-coin dealer (Episode 138: "Survivor"), and Briscoe facing a corrupt cop who stood by him in his drinking days (Episode 139: "Corruption"). Also, there is a sequel to the fabulous Episode 46: "Conspiracy" that now looks into the issue of government informants (Episode 143: "Entrapment"), a serial rapist who gets out on parole and is hounded by McCoy (Episode 152: "Mad Dog"), and a much better season closer about the death penalty and mortality (Episode 157: "Terminal").

However, the show suffers from some creative low points (Episode 142: "Family Business" and Episode 147: "Matrimony"), some very familiar tales (Episode 137: "Good Girl"), and a three-part soap opera that the network dubs "Judgment in L.A." For the first time, *Law & Order*'s fiction goes bicoastal, which is a geographic reality for the production of the program itself. Given that NBC spotlights this much-hyped trilogy in the Thursday night slot usually reserved for *ER*, a larger-than-usual audience is expected to tune in to the proceedings. This miniseries device may attract more viewers but, for some fans, it proves to be a big disappointment.

Critically speaking, 1996–97 might not be a banner year for *Law & Order*, but the show is finally earning the kind of TV viewer attention it has deserved all along, with the big prize just ahead.

Episode Descriptions

Episode 135: *Causa Mortis*

Original air date: September 18, 1996
Teleplay by Rene Balcer, directed by Ed Sherin, cinematography by Christopher Misiano

Additional Cast and Guest Stars: George Martin (Abe Mercer), Cyndi Cartagena (Anna Galvez), Victor Sierra (Fernando Salva), Louise Sorel (Marcy Wrightman), Ted Kazanoff (Ian Rankin), Hugh O'Gorman (Chuck Rodman), Rebecca Nelson (Maureen Rankin), DeAnn Mears (Judge Ganz), Lawrence Arancio (Judge Scarletti)

Reviewing the Case: McCoy is assigned a new ADA, Jamie Ross, who is determined to prosecute carjacker/murderer Fernando Salva as harshly as possible by using an audio tape made by one of his victims as she begged for her life. Without any lingering details, the regular characters are picking up the pieces of their lives following the devastation depicted in Episode 134: "Aftershock" at the end of Season Six. Those events have made Jack McCoy a much different person today. He looks weathered, weighed down with sorrow, and is completely implacable in the performance of his duties. At first, he wants nothing to do with Jamie Ross. Then he battles her at every turn. This segment is a legal and moral struggle either to find Salva guilty of second-degree murder with depraved indifference or to convict him of a capital offense because he left the woman for dead. This offering also introduces Assistant U.S. Attorney Rodman (played with a hilarious "Dudley Do-Right" efficiency by Hugh O'Gorman), who becomes a pawn in the game. Once the death tape is played in court, "Causa Mortis" finds its cathartic sting.

Noteworthy Discoveries: Jamie Ross used to work as a defense attorney at Gorton & Steinhart and was once married to hotshot attorney and partner Neal Gorton. They have a child.

Relevant Testimony: RENE BALCER (writer): "I wanted to provide a reason for Jamie Ross to change sides from being a defense attorney into a prosecuting attorney. [When Ross tells McCoy that story about believing in monsters and things that go bump in the night] . . . that anecdote came from a friend of mine who is a defense attorney in Pittsburgh. Fifteen years ago, he told me that he was defending a sexual killer and, as the prosecutor was describing the crime in detail to the jury, he noticed his client was getting an erection and he put his coat over the client's lap so that no one would see it. So her story to McCoy is based on that."

Episode 136: I.D.
Original air date: September 25, 1996
Teleplay by Ed Zuckerman, directed by Constantine Makris, cinematography by Christopher Misiano

Additional Cast and Guest Stars: Pamela Gray (Joanne Sullivan), Jerry Adler (Judge Parks), Gerry Bamman (Stan Gillum), Aida Turturro (Yvonne), Stephen Mendillo (Lieutenant London), Dicky Fine (Perkles), Billy Gillespie (Larry), Alan Manson (Chief Judge)

Reviewing the Case: While the detectives try to identify a nude corpse in an elevator, a trial judge (Jerry Adler, in a quirky role) hampers the prosecution by sexually harassing Jamie Ross. Considering the subject matter, this is an energetic, multi-layered, and often idiosyncratic episode. The main drama is about a woman who kills her own sister in order to assume the sibling's identity, but scattered throughout the story line are funny characters. They include Perkles, the bizarre maintenance man who lectures Briscoe and Curtis on the secret life of elevators; Yvonne, the receptionist who chatters away even when there isn't anyone there; and Harry Shapiro, who can't believe he's buying butter from farmers and selling it to the Arabs. The nuttiness continues when McCoy is arrested for contempt of court (Schiff visiting him in his jail cell is one of Steven Hill's funniest scenes ever on the series). "I.D." is about people who are everything they say they are and others who are not even close.

Noteworthy Discoveries: It is revealed that Jamie Ross has two brothers.

Episode 137: Good Girl
Original air date: October 2, 1996
Teleplay by Jeremy Littman, directed by Jace Alexander, cinematography by Constantine Makris

Additional Cast and Guest Stars: Dennis Boutsikaris (Al Archer), Chelsea Altman (Danielle Mason), Giancarlo Esposito (Dwayne Baylor), Tommy Hollis (Ed Monroe), Myra Lucretia Taylor (Jane Monroe), Jennifer Esposito (Gina Tucci), John MacKay (Henry Mason), Robin Mosley (Dorothy Mason), David Rosenbaum (Judge Berman), Hope Clarke (Judge Reynolds), Joan Copeland (Judge Stein)

Reviewing the Case: After the death of Charley Monroe, a young black man, Briscoe and Curtis suspect his white girlfriend, Danielle Mason, of the crime. Monroe's angry parents push McCoy to indict her, although Mason claims it was self-defense as their son was about to rape her. Crime between blacks and whites can become politicized, a familiar topic on *Law & Order*. Here, when defense attorney Al Archer maintains that his white client is being persecuted by the black power structure, it becomes a new twist on an old subject. When the Monroe family complains that McCoy is slow to gather evidence because their son was black, a racial war starts to brew. Giancarlo Esposito delivers a shrewd performance as the Monroes' lawyer who plays with a stacked deck and hopes his prize will be a hung jury. Although the color lines are drawn, the story turns out to be a simple one about a young girl's violent response to rejection. In "Good Girl" a crime of passion has become a political circus.

Episode 138: Survivor

Original air date: October 23, 1996
Teleplay by Barry Schkolnick, directed by Vincent Misiano, cinematography by Constantine Makris

Additional Cast and Guest Stars: Karen Allen (Judith Sandler), Tovah Feldshuh (Danielle Melnick), Michael Willis (Richard Peterson), Larry Keith (Francis Dunlap), Lenka Peterson (Ann Schoenberg), Darrell Larson (Mark Lehmann), Lynn Cohen (Judge Mizener)

Reviewing the Case: Millionaire coin dealer Richard Peterson is the initial suspect in Briscoe and Curtis's investigation into the murder of Stephen Campbell, who also was in the rare-coin business. Evidence in the crime leads to Judith Sandler, the daughter of Holocaust survivors. In the last third of the episode, an emotional punch is delivered unexpectedly. Most of the vitality of these later scenes comes from Karen Allen's searing performance as an art restorer whose life is as damaged as the works she repairs. Some lost coins from a family collection have become an obsession for Sandler, leading her to Peterson and the murder victim. The story line also concerns itself with Peterson, a self-involved, spoiled kid who has no sense that his game of fraud could lead to such tragic conclusions. "Survivor" contrasts a man who has the world at his feet with a woman whose world became a rug that was pulled out from under her.

Episode 139: Corruption

Original air date: October 30, 1996
Teleplay by Gardner Stern, story by Rene Balcer and Gardner Stern, directed by Matthew Penn, cinematography by Christopher Misiano

Additional Cast and Guest Stars: Kevin Conway (Lt. John Flynn), Josef Sommer (Judge Sullivan), Tim Ransom (Det. Andy Sullivan), Jeff Williams (Det. Kenny Edwards), Caroline Kava (Betty Abrams), Manuel Antonio Estrella (Ruben Morales), Kirk Acevedo (Richie Morales), Nancy Ticotin (Club Bahia Hostess), Dupree Kelly (Two-Tone).

Reviewing the Case: Curtis uncovers evidence of police corruption involving Briscoe's old friend and colleague, Lieutenant Flynn, after a reputed drug dealer is killed in a sting. When the DA's office vies with an ambitious judge for Flynn's testimony, he accuses Briscoe of stealing evidence years earlier while still an alcoholic. The segment bears a slight resemblance to Episode 22: "The Blue Wall" in the way it explores the complicated loyalties of police officers put to the test when one cop turns bad. Along with Episode 119: "Angel," this installment gives Benjamin Bratt some dramatic range as Rey Curtis. His ethical, straight-arrow persona develops deeper purpose when he has to implicate another cop who was his partner's friend. Orbach brings lovely, subtle touches to his scenes, especially that look of pain when a former lover is raked over the coals at a hearing on police misdeeds, and the moment when he finally realizes that Flynn is crooked and has to face him. Kevin Conway doesn't do anything spectacular on camera, but he's convincing as a man drowning in his own deceptions. The ending is somewhat predictable, but it finally establishes Briscoe and Curtis as partners who can trust one another.

Noteworthy Discoveries: It is mentioned that Curtis's mother is Peruvian.

Relevant Testimony: RENE BALCER: "Originally, we wanted Claire Kincaid to return in this one to help out Briscoe by providing some background information that would help him clear himself.... But Jill Hennessy didn't want to come back. So I had to think of another way for Briscoe to clear himself. Then I remembered the song 'Long Black Veil,' from The Band's *Music From Big Pink* [album], about the woman who walks the hills where [her lover] was executed because he was in the arms of his best friend's wife. So I thought of that and decided to put Briscoe in a similar situation where he would have to betray a confidence."

Episode 140: Double Blind

Original air date: November 6, 1996
Teleplay by Jeremy Littman and William Fordes, directed by Christopher Misiano, cinematography by Constantine Makris

Additional Cast and Guest Stars: John Bedford Lloyd (Dr. Christian Varrick), Mark Bateman (Alan Sawyer), Daniel Ziskie (Fred Sawyer), E. Katherine Kerr (Ilene Sawyer), Randell Mell (Aaron Blum), Richard Hamilton (James "Jimmy the Pin" Poulos), Tom O'Rourke (Peter Behrens), Jennifer Van Dyck (Jill Perry), Christine Farrell (Schier), Susan Blommaert (Judge Steinman), Ben Hammer (Judge Mooney) Fred J. Scollay (Judge Barsky)

Reviewing the Case: The murder of a janitor in a university laboratory leads back to student employee Alan Sawyer, whose participation in a drug study may have prompted the crime. Christian Varrick is the ambitious psychiatrist who conducted the research. Here, *Law & Order* returns forcefully to the subject of dishonesty and careerism in the medical profession. Mark Bateman gives a thoughtful performance as the young man who heard voices that told him to kill, yet he has an iridescent, detached quality that makes him oddly sympathetic. However, little sympathy need be expended for the doctor who lies about the boy's true condition (he's not schizophrenic) in order to fund his study. When Sawyer confronts Dr. Varrick with the truth about his condition, the young man's voice is finally his own.

Episode 141: Deadbeat

Original air date: November 13, 1996
Teleplay by Ed Zuckerman and I. C. Rapoport, directed by Constantine Makris, cinematography by Christopher Misiano

Additional Cast and Guest Stars: Val Avery (Max Schaeffer), Deborah Hedwall (Arlene Webber), Jerry Stiller (Sam Pokras), Rene Props (Victoria Lewis), Scott Sowers (Joe Kirby), Vincent Pastore (Jimmy Pogosian), Nick Sandow (Pete Pogosian), Barbara Eda-Young (Betsy Graves), Zachary Kady (Billy Webber), Larry Sherman (Judge Fraiser), Madeline Lee (Judge Connors)

Reviewing the Case: The murder of Michael Malone, a "deadbeat dad" whose son is dying of leukemia, presents McCoy and Ross with both a sympathetic suspect and a moral dilemma. The subject of fathers who do not pay alimony after leaving their wives and children is a relatively new one to television drama. This episode is an intricate tale of deception in which all the characters have something to hide, and very good reasons for doing so. Michael's wife, Arlene, claims that her husband refused to cooperate when she discovered that he was a match for their son's bone marrow transplant. It is discovered, however, that not only wasn't he a match, but also that he possibly wasn't even the real father. Ross's empathy for Arlene has much to do with being a single mother herself. "Deadbeat" ponders a despicable man's actions and how he inspired unsavory behavior in some basically decent people.

Noteworthy Discoveries: This episode won the esteemed Edgar Allen Poe Award.

Episode 142: Family Business
Original air date: November 20, 1996
Teleplay by Gardner Stern and Barry Schkolnick, directed by Lewis H. Gould, cinematography by Constantine Makris

Additional Cast and Guest Stars: Anne Twomey (Kate Bergreen-Spiegel), Jean DeBaer (Laura Bergreen), Joseph Wiseman (Seymour Bergreen), Bill Moor (Paul Medici), Richard Venture (Doug Greer), James Murtaugh (David Solomon), Victor Slezak (Jeffrey Arbaugh), Gene Silvers (Clarence Gray), Rochelle Oliver (Judge Larkin)

Reviewing the Case: Blame for the murder of Richard Spiegel, chief financial officer for an exclusive, family-owned department store, shifts from his co-workers to the two daughters of the company president. Of all the upscale, yuppie crime episodes *Law & Order* has done, this one seems the most bankrupt. After a coy opening, featuring a security guard at play with his girlfriend, the drama loses its playfulness very fast. The sisters in the story don't get along. One sleeps around, and the other runs the company into the ground. Unfortunately, there is nothing here that is substantially different from any number of daytime soaps.

Episode 143: Entrapment
Original air date: January 8, 1997
Teleplay by Rene Balcer and Richard Sweren, directed by Matthew Penn, cinematography by Constantine Makris

Additional Cast and Guest Stars: Michelle Hurd (Angela Roney), Ron Cephas Jones (Roland Books), Chris McKinney (Huey Tate), Michael Gaston (Agent Fletcher), Robert Hogan (Agent Carlin), Gloria Foster (Satima Tate), Joseph Siravo (Lou Shore), Donna Hanover (Judge Bourke), Michael Marcus (Judge Russo)

Reviewing the Case: Huey Tate is a young man accused of shooting Roland Books, the African-American Congress activist he believes murdered his father years earlier. The case comes undone when authorities learn that their chief witness was once an FBI informant and is still under that agency's protection. This installment, a multi-faceted sequel to Episode 46: "Conspiracy," does more than merely continue the story about officials in a movement organization who might have arranged the assassination of their leader, Marcus Tate. It also ventures into the murky world of government informants, used during the 1960s and early 1970s to infiltrate and undermine leftist groups. McCoy and Ross are unable to prosecute anybody. Once again, the African-American Congress circles the wagons around one of its own.

Relevant Testimony: RENE BALCER (writer): "This is the sequel to [Episode 46:] 'Conspiracy,' except that we couldn't get Joe Morton to do the show because he was doing another series at the time. In this one, we wanted to highlight the issue of entrapment and the way the FBI—and, by extension, other law enforcement authorities—use informers and abuse them. There were also elements of the World Trade Center bombing, where the FBI had tossed aside an informer's information that turned out to be accurate. It was a fun episode because it gave McCoy the chance to have a d***-measuring contest with the FBI."

Episode 144: Legacy

Original air date: January 15, 1997
Teleplay by Ed Zuckerman and Jeremy Littman, directed by Brian Mertes, cinematography by Christopher Misiano

Additional Cast and Guest Stars: Bradley White (Jim Shepherd), Charlotte Moore (Robin Shepherd), Frances Sternhagen (Estelle Muller), Tom Riis Farrell (Howard Phillips), Mark Margolis (Bronson), Jere Shea (Mr. Goldman), Hugh O'Gorman (Chuck Rodman), Christine Farrell (Schier), Leslie Hendrix (Rogers), David Lipman (Judge Torledsky), Becky London (Judge Webber)

Reviewing the Case: A hit man shoots Jim Shepherd in the street and all the evidence points to his wife's former mother-in-law, Estelle Muller. She felt that Shepherd was responsible for her son's death. This episode starts out with a revenge plot and turns into a narrative about romantic denial, in which a woman comes to realize that she has married her own stalker. Actor Bradley White here has the same ethereal quality he displayed as the obsessed fan in Episode 34: "Star Struck." Charlotte Moore's performance gets better as the story advances (her face registers all the horrible pieces falling into place). However, it's the elegant actress Frances Sternhagen (her character engineers the revenge) who provides "Legacy" with the flavor that it needs. For example, when she walks in

Riverside Park with Briscoe, believing him to be a hit man rather than a cop, she's as casual in her choice of a murder scenario as someone trying to decide on dinner.

Noteworthy Discoveries: Briscoe and Curtis smoke stogies in their car parked outside the Village Cigar Store in Greenwich Village and discuss how the CIA tried to assassinate Cuban president Fidel Castro.

Episode 145: Menace
Original air date: February 5, 1997
Teleplay by I. C. Rapoport, story by I. C. Rapoport and Barry Schkolnick, directed by Constantine Makris, cinematography by Christopher Misiano

Additional Cast and Guest Stars: John Cullum (Harold Dorning), Christopher Cousins (Robert Dorning), John Ellison Conlee ("Crazy" Mike Dugan), Tony LoBianco (Sal DiMarco), Caitlin Clarke (Linda Walsh), James Georgiades (George Marsh), Katherine Narducci (Mrs. Marsh), Rusty DuWees (Dave Randall), Marilyn Rockafellow (Mrs. Watney), John Ramsey (Judge Schreiber), Francine Beers (Judge Silver), John Fiore (Det. Anthony Profaci)

Reviewing the Case: Karen Watney's apparent suicidal leap off the Brooklyn Bridge leads Detectives Briscoe and Curtis to a known bully who may have terrorized her because of knowledge she had about a business fraud. This is a well-crafted story, with many entertaining twists, but the resolution at which it arrives is rather weak. The first third of the installment, based on the real-life case of a woman in Detroit who jumped from a bridge to escape an assailant, is compelling because witnesses are held accountable for their failure to act. When the episode reveals the business malfeasance behind the plot, it proves to be another obvious father-son conflict. "Menace" unfortunately loses touch with the more universal peril at the heart of the drama.

Noteworthy Discoveries: Curtis's wife leaves him after he confesses his affair (from Episode 134: "Aftershock").

Episode 146: Barter
Original air date: February 12, 1997
Teleplay by Rene Balcer and Eddie Feldman, directed by Don Karlok, cinematography by Constantine Makris

Additional Cast and Guest Stars: George DiCenzo (Sam "Bunny" Russo), Scott Bryce (Steven Tashjian), Victor Argo (Enrique Flores), Dana Reeve (Susan Tashjian), Meg Mundy (Mrs. Harriet Keenan), Alec Phoenix (Peter Messina)

Reviewing the Case: Sally Gans is shot to death in a parking garage, but she might have been mistaken for another woman. Somehow, it's all connected to loan shark Sam "Bunny" Russo, a man well-versed in unscrupulous collection methods. He always finds violent ways to recoup his money, including persuading one debtor to kill another in return for release from liability. Russo discovers the perfect patsy in Steven Tashjian, who is up to his eyelids in arrears. This situation poses an interesting dilemma for McCoy when he gives Tashjian immunity so he can convict Russo. George DiCenzo offers a peacock-style performance as Russo, a man who basks in the limelight. Victor Argo, as Russo's hit man, expresses states of terror very eloquently, considering the occupation of his character. Scott Bryce, as Tashjian, has a magnetic moment on the stand when guilt and terror merge during a confession. In "Barter" the bad guy is convicted, but his bad deeds linger long after the jail door clangs shut.

Noteworthy Discoveries: Dan Karlok had worked earlier on *Law & Order* as a best boy [errand-runner] before directing this episode, his first on the TV series.

Episode 147: Matrimony
Original air date: February 19, 1997
Teleplay by Ed Zuckerman and Richard Sweren, directed by Lewis Gould, cinematography by Constantine Makris

Additional Cast and Guest Stars: Arija Bareikis (Kim Triandos), George Grizzard (Arthur Gold), Anna Holbrook (Velma Darcy), Michael Lombard (Robert Mellors), Boyd Gaines (Oliver Shain), Stephen Bradbury (Victor Henckel), Mark Kenneth Smaltz (Elias Bunch), Roger Serbagi (Judge Quinn)

Reviewing the Case: The murder of Peter Triandos, a wealthy philanthropist, is initially laid at the door of his pretty young wife. Before long, a would-be thief helps prosecutors to consider the motives of Triandos's lawyer and the mother of that pretty young wife. Although this episode is about the great American appetite for greed, in this story it suffers more from fatigue. Actress Anna Holbrook, looking like a matronly Tanya Tucker, is funny and appealing in a down-home way, but Arija Bareikis plays the spoiled widow in an all-too-familiar episodic television manner that just doesn't work. Even the repeat appearance of Arthur Gold, the wonderfully feisty defense attorney, fails to enliven the proceedings. Gold's battles with McCoy don't offer the excitement of his matches with Ben Stone, probably because McCoy isn't as vulnerable an adversary.

Noteworthy Discoveries: Curtis is now living at his sister's place, after being kicked out of his home because of that extramarital affair.

Episode 148: Working Mom

Original air date: February 26, 1997
Teleplay by Jeremy Littman and I. C. Rapoport, directed by Jace Alexander, cinematography by Christopher Misiano

Additional Cast and Guest Stars: Elaine Stritch (Lanie Stieglitz), Felicity Huffman (Hillary Colson), Jodie Markell (Sondra Benton), Richard Poe (Mac Burnum), David Chandler (Louis Colson), Pamela Stewart (Jane Tennick), John Cunningham (Metzler), Richard Bright (Clay), Billy Strong (Gino Ricardo), William Severs (Judge Fillmore)

Reviewing the Case: The murder of Gilbert Keene, an ex-cop with a propensity for blackmail and illicit sex, brings feminist lawyer Lanie Stieglitz into court against McCoy. She is defending Hillary Colson, a suburban housewife and mother moonlighting as a prostitute, who claims she killed the victim in self-defense to ward off a rape. The episode plays with the perception that those who live a so-called normal life might have darker depths and desires that they wish to express openly. However, the true ingenuity of this narrative is the realization that, no matter how much people wish to escape from the drudgery of middle-class existence, they still rely on the security it offers them. McCoy insists that Colson killed Keene when he threatened to expose her secret. Felicity Huffman is hardly recognizable here compared with her role as the fragile young woman raped by a gynecologist in Episode 50: "Helpless." In that

Episode 148: "Working Mom" (Season Seven), featuring feisty defense attorney Lanie Stieglitz (Elaine Stritch) having words with EADA Jack McCoy (Sam Waterston) about her client, a housewife moonlighting as a prostitute. [courtesy of NBC/Copyright ©1997 by Universal City Studios, Inc. Courtesy of Universal Publishing Rights, a Division of Universal Studios Licensing, Inc. All rights reserved.]

installment, the actress demonstrated feelings that were so raw you could see right through her. Here her character's emotions are completely hidden. Returning as the vehement Stieglitz after an Emmy-winning performance in Episode 53: "Point of View," Elaine Stritch is wonderful as the crusty crusader who loves to shake the foundations of the legal system.

Noteworthy Discoveries: Jamie Ross cross-examines a witness for the first time.

Episode 149: "D-Girl"

NOTE: This episode is the first segment of a three-part consecutive story line.
Original air date: March 13, 1997
Teleplay by Rene Balcer, Ed Zuckerman, and Gardner Stern, directed by Ed Sherin, cinematography by Constantine Makris

Additional Cast and Guest Stars: Lauren Graham (Lisa Lundquist), Keith Szarabajka (Neal Gorton), Scott Cohen (Eddie Newman), Jeffrey Sams (Evan Grant), Dick Latessa (Mitchell Klein), Paul Hecht (Dr. Duval), Janeane Garofalo (Greta Heis), Michael Zaslow (Ben Hollings), Don Creech (Carl Thurston), Robert Culp (as himself), Leslie Hendrix (Rogers), John Newton (Judge Caffey), Norma Fire (Judge Jensen), John Fiore (Det. Anthony Profaci)

Reviewing the Case: A torso fished out of the Hudson River is identified as Heidi Ellison, a mogul at Mattawin Studios. This discovery sends Curtis and Briscoe to Los Angeles to obtain a blood sample from Ellison's physical trainer, Evan Grant. The first part of this trilogy is as shallow as the title. While the underlying murder mystery is interesting in the New York locales, once "D-Girl" shifts to Los Angeles the sun-and-surf atmosphere seems to go to everyone's head. This installment is filled with non-essential material. For example, Curtis is estranged from his wife, yet manages to fend off some bold advances from Lisa Lundquist, the studio's seductive vice president of production. She keeps batting her eyelashes for naught. In addition, there's something almost pimp-like about Briscoe constantly urging Curtis to give in to temptation. At the same time, Jamie's ex-husband, Neal Gorton, is introduced as the defense attorney for filmmaker Eddie Newman, husband of the dead woman and a key suspect. Instead of transcending the headlines that attract our prurient interest in crime, "D-Girl" indulges in the ho-hum.

Noteworthy Discoveries: Curtis and his wife are still separated. The veteran film and television actor Robert Culp (star of such TV series as *Trackdown* [1957–59] and *I Spy* [1965–68], as well as such recent feature films as *The Pelican Brief* [1993] and *Mercenary* [1996]) shows up, as himself, on a Los Angeles beach.

Relevant Testimony: RENE BALCER (writer): "The network wanted it to be a four-parter but I didn't think we could sustain four parts. I had the idea of doing one about the film business because I worked in features for twelve years, and [writers] Ed Zuckerman and Gardner Stern also worked in that world and had a jaundiced view of it. We thought that we could get our jabs into biting the hands that feed us. The inspiration was the death of the producer Don Simpson, his personality, plus others I'd rather not name, and [we] also play upon the huge egos that flourish in this business. It was a self-reflexive piece."

Episode 150: Turnaround
NOTE: This episode is the second segment of a three-part consecutive story line.
Original air date: March 20, 1997
Teleplay by Rene Balcer, Ed Zuckerman, and Gardner Stern, directed by Ed Sherin, cinematography by Constantine Makris

Additional Cast and Guest Stars: Keith Szarabajka (Neal Gorton), Lauren Graham (Lisa Lundquist), Scott Cohen (Eddie Newman), Jeffrey Sams (Evan Grant), Jeffrey Force (Chasen Martell), Paul Hecht (Dr. Duval), Kevin O'Rourke (Deputy District Attorney Weiss), Jude Ciccolella (Sherrick), Michael Harney (Detective Miller), Mark Joy (LAPD Detective Dunlevy), Glenn Kubota (Hayashi), George Guidall (Mr. Ellison), Donald Corren (Medill), John Carter (Judge Van Ness), DeAnn Mears (Judge Ganz)

Reviewing the Case: Briscoe and Curtis arrive back in New York with the suspect, Evan Grant, and they try to pin down his schedule on the night of the murder. It turns out that the victim's ex-husband, Eddie Newman, was also in the area at the time, and might have an even stronger motive for commiting the crime. McCoy and Ross fly to L.A. to defend a new arrest warrant against a legal attack by Newman's attorney, Neal Gorton, who is Ross's ex-husband. Borrowing heavily from the O. J. Simpson case (a dream-team defense, media frenzies, an officer who once arrested Newman for assaulting his wife), this episode offers nothing fresh or exciting with the material at hand. In addition, Scott Cohen's performance as Newman has enough tics and mannerisms to qualify for another charge, that of overacting. McCoy seems like a man totally at odds with his new surroundings in La La Land, and "Turnaround" lacks even the suspense of good legal drama.

Relevant Testimony: CAREY LOWELL (actor): "In the trilogy, they did bring [in] my ex-husband, which I think was a little bit hard to swallow.

Everybody was saying, 'Why were you married to him? He's so rotten and abusive—what were you thinking?' So, it seemed a little far-fetched. But I enjoy that it's not a soap opera, and it's not overly dramatic, and we don't have to take our clothes off. There are no love scenes; it's just implied. That challenges the audience to use their imagination, which is much more interesting anyway."

Episode 151: Showtime

NOTE: This episode is the third segment of a three-part consecutive story line.
Original air date: March 27, 1997
Teleplay by Rene Balcer, Ed Zuckerman, and Gardner Stern, directed by Ed Sherin, cinematography by Constantine Makris

Additional Cast and Guest Stars: Keith Szarabajka (Neal Gorton), Lauren Graham (Lisa Lundquist), Scott Cohen (Eddie Newman), Paul Hecht (Dr. Duval), Michael Zaslow (Ben Hollings), Janeane Garofalo (Greta Heis), Stuart Feldman (Kevin), Stephanie Lane (Denise), Bernie McInerney (Judge Callahan)

Reviewing the Case: As Eddie Newman's trial begins, Neal Gorton puts personal pressure on Jamie Ross by threatening to demand custody of their child. The case hinges on the role of Dr. Duval in the lives of both Eddie Newman and Heidi Ellison. As in Episode 149: "D-Girl" (the first part of this trilogy), the basic drama is continually circumvented by peripheral details. Curtis still refuses to sleep with Lisa Lundquist. However, he manages, somehow, to have the best of both worlds. Lisa provides him with valuable information about the case, while he attempts to reconcile with his wife. There are no surprises when we get to the trial (except perhaps that standup comic Janeane Garofalo's character doesn't seem to have been created for any logical purpose). This installment does have a few humorous moments, such as when McCoy, who has been complaining about the media circus, is seen checking a televised commentary show similar to CNN's *Burden of Proof* to see how they rate his performance at the trial. The ending of this three-parter has a tinge of melancholy, as McCoy sits alone at his desk with a drink and thinks about Kincaid. After this poorly executed three-headed monster, it's time for *Law & Order* to move on.

Episode 152: Mad Dog

Original air date: April 4, 1997
Teleplay by Rene Balcer, directed by Christopher Misiano, cinematography by Constantine Makris

Additional Cast and Guest Stars: Burt Young (Lewis Darnell), David Wolos-Fonteno (Munro), Lisa LoCicero (Janeane Darnell), Ned Eisenberg (James Granick), Anthony Ruivivar (Raymond Cartena), Eden Riegel (Natalie), Sarah Burke (Natalie's mother), Leslie Hendrix (Rogers), Stephen Henderson (Judge Mowat), Laurie Kennedy (Judge Shields)

Reviewing the Case: McCoy is obsessed with nailing Lewis Darnell, a serial rapist recently released on parole, but the prosecutor comes close to harassing the cops as he urges them to connect this suspect to a new rape and murder. The engrossing episode explores some of the more questionable aspects of McCoy's single-mindedness. Darnell (Burt Young in tip-top form) is definitely on the precipice of falling back into his old habits. Obsessed about having failed to keep this creep off the streets in the parole hearing, McCoy walks an ethical tightrope as he pursues Darnell mercilessly. Waterston gives an ingenious performance that manages to keep the audience with him even though his actions are almost reprehensible. Lisa LoCicero is quite memorable as Darnell's daughter, especially in the haunting and inevitable conclusion. "Mad Dog" is a tale of two men driven by obsessions that put them on a collision course.

Noteworthy Discoveries: Constantine Makris won an Emmy for his cinematography (which is magnificent) in this episode.

Episode 153: Double Down
Original air date: April 16, 1997
Teleplay by Ed Zuckerman and Shimon Wincelberg, story by Richard Sweren and Shimon Wincelberg, directed by Arthur Forney, cinematography by Constantine Makris

Additional Cast and Guest Stars: Luke Reilly (Henry Harp), Edie Falco (Sally Bell), Theresa Merritt (Ruth Titus), Hilda Harp (Mary Fogarty), David Lipman (Judge Torledsky), Nancy Addison (Judge Davis), Shawn Elliott (Judge Santos), John Fiore (Det. Anthony Profaci)

Reviewing the Case: A liquor store robbery goes awry when an off-duty policeman is killed and a limousine driver, Mitchell Titus, is kidnapped. McCoy agrees to give immunity to Henry Harp, one of the wounded thieves, in return for locating the kidnapped driver. However, the prosecutor is torn between the cops who want Harp convicted and Titus's wife, who is primarily concerned about her husband's welfare. "Double Down" sets up this fascinating dilemma and then begins a race against the clock (as in Episode 83: "Mayhem," time actually ticks by on the screen). This segment makes it clear how crucial deal-making is to the American justice system.

Noteworthy Discoveries: It is learned that McCoy has been a prosecutor for twenty-two years. This is also the first time that his apartment is seen by *Law & Order* viewers.

Episode 154: We Like Mike

Original air date: April 30, 1997
Teleplay by Gardner Stern and I. C. Rapoport, directed by David Platt, cinematography by Christopher Misiano

Additional Cast and Guest Stars: Frank John Hughes (Mike Bodak), Casey Siemaszko (Shuman), Benny Nieves (Ricky Garcia), Fernando Lopez (Tony Garcia), John Donan (Sgt. Frank Gottlieb), Dina Pearlman (Ruth Gottlieb), Ron Frazier (Judge Iannello)

Reviewing the Case: Mike Bodak, who claims to have helped a young man change a flat tire, is initially the suspect when the motorist is found murdered. However, as evidence mounts against Ricky Garcia, who was spotted at the scene, Bodak becomes the prosecutor's reluctant witness. This segment is a gently optimistic episode about a luckless fellow being given a hard time by the police and the DA, yet still agreeing to testify against a killer because it is the right thing to do. Frank John Hughes (who had a funny cameo as the gabby parking lot attendant in Episode 35: "Severance") fully inhabits the role of an ordinary man who works for a bookie but doesn't have a menacing bone in his body. "We Like Mike" is hardly amazing, but the viewer comes to really appreciate the guy.

Episode 155: Passion

Original air date: May 7, 1997
Teleplay by Barry Schkolnick, story by Barry Schkolnick and Richard Sweren, directed by Constantine Makris, cinematography by Richard Dobbs

Additional Cast and Guest Stars: Sara Botsford (Diane Posner), Cynthia Harris (Selma Diamond), Robert Foxworth (Charles Evans), John Coughlin (Timothy Stevens), Oren J. Sofer (Austin Posner), MacIntyre Dixon (Prof. Peter Hilligan), Ryan Dunn (Jane), Everett Quinton (Jeffery Weiss), John Coughlin (Judge Williams), Patti Karr (Judge Haines), Ira Wheeler (Judge Hopper)

Reviewing the Case: Briscoe and Curtis investigate the death of book editor Joni Timberman, who reportedly was having an affair with one of her authors, Charles Evans. His longtime companion, Diane Posner, denies that their relationship was rocky. This average episode pivots on a woman's passion for a man, which overrides every other concern, including her son who feels neglected. Sara Botsford makes Posner credible but doesn't offer the kind of spectral intensity that, say, Frances Fisher brought to Episode 61: "Animal Instinct." Actor Robert Foxworth provides just the right amount of vanity for a best-selling author who thinks his personality is as popular as his books.

Episode 156: Past Imperfect
Original air date: May 14, 1997
Teleplay by Janis Diamond, directed by Christopher Misiano, cinematography by Richard Dobbs

Additional Cast and Guest Stars: Rene Augesen (Sonja Harland), Bray Poor (Grant Silverman), Katherine Borowitz (Marjorie Larson), Paul Lieber (Jimmy Burke), David McCallum (Craig Holland), Adam Kaufman (Doug Burke), Fiona Gallagher (Sheila Mullins), Mimi Wedell (Mrs. Sandinsky), Clark Middleton (Ellis), Bob Kaliban (Judge Kelman), Kitty Chen (Judge Yee)

Reviewing the Case: A blood stain found where former model Christine Sandler was murdered is determined to be from a blood relative and, ultimately, leads detectives to her illegitimate child. Part of the quirky nature of this episode is that just about every character under suspicion has a questionable history and a solid reason to kill Sandler. For such a tragic story, the elements are often quite light and funny. David McCallum's fey fashion photographer is endearingly flamboyant, especially when he gives Curtis the eye. Actor Paul Lieber—a dead ringer for Flea, who plays bass with the Red Hot Chili Peppers—gives rock'n'roll burnout a whole new meaning (he and Briscoe are the ultimate odd couple during some of the questioning). Rene Augesen shows equal amounts of disbelief and rage as Sonja, the unwanted daughter. In "Past Imperfect" the love child turns out to be anything but loved or lovable.

Episode 157: Terminal
Original air date: May 21, 1997
Teleplay by Rene Balcer and Ed Zuckerman, directed by Constantine Makris, cinematography by Christopher Misiano

Additional Cast and Guest Stars: Kent Williams (Henry Coburn), Roy Thinnes (Victor Panatti), Liana Pat (Carolyne Trang), Jack Gilpin (Jeff Aktell), Dani Klein (Susan Beckner), Ava Haddad (Sally Jacobs), Donald Corren (Medill), Charlotte Colavin (Judge Pongracic), Michael Moran (Judge Barclay)

Reviewing the Case: Two accidental deaths from a shooting near a docked singles' cruise ship lead to suspect Hank Coburn, who becomes the center of a capital case for which the governor wants the death penalty. Adam Schiff doesn't think the crime's legal implications point to such an extreme measure. This installment delivers on what Episode 134: "Aftershock" could only promise. The personal lives of the characters dovetail with the issues, without resorting to sensationalism. During the proceedings here, Steven Hill gives his most exquisite performance to date. For once, the issue is not the moral collapse of a friend, but rather the possible loss of a loved one who has had a stroke. The great irony of this offering is how Schiff's battle against the governor inadvertently spares Coburn, with Schiff left to face his own trial: whether or not to keep his wife on life-support. "Terminal" asks very tough questions and doesn't blink once.

Relevant Tetimony: RENE BALCER (writer): "I had the idea a year earlier to put Schiff in conflict with the governor. It was based on a [situation] where the Bronx DA was removed from a case by the governor and I wanted to contrast that public action with this private dilemma that Schiff was facing. Steven Hill wanted it to be clear that by pulling the plug on his wife he wasn't sentencing his wife to death; he was turning the decision over to a higher power."

Season Eight
October 1997–May 1998
60-minute episodes

Production Team:

Dick Wolf (Executive Producer), Ed Sherin (Executive Producer), Rene Balcer (Executive Producer), Kathy McCormick (Co-Executive Producer), David Shore (Producer), Lewis H. Gould (Producer), Billy Fox (Producer), Jeffrey Hayes (Producer), David Black (Consulting Producer), Arthur Forney (Supervising Producer), Barry Schkolnick (Executive Story Editor), Lewis H. Gould (Unit Production Manager), Richard Bianchi (Production Designer), Mike Post (Music), Lynn Kressel C.S.A. (Casting), Suzanne Ryan (Casting), Richard Dobbs (Camera Operator), Moe Bardach (Location Manager), Toni Morgan (Editor), Neil Felder (Editor), Monty DeGraff (Editor), Mike Struk (Technical Advisor), Bill Fordes (Technical Advisor), Park Dietz, M.D. (Technical Advisor)

Regular Cast:

Benjamin Bratt (Det. Reynaldo Curtis), Steven Hill (District Attorney Adam Schiff), Carey Lowell (Assistant District Attorney Jamie Ross), S. Epatha Merkerson (Lt. Anita Van Buren), Jerry Orbach (Det. Lennie Briscoe), Sam Waterston (Executive Assistant District Attorney Jack McCoy)

Eighth Season Overview

It took eight years but finally, in what came as a total surprise to virtually everyone, *Law & Order* wins the Emmy Award for Outstanding Dramatic Series. This honor arrives when, remarkably, there is no cast change of a major character on the show, other than J. K. Simmons replacing Carolyn McCormick as the resident psychiatrist. Dr. Emil Skoda is introduced in Episode 159: "Denial." Also, Christopher Misiano bequeaths his regular position as camera operator to Richard Dobbs, who has alternated with him in this job for the last few seasons. Henceforth, Misiano either directs or works as cinematographer on *Law & Order*.

When the show had experienced dramatic and controversial cast departures in the past, the writers had to dream up innovative ways for them to exit the series. In Season Eight, however, they devise ways to leave the characters dangling: Van Buren launches a lawsuit (which she loses) against the department when a white woman with the same score on a qualifying exam is promoted to captain; McCoy is cited for unethical behavior, after covering up a witness report in Episode 168: "Under the Influence"; a friend betrays Jamie Ross (Episode 165: "Shadow"), and later Ross receives a marriage proposal that tempts her to think about finding another line of work. (She does just that, after actress Carey Lowell decides to leave the show following the season finale on May 20, 1998.) Then there's Curtis, whose wife's struggle with multiple sclerosis leaves him wondering whether he will continue as a detective. Adam Schiff faces an election campaign against the judge who McCoy double-crossed in Episode 168: "Under the Influence," and his old friend Carl Anderton (Episode 166: "Burned") works to defeat him. And Briscoe is plagued by his worst crisis since he got into the car with the doomed Claire Kincaid (Episode 134: "Aftershock"). Rest assured, none of these loose ends will be tied up until the ninth season of *Law & Order*.

Following the success of an earlier crossover with *Homicide: Life on the Street*, the New York contingent heads to Baltimore again in a two-part production (Episode 163: "Baby, It's You" being the first part on *Law &*

Order) about a teenage model who dies of toxic shock after a sexual assault. Apparently, this cross-pollination has become so popular with fans of both TV shows that yet another one is planned for the 1998–99 season.

Many strong subjects are addressed in this season, including child abuse (Episode 159: "Denial"), female circumcision (Episode 167: "Ritual"), antigovernment militias (Episode 162: "Nullification"), serial killers (Episode 170: "Castoff"), and cop killers ("Bad Girl"). On the whole, it is a strong season that includes the welcome return of David Black, a head writer in the first two years of *Law & Order*. The only significant complaint about Season Eight might be the unusually dark quality of the image, which makes a viewer want to shine a flashlight on the TV screen to see what's really going on.

Episode Descriptions

Episode 158: Thrill

Original air date: October 1, 1997
Teleplay by Rene Balcer, directed by Martha Mitchell, cinematography by Christopher Misiano

Additional Cast and Guest Stars: Rob McElhenney (Joey Timon), Michael Maronna (Dale Kershaw), James Handy (Mr. Wheeler), Suzanne Costallos (Mrs. Wheeler), Sig Libowitz (Stan Shatenstein), Jan Munroe (James Galva), Donna Murphy (Carla Tyrell), Susan Blommaert (Judge Steinman), Nick Wyman (Judge Mickerson), John Fiore (Det. Anthony Profaci)

Reviewing the Case: When delivery boy Matthew Wheeler is shot by two young men in a "thrill killing," the Catholic Church steps in to protect the confession one of them made to his uncle, who just happens to be a priest. This episode depicts the terrifying kind of murder without passion or true motivation that has become far too common in today's society: Random victims are chosen just for the kick of watching someone die. The two suspects, Joey Timon and Dale Kershaw, are two inordinately vacant sociopaths. The legal argument about the confession is fascinating because McCoy is a Catholic, and he must decide whether or not to challenge the church. His shrewdest move is asking for simultaneous trials in the hope that one conviction might force a plea from the other suspect. However, the episode's emotional epiphany comes with Mrs. Wheeler telling the boys that she forgives them.

Noteworthy Discoveries: Curtis's wife, Deborah, is diagnosed with a latent form of multiple sclerosis.

Relevant Testimony: RENE BALCER (writer): "Two guys killed a pizza delivery guy in New Jersey, and also a guy was killed in Central Park. That's what inspired [the story]. There is the confession [in 'Thrill'] but also the Christian notion of forgiveness, and forgiving the most horrific acts. [Contrasted with] the mother who forgives her son's killer, we have McCoy saying that he can't.... It wasn't a slam against the church, it was an examination of beliefs. It is also about the randomness of life."

Episode 159: Denial
Original air date: October 8, 1997
Teleplay by David Shore, story by David Shore and Rene Balcer, directed by Christopher Misiano, cinematography by Constantine Makris

Additional Cast and Guest Stars: Mags Chernok (Christina Talbert), Zach Chapman (Tommy Horton), Benjamin Hendrickson (Warren Talbert), Jan Maxwell (Sarah Talbert), James Rebhorn (Charles Garnett), J. K. Simmons (Dr. Emil Skoda), Evalyn Baron (Rachel Shelton), Mark Zimmerman (Judge Murray), Barbara Tirrell (Judge Markham), Doris Belack (Judge Barry)

Reviewing the Case: A hotel cleaning staff finds a bloody towel in a vacant room and this evidence of foul play implicates two college students, Christina Talbert and Tommy Horton. She has given birth to a baby they insist was stillborn, a claim that is disputed when the medical examiner's report indicates a living infant emerged from the womb. The word *denial* becomes something of an understatement in considering the actions of the teenagers. The segment maps out the narcissism that lies at the heart of their love affair, shaping a brutal indifference to others. (This chilling detachment is similar to that of the killer kids in the previous episode, "Thrill.") The other true horrors in this drama are the collusion of Christina's father and the jury's willingness to look the other way.

Episode 160: Navy Blues
Original air date: October 15, 1997
Teleplay by Kathy McCormick, story by Dick Wolf and Kathy McCormick, directed by Jace Alexander, cinematography by Constantine Makris

Additional Cast and Guest Stars: Kate Walsh (Lieutenant Blair), Patti LuPone (Ruth Miller), Molly Price (Quarter Master Stroud), Daniel Von Bargen (Sergeant Commander Billings), Jack Gwaltney (Jack Young), Lee

Episode 160: "Navy Blues" (Season Eight), with defense attorney Ruth Miller (Patti LuPone) and her client Lt. Blair (Kate Walsh) waiting for the jury's verdict on a murder charge. [courtesy of NBC/Copyright ©1997 by Universal City Studios, Inc. Courtesy of Universal Publishing Rights, a Division of Universal Studios Licensing, Inc. All rights reserved.]

Shepherd (Lieutenant Commander McIntyre), Joyce Reehling (Lieutenant Commander Coleman), Reuben Jackson (Lieutenant Lopez), John Speredakos (William T. Ottenberg), Bill Parry (Commander Halibert), Kurt Knudson (Judge Waxman), Helmar Augustus Cooper (Judge McNeil)

Reviewing the Case: The investigation into navy pilot Robert Stroud's death leads to Lieutenant Blair, the deceased's lover. She has been an emblem for equal rights in the service, and McCoy encounters difficulty prosecuting her due to disagreements about jurisdiction in the case. This episode is clearly inspired by Kelly Flinn, the air force officer caught up in a 1997 adultery scandal. This uncomplicated story, about how heroes may be seen in a more human light, offers a fascinating contrast: Jamie Ross idealizes Blair but McCoy remains skeptical. Actress Kate Walsh, who has the same type of opaque coolness as famed French actress Catherine Deneuve, is skilled at keeping Blair's thoughts and feelings in check until the final revelation. What is interesting about "Navy Blues" is that, while many men have been disillusioned by their role models, the process may be just starting for women.

Episode 161: Harvest

Original air date: October 29, 1997
Teleplay by I. C. Rapoport, story by Rene Balcer and I. C. Rapoport, directed by Matthew Penn, cinematography by Richard Dobbs

Additional Cast and Guest Stars: Michael Nouri (Dr. Donald Cosgrove), Carlos Pizzaro (Elias Camacho), Robert Stanton (Jason Sutter), Marty O'Neal (Armand Schultz), David Marshall Grant (Charlie Harmon), Andrew Pang (Dr. Hsu), John Ramsey (Judge Schreiber), David Lipman (Judge Torledsky)

Reviewing the Case: A mother is shot while in the car with her family and the case leads not only to Elias Camacho, the man who fired the gun, but also to Dr. Cosgrove, who declared the woman brain-dead. It turns out that the doctor may have had ulterior motives. This episode continues the *Law & Order* tradition of rooting out the worst medical practitioners in America. If they're not alcoholics (Episode 1: "Prescription for Death"), stealing kidneys (Episode 21: "Sonata for Solo Organ"), or populating the world with their own sperm (Episode 103: "Seed"), these healers seem to be harvesting organs from people not officially dead, as part of a career move. Actor Michael Nouri makes an ideally arrogant and indifferent doctor, so there's a certain pleasure in watching McCoy take him on. It's also oddly comic when McCoy and Ross try Camacho and Cosgrove together as the murderers, in that these men come from such diverse backgrounds. The most alarming thought coming from "Harvest" is that, given the opportunity, Cosgrove would do it again.

Noteworthy Discoveries: It is discovered that Charlie Harmon in the DA's office is a friend of Jamie Ross's. He will figure prominently in Episode 165: "Shadow."

Relevant Testimony: RENE BALCER (writer): "This was based on a *60 Minutes* piece where a woman who was shot had the plug pulled . . . so her organs could be harvested. [We also used] the story from L.A. where some people drove into a gang-controlled alley by mistake and had their car riddled with bullets."

Episode 162: Nullification

Original air date: November 5, 1997
Teleplay by David Black, directed by Constantine Makris, cinematography by Christopher Misiano

Additional Cast and Guest Stars: Denis O'Hare (Phil Christie), Gerry Becker (Thomas Robbins), Betsy Aidem (Kay Brant), Jess Tendler

(Matthew Brant, Jr.), Leslie Hendrix (Rogers), Christine Farrell (Shrier), Ted Kazanoff (Judge Scarlatti), Victor Truro (Judge Spivak), Barbara Spiegel (Judge Doremus)

Reviewing the Case: When an armored truck robbery at an offtrack betting parlor leads to three shooting deaths, a clandestine militia group is uncovered. As McCoy tries to bring them to trial, the indicted and indignant patriots declare themselves POWs in a war against the U.S. government. Their plan is to convince the jury to nullify a verdict on those grounds. This segment qualifies as the most hair-raising political drama *Law & Order* has done since Episode 93: "White Rabbit." While tapping into some of the unresolved issues from Waco, Ruby Ridge, and the Oklahoma City bombing, it also tries to establish a context for a type of civil disobedience that is totally different from the kind America experienced in the 1960s. When such a group turns a courtroom into a theater of the absurd, it might seem unthinkable that a jury could consider sympathizing with them. Yet it was only a few decades ago that The Chicago Seven helped turn an Illinois courtroom upside down in response to an inane and biased judge (some members of that jury sympathized with the defendants). David Black's savvy script presents the militia groups as a darker mirror image of the radicals from yesteryear. Sam Waterston gives an impassioned performance, with McCoy drawing on his instincts as a former activist who cut his teeth on the turmoil of the Vietnam War era. The astonishing Denis O'Hare, as the militia leader, plays McCoy's doppelgänger to perfection. "Nullification" demonstrates that times may have changed, but some of the means stay the same.

Relevant Testimony: DAVID BLACK (writer): "[A]s I researched 'Nullification,' I really began examining my feelings about the militia. There are parts of the militia movement that are bigoted, and which I have no patience with; there are other parts...which sound to me like the original revolutionists of America. They do sound like Tom Paine and [Thomas] Jefferson.... I don't think they should use terrorist tactics, but philosophically I have some sympathy. It was good for the drama to have their case presented soundly."

Episode 163: "Baby, It's You"
Original air date: November 12, 1997
NOTE: This episode is the first part of another joint two-part production with NBC-TV's *Homicide: Life on the Street.*
Teleplay by Jorge Zamacona, directed by Ed Sherin, cinematography by Constantine Makris

Additional Cast and Guest Stars: Tom Tammi (Steven Janaway), Maureen Anderman (Gayle Janaway), Dan Hedaya (Leslie Drake), Richard Belzer (Det. John Munch), Jon Seda (Det. Paul Falsone), Zeljko Ivanek (Assistant State's Attorney Ed Danvers), Yaphet Kotto (Lt. Al Giardello), Sam Valle (Johnny Ramirez), J. K. Simmons (Dr. Emil Skoda), Leslie Hendrix (Rogers), Dan Frazer (Judge McLellan), John Fiore (Det. Anthony Profaci)

Reviewing the Case: Brittany Janaway, a fourteen-year-old fashion model, dies from toxic-shock syndrome and an autopsy reveals she had been raped two weeks earlier. Since the assault took place in Baltimore, Briscoe calls upon Detective Munch. Meanwhile, the girl's parents hire an aggressive lawyer who offers a $250,000 reward that starts a media frenzy McCoy fears will poison the jury pool. This episode, based loosely on the JonBenet Ramsey case, is somewhat better than the first full crossover production (*Law & Order* Episode 124: "Charm City" and *Homicide* Episode 46: "For God and Country") but it still feels too much like a ratings gambit. The main story is absorbing enough, but who really cares about revisiting the tiresome rivalry about Munch's ex-wife? When Curtis and Falsone discuss their respective families, dullness sets in. Dan Hedaya livens things up as the Janaway lawyer, and Tom Tammi and Maureen Anderman are also quite convincing as parents who keep the family secrets to themselves. "Baby, It's You" concludes on *Homicide* (Episode 83, aired on November 12, 1997), but the revelations are rather baffling because they don't provide sufficient motivation for the killer.

Noteworthy Discoveries: It is discovered that Curtis is part English-German, along with being of Peruvian Indian descent. His sister died in a car accident when she was ten.

Episode 164: Blood
Original air date: November 19, 1997
Teleplay by Craig Tepper, story by Rene Balcer and Craig Tepper, directed by Jace Alexander, cinematography by Christopher Misiano

Additional Cast and Guest Stars: Stephen Mendillo (Josh Burdett), Deborah Rush (Frances Houston), Harry O'Reilly (Jerry O'Brien), Lou Liberatore (Dale Brody), Kent Broadhurst (Harry Stokley), Mike Hodge (Leonard Hill), Keith Randolph Smith (Morris Keach), Joan Copeland (Judge Stein)

Reviewing the Case: Briscoe and Curtis investigate the apparent suicide of a woman who had just given up her baby for adoption. When the detectives locate the child, they discover that the mother's death might have been a murder that is related to her husband's long-held secret.

This is an intriguing episode about a black man who denies his racial heritage, then pays dearly for that decision. Josh Burdett began passing for white at a time when drinking fountains were still segregated. Although racism is more implicit now than in the days of segregation, it still finds insidious ways to resurface. Burdett's ex-wife, Frances, is a prime suspect who shrewdly hires a black lawyer named Alanis Joyner. "Blood" is about the same kind of self-deceptions explored in such stories as Episode 128: "Deceit," only this time the closet has racial rather than sexual implications.

Noteworthy Discoveries: Lieutenant Van Buren reveals that she is taking the exam that would allow her to be promoted to captain.

Relevant Testimony: RENE BALCER (writer): "This was inspired by the story of the New York literary figure Anatole Broyard, who was discovered to be black after he died, and the kind of racism that isn't the Ku Klux Klan...cross-burning, but something much more subtle."

Episode 165: Shadow
Original air date: November 26, 1997
Teleplay by Richard Sweren, directed by Matthew Penn, cinematography by Christopher Misiano

Additional Cast and Guest Stars: David Marshall Grant (Charlie Harmon), Bruce MacVittie (Arvin Baker), Jacinto Tara Riddick (Oscar Liriano), Roger Pretto (David Baez), Don Billett (Ed Richter), Alexandra Neil (Lisa Harmon), Michael K. Williams (Delmore Walton), Dominic Chianese (Judge Kaylin), Rosemary DeAngelis (Judge Goldman), Bruce Katzman (Judge Denham)

Reviewing the Case: A murder investigation into the death of a bail bondsman leads to Arvin Baker, a lawyer fixing cases for high fees, as well as to his accomplice in the district attorney's office. When McCoy and Ross set up a "shadow" trial to determine this person's identity, it points to her pal Charlie Harmon. She goes through what Adam Schiff experiences practically on a yearly basis: betrayal by a corrupt friend. While the proceedings here are fairly predictable, it provides a fascinating look into how a fake hearing can be used to weed out a possibly guilty person. The episode would be better if actor David Marshall Grant didn't infuse Harmon with such obvious dishonesty. Nonetheless, Carey Lowell has some enjoyable scenes with Harmon's wife (Alexandra Neil) and an intense one with Michael K. Williams. He's a prison inmate who asks Ross to take off her jacket in return for the information she wants. Apart from that battle of wills, "Shadow" doesn't cast a very long one.

Relevant Testimony: CAREY LOWELL (actor): "[I] go into Sing Sing to question a suspect because we think his lawyer is selling pleas, and this prisoner wants me to take off my jacket and I say, 'No, I'm not going to do that. Maybe I can help you some other way.' He says, 'How about a letter to my parole officer?' I say, 'I can do that.' And then I ask him [another] question that he's reticent to answer. So I take off my jacket and he starts talking again. I fought a lot not to have to take my jacket off. I felt there was a fine line there; why should she give this guy that? I lost that fight. That was one example where I think the writers did me a disservice."

Episode 166: Burned

Original air date: December 10, 1997
Teleplay by Siobhan Byrne, directed by Constantine Makris, cinematography by Christopher Misiano and Richard Dobbs

Additional Cast and Guest Stars: Robert Vaughn (Carl Anderton), Bob Dishy (Lawrence Weaver), Sam Huntington (Terry Lawlor), Mia Dillon (Elaine Anderton Lawlor), Joseph Siravo (Stan Kaminsky), Michael O'Hare (Roy Lawlor), J. K. Simmons (Dr. Emil Skoda), Sylva Kelegian (Sandra Lawlor), Anne Jackson (Judge Simons)

Reviewing the Case: When an answering machine message contains a confession of murder, the investigation leads to Terry Lawlor, a teenage boy who admits to setting the fire that killed his step-sister two years earlier. The young man lives with his wealthy, influential grandfather, Carl Anderton, who is another in a long line of Adam Schiff's friends trying to make a case disappear before McCoy can even prosecute it. This segment is a promising idea for a story that is never adroitly developed. Robert Vaughn's Anderton seems too one-dimensional for a manic-depressive. He's supposed to be charming one minute and sinister or aggressive the next, but the captivating part never seems to shine. (Why would Schiff be this guy's friend and political ally in the first place?) More importantly, we don't see the emotional connection between Anderton and his grandson Terry, whose problematic mental condition—seemingly inherited—also never emerges in a cinematic fashion. When we reach Anderton's bipolar breakdown, the collapse has no more depth than if he'd been upset about someone stealing his parking space. "Burned" is exactly how the viewer feels when it's over.

Episode 167: Ritual

Original air date: December 17, 1997
Teleplay by Kathy McCormick and Richard Sweren, directed by Brian Mertes, cinematography by Constantine Makris

Additional Cast and Guest Stars: Cotter Smith (Eric Martin), Ava Haddad (Nari Martin), Emmy Rossun (Alison Martin), Steve Landesburg (Howard Cahill), Maryann Urbano (Hamida Wazir), Ramsey Faragallah (Mr. Tobak), Ray Genadry (Jeff Mohammed), Ed Setrakain (Judge O'Hara)

Reviewing the Case: Josef Moussad is an Egyptian whose murder uncovers a planned female circumcision of the pre-pubescent Alison Martin. Her angry father, Eric Martin, an American, may have had a hand in the killing. This episode is concerned with the specific controversial issue of clitoridectomy, and it reflects the wide gap between traditional Egyptian and American cultures. Although it's difficult to understand Eric Martin's apparent lack of awareness that this operation is customary in his wife's family and native land, actor Cotter Smith gives such a persuasive performance in the part that this improbability can almost be forgiven. Maryann Urbano is extremely convincing as the traditional Egyptian grandmother who insists on this "protection" for her granddaughter because of the decadence she perceives in Western society.

Noteworthy Discoveries: It is revealed that Van Buren is suing the police department for racism after being refused a promotion.

Episode 168: Under the Influence
Original air date: January 7, 1998
Teleplay by Rene Balcer, directed by Adam Davidson, cinematography by Richard Dobbs

Additional Cast and Guest Stars: Cliff Gorman (Judge Feldman), Daniel McDonald (Dressler), David Garrison (Billings), Kathryn Meisle (Susan Young), Gene Canfield (Norris), Melanie Ray (Luisa), Pat Moya (Deborah Curtis), Arielle Kaplan (Serena), Lauren Kaplan (Isabel), Claywood Sempliner (Fischer), Elana Renderos (Tena Galvaz), Matthew Lewis (Arraignment Judge), John Fiore (Det. Anthony Profaci)

Reviewing the Case: Can a drunk driver who has mowed down three people receive a fair trial? The murder case is compromised when Judge Feldman, who has a secret agenda, and McCoy, who has a hidden motive, conspire to bury vital information in order to guarantee a conviction. This prosecutor has walked a fine line of ethical propriety before, such as in Episode 94: "Competence," Episode 97: "Scoundrels," and Episode 146: "Barter." However, in those situations, he was cleverly testing both his own limits and those of the legal system. Here, McCoy's cleverness masks a deep spiritual malaise that prompts him to seek vengeance for the death of Claire Kincaid, killed in Episode 134: "Aftershock" by a drunk driver who got off with a light sentence. Waterston brilliantly reveals the rage and guilt that has been buried behind McCoy's haggard face since the tragedy. Cliff Gorman, as an ambitious man with a beady eye on District Attorney Adam Schiff's job, turns political expedience into a deft little two-step. Finally, Daniel McDonald, as the suspect, succeeds in the difficult task of putting a haunted face on a repulsive drunk. "Under the Influence" offers a sober look at the cost of trying to satisfy our darker impulses.

Noteworthy Discoveries: Deborah Curtis is seen visiting her husband, Rey, at the precinct. Afflicted with multiple sclerosis, she is walking with a leg brace and a cane.

Episode 169: Expert

Original air date: January 21, 1998
Teleplay by I. C. Rapoport and David Shore, directed by Lewis Gould, cinematography by Constantine Makris

Additional Cast and Guest Stars: Stephen Pearlman (Dr. Leon Mayer), Vera Farmiga (Lindsay Carson), Joanna Merlin (Jane Verdon), Fred Burrell (Arthur Rigg), Matthew Sussman (Peter Bronner), Judy Kuhn (Beth Prentiss), J. K. Simmons (Dr. Emil Skoda), Christine Farrell (Shrier), Ben Hammer (Judge Mooney)

Reviewing the Case: Someone tries to assassinate Dr. Leon Mayer, who is an "expert" witness making a career of peddling insanity pleas at murder trials. Briscoe and Curtis discover that the assailant is Lindsay Carson, an angry woman whose father went to prison after paying Mayer to testify for the defense at his murder trial. There's a promising (but largely underdeveloped) idea lurking in this plot line: Lawyers who retain questionable specialists essentially exploit the justice system by buying testimony that may not be relevant to the truth of the case. What this episode actually delivers, however, is a predictable drama in which the suspect blames her behavior on an inherited problem, a form of the dissociative disorder that her father had claimed was the reason for his crime.

Usually when *Law & Order* explores unorthodox motives—like the genetic disposition for violence in Episode 75: "Born Bad" or the battered-woman syndrome in Episode 91: "Blue Bamboo"—there is a logic that connects the character to the trial. The crime then points to larger issues at work in society. However, this time, the motive seems to have been an afterthought on the part of the scriptwriters, because there is nowhere else for the story to go. The only credible, and witty, moment in "Expert" occurs when the two shrinks, Skoda and Mayer, discuss the validity of a diagnosis while struggling with their own barely-disguised desires to clobber each other.

Episode 170: Castoff

Original air date: January 28, 1998
Teleplay by David Black and Harold Schechter, directed by Gloria Muzio, cinematography by Constantine Makris

Additional Cast and Guest Stars: Mitchell Lichtenstein (Edward Chandler), Dennis Boutsikaris (Pressman), Dennis Kelly (Congressman Maxwell), Jon DeVries (Gaylin), John Benjamin Hickey (Thatcher), Jerry Mayer (Greenwald), Gene Saks (Judge Samuel)

Reviewing the Case: The murders of two people are linked to drugs and kinky sex. A serial killer, Eddy Chandler, claims that too much television made him commit his crimes. This installment seems to have a split personality. Its first half is clearly a mediocre adaptation of the infamous Andrew Cunanan case, while the second half sports an excellent debate on the impact of TV violence on our culture. Unfortunately, the two stories never mesh successfully. As seen in Episode 12: "Life Choice," Episode 27: "God Bless the Child," and Episode 162: "Nullification," writer David Black has an uncanny gift for turning polemical subjects into richly complex drama. Here, however, the issues don't emerge from within the central character; they seem to be imposed upon him. Lichtenstein's performance is so twitchy that an infestation of fleas could be as much to blame for Chandler's actions as the Road Runner cartoons he cites in court. McCoy does engage in some fascinating legal arguments with defense attorney Pressman, as well as with a congressman who deplores Chandler's murderous behavior but supports censorship.

Episode 171: Grief

Original air date: February 4, 1998
Teleplay by Suzanne Oshry, directed by Christopher Misiano, cinematography by Constantine Makris

Additional Cast and Guest Stars: Cecilia Hart (Greta Singer), Erik Jensen (George Harding), Edie Falco (Sally Bell), Marin Hinkle (Leslie Russo), George Bamford (Harry Singer), Jonathan LaPaglia (Frank Russo), George Palermo (Joe Russo)

Reviewing the Case: Found severely beaten, George Harding might be guilty of raping the comatose Wendy Singer, but at the instigation of her own mother. This episode is one of those stories, like Episode 159: "Denial," that gets creepier as it progresses. What begins as a possible sexual assault of a woman, the mentally-ill Leslie Russo (hauntingly portrayed by Marin Hinkle), turns instead into a harrowing tale of a self-centered parent who sacrifices her daughter's life in order to have a grandchild she can show off. Unfortunately, Cecilia Hart's performance is pitched a little too high to be truly effective, but George Bamford, as her husband, gives the growing awareness of his wife's motives a subtle and compelling reading. As in Episode 160: "Navy Blues," McCoy and Ross are in disagreement on the case, and the viewer is left to sort out who is the more "sympathetic" suspect, Harding or Mrs. Singer. One might say that such a choice is akin to wondering which shark has sharper teeth.

Noteworthy Discoveries: In Episode 97: "Scoundrels," it was learned that Sally Bell, who is Greta Singer's attorney here, was a former assistant and lover of Jack McCoy's. Yet, in Episode 153: "Double Down" and even more so here, they act as if they've never met before. Is this an oversight on the part of *Law & Order*'s writers or planned that way?

Relevant Testimony: RENE BALCER (writer/co-executive producer): "Well, I think that [Edie Falco] was probably cast at the last minute out of New York and her backstory as Sally Bell wasn't checked out. So, let's just imagine that her relationship with McCoy has chilled over the years. Maybe she even got hit with a large object and developed amnesia."

Episode 172: Faccia á Faccia
Original air date: February 25, 1998
Teleplay by Rene Balcer and Eddie Feldman, directed by Martha Mitchell, cinematography by Christopher Misiano

Additional Cast and Guest Stars: Philip Bosco (Vincent Dobbs), Michael Rispoli (John DiMaio), Frank Savino (Alberto Napoli), Katherine Narducci (Vicky Grant), Rocco Sisto (Brendan Hall), John O'Leary (Ronny Napoli), J. K. Simmons (Dr. Emil Skoda), Ken Marks (Agent Ruggiero), Jack Willis (Duane Wheeler), David Lipman (Judge Torledsky)

Reviewing the Case: The body of Nick LaGressa, a former hit man in the Witness Protection Program, is found in Central Park Lake. Briscoe and Curtis come upon another hit man, John DiMaio, who claims to have been acting on orders from Alberto Napoli, the mobster against whom LaGressa once testified. McCoy and Ross, however, turn up evidence that DiMaio may be covering up for someone with an entirely different motive for wanting LaGressa dead. The episode is both a darkly comic and incisive examination of how law enforcement agencies attempt to use the Witness Protection Program to convince mob conspirators to squeal on their bosses. The amusing part of this particular story is that *everybody* wants to make a deal, especially if a confession can lead to a bestseller or a possible movie deal.

One of the ironies of "Faccia á Faccia" is that LaGressa's killer is not a member of a Mafia clan. Instead, a family that LaGressa victimized resents that he might profit from a book about his exploits. Michael Rispoli plays DiMaio as a happy-go-lucky guy who sees his role as an enforcer as star-making material. Frank Savino, as Napoli, brings back fond memories of the late William Hickey's sly, wormy don in the film *Prizzi's Honor* (1985). Since gangsters are a prominent part of the popular imagination, this clever episode reveals how, by striking a bargain with the DA, the mob can both kill and make a killing at the same time.

Noteworthy Discoveries: The Masucci Family (who figured in the pilot, Episode 6: "Everybody's Favorite Bagman," and featured in Episodes 15 and 16: "The Torrents of Greed") is mentioned once again here. In a departure from his usual fearlessness, Curtis shows signs of self-doubt when he and Briscoe try to apprehend DiMaio.

Relevant Testimony: RENE BALCER (writer): "The idea came from reading in the news about a mobster, Sammy "The Bull" Gravano. He was being sued by family members of his victims. I wanted to explore the kind of fascination and media attention he got, which was somewhat odious to me. One of my nephews, who was fifteen or sixteen, was very taken by that whole rap, gangsta-goomba, wiseguy thing. We originally thought of casting Tom Arnold. We wrote the part of DiMaio with him in mind, but there were scheduling problems. The episode is really a comic opera."

NOTE: The remainder of Season Eight (1997–98) of *Law & Order* aired too late for inclusion in this book.

EPISODE CHECKLIST

This episode checklist is presented in alphabetical order by episode name. Each name is then followed by the date of its airing and by its episode number in bold. The list is for Seasons One to Eight (up to date of publication of this book).

For the convenience of readers, the following list indicates the numbered episodes to be found in each season:

SEASON 1: Episodes 1–22
SEASON 2: Episodes 23–44
SEASON 3: Episodes 45–66
SEASON 4: Episodes 67–88

SEASON 5: Episodes 89–111
SEASON 6: Episodes 112–134
SEASON 7: Episodes 135–157
SEASON 8: Episodes 158–

Act of God (3/22/95) **105**
Aftershock (5/22/96) **134**
American Dream (11/10/93) **74**
Angel (11/29/95) **119**
Animal Instinct (3/17/93) **61**
Apocrypha (11/3/93) **73**
Aria (10/1/91) **25**
Asylum (10/8/91) **26**
Atonement (4/10/96) **129**
Baby, It's You (11/12/97) **163**
Bad Faith (4/26/95) **108**
Barter (2/12/97) **146**
Benevolence (5/19/93) **66**
Big Bang (3/2/94) **82**

Bitter Fruit (9/20/95) **112**
Black Tie (10/20/93) **71**
Blood (11/19/97) **164**
Blood Is Thicker... (2/4/92) **36**
Blood Libel (1/3/96) **120**
Blue Bamboo (10/5/94) **91**
Blue Wall, The (4/9/91) **22**
Born Bad (11/17/93) **75**
Breeder (1/12/94) **79**
Burned (12/10/97) **166**
By Hooker, By Crook (11/13/90) **7**
Castoff (1/28/98) **170**
Causa Mortis (9/18/96) **135**
Censure (2/2/94) **80**

DICK WOLF FILMOGRAPHY

FEATURE FILMS

Skateboard (1977), *Gas* (1981), *No Man's Land* (1987, co-produced with his eventual *Law & Order* partner Joe Stern), *Masquerade* (1988), *School Ties* (1992)

TELEVISION SERIES

Gideon Oliver (1989), *Christine Cromwell* (1989–90), *Nasty Boys* (1990, with Benjamin Bratt), *H.E.L.P.* (1990), *Law & Order* (1990–), *The Human Factor* (1992), *Mann & Machine* (1992, with S. Epatha Merkerson), *Crime & Punishment* (1993), *South Beach* (1993), *New York Undercover* (1994–), *The Wright Verdicts* (1995), *Swift Justice* (1996), *Feds* (1997), *Players* (1997–)

THE AWARDS AND NOMINATIONS

AWARDS

Season One (1990–91)

D. W. Griffith Award
- Best TV Series

TV Guide's Best & Worst Awards
- Best New Series

Season Two (1991–92)

Emmy Award
- For Outstanding Individual Achievement in Sound Editing for a Series

Silver Gavel Award
- Dick Wolf

Season Three (1992–93)

Crystal Apple Award
- Dick Wolf

Edgar Award
- For Outstanding Series

Emmy Award
- For Outstanding Guest Actress in a Drama Series (Elaine Stritch)
- For Outstanding Individual Achievement in Cinematography (Constantine Makris)

Silver Gavel Award
- Dick Wolf

Season Four (1993–94)

There were no awards given *Law & Order* during this season

Season Five (1994–95)

Big Apple Award
  • Dick Wolf

Edgar Award
  • For Outstanding Series

New York Chapter/NATAS Governor's Award
  • Dick Wolf

Season Six (1995–96)

Nancy Susan Reynolds Award
  • For Dramatic Series: Episode 102: "Performance"

Silver Gavel Award
  • Dick Wolf

Season Seven (1996–97)

Golden Laurel Award
  • For Episodic Television

Peabody Award
  • For Entertainment Series

Writers Guild of America
  • For Best Teleplay in an Episodic Series: Episode 143: "Entrapment" (Rene Balcer and Richard Sweren)

Season Eight (1997–98)

Emmy Awards
  • For Outstanding Drama Series
  • For Outstanding Achievement in Cinematography (Constantine Makris)

Publicists Guild of America TV Showmanship Award
  • Dick Wolf

NOMINATIONS

From 1990 through 1998, *Law & Order* has received the following nominations:

Emmy Awards: Twenty-three

Edgar Allen Poe (Mystery Writers of America) Awards: Eight

Screen Actors Guild Awards: Five

Image Awards: Four

Golden Globe Awards: Three

Viewers of Quality Television: Three

Writers Guild Awards: Three

EDI (Equality, Dignity, Independence) Awards: Two

Angel Awards: One

Casting Society of America Awards: One

GLAAD/LA: One

Humanitis Awards: One

Jewish Televimage Awards: One

Laurel Award (Producers Guild of America): One

Planned Parenthood Distinguished Service Awards: One

Television Critics Association Awards: One

ADDRESSES: CYBERSPACE AND POSTAL

OFFICIAL WEB SITES

NBC
   http://www.nbc.com

UNIVERSAL STUDIOS
   http://www.mca.com/tv/laworder/
   http://www.univstudios.com/tv/laworder/
   http://www.universalstudios.com/tv/laworder/prodteam/wolf.html

WOLF FILMS OFFICIAL *LAW & ORDER* WEB SITE
   http://www.wolffilms.com/laworder.html

FAN SITES

Brett's *Law & Order* Page:
   http://www.i2.i-2000.com/~ru/law.html

David's *Law & Order* Page:
   http://www.cs.mun.ca/~david12/laworder.html

Law & Order Episode Guide:
   http://www.dickinson.edu/~buchan/docs/lo/law-and-order.html

Law & Order Mailing List Page:
   http://members.aol.com/lomail/index.html

Law & Order News:
   http://people.delphi.com/shadow1and2/lonews.html

Law & Order Page Links:
   http://members.tripod.com.~Napua/Orderlaw.html

Law & Order Titles and Air Dates Guide:
http://www.dickinson.edu/~djk/LawandOrder_1.shtml

Law & Order Trivia Game:
http://lotrivia.html

Michael's *Law & Order* Page:
http://members.aol.com/mlovato810/law/law.html

Tim's *Law & Order* Page:
http://www.geocities.com/TelevisionCity/5039/lostuff.html

Usenet:
alt.tv.law-and-order

MAILING ADDRESSES:

Arts & Entertainment Network
235 East 45th Street
New York, New York 10017

Law & Order Production Office
Pier 62; West 23rd Street
New York, New York 10011

MCA-Universal Television
100 Universal City Plaza
Universal City, California 91608

NBC – National Broadcasting Co., Inc.
10 Rockefeller Plaza
New York, New York 10112

NBC – National Broadcasting Co., Inc.
3000 West Alameda Avenue
Burbank, California 91523

Wolf Productions
100 Universal City Plaza
Building 69
Universal City, California 91608

BIBLIOGRAPHY

PERIODICALS

Blosser, John. "'*Law & Order*' Star: I'm a Drunk—and Proud of It!" *National Enquirer*, September 9, 1997, p. 33.

Buck, Jerry. "*Law & Order* series stretches actor's talents as Yale theater once did." *The Arizona Republic*, June 19, 1992.

Buckley, Michael. "New York Actors on TV: *Law & Order* Casts the Big Apple's Best." *Theater Week*, July 22–28, pp. 15–19.

Burlingame, Jon. "He Makes TV Sound the Way It Sounds." *Washington Post*, July 24, 1994, p. 46.

"Chris Noth: brooding detective of *Law & Order*." *Entertainment Weekly*, June 25, 1992.

Cuff, John Haslett. "Grimily authentic cops and courts." (Toronto) *Globe and Mail*, September 11, 1990.

_____. "*Law and Order* still arresting." (Toronto) *Globe and Mail*, February 15, 1995.

_____. "The trouble with being Michael." (Toronto) *Globe and Mail*, January 3, 1998, p. C2.

Doyle, John. "*Law and Order*, so ordinary, works." (Toronto) *Globe and Mail*, March 2, 1991.

Gay, Verne. "Sorvino Comes Out of the Cold." *New York Newsday*, November 8, 1992, p. 55.

Gliatto, Tom and Maria Eftimiades. "The Singing Ex-Detective." *People*, November 23, 1992, pp. 115–118.

Greppi, Michele. "New Yorker Orbach in sole drama made here." *New York Post*, November 24, 1992, p. 61.

Horowitz, Simi. "*Law & Order* in New York City." *Los Angeles Times*, June 28, 1992, p. 80.

_____. "More Like Naked City." *Houston Chronicle*, June 7, 1992, p. 4.

Johnson, Allan. "Star of the Story." *Chicago Tribune*, February 20, 1996, p. C3.

Kalbacker, Warren. "Twenty Questions: Michael Moriarty." *Playboy*, July 1994, pp. 139–142.

Kaplan, Michael. "True Grit." *Us*, July 1992, pp. 73–76.

Kennedy, Dana. "Law & Disorder." *Entertainment Weekly*, April 14, 1995, pp. 33–35.

Knutzen, Eric. "Much ado about Noth." *Starweek*, October 1992, p. 7.

March, Al. "A World of Series." *San Francisco Examiner*, August 13, 1992, p. C1.

Moore, Frazier. "'*Law & Order*' not your everyday channel-zapper kind of show." *Richmond Times-Dispatch*, November 23, 1992, p. C7.

"Outing." Chris Noth quote. *USA Today*, April 27, 1992.

Plummer, William. "Taking It to the Street." *People*.

Roush, Matt. "A Richer '*Law & Order*'." *New York Daily News*, November 25, 1992.

Rudolph, Illeane. "'*Law & Order*' Finally Stands." *TV Guide*, November 19, 1994, pp. 40–41.

Salutin, Rick. "Cross Current: Media." (Toronto) *Globe and Mail*, December 4, 1992.

Schwartzbaum, Lisa. "Chris Noth." *Entertainment Weekly*, summer 1992.

_____. "A Series of Ins and Outs." *People*, July 22, 1996, p. 16.

Solni, Claude. "Exit From Law & Order; Paul Sorvino Departs." *The Villager*, November 18, 1992, p. 6.

Tucker, Ken. "'Crime' Doesn't Pay." *Entertainment Weekly*, February 26, 1993, pp. 46, 48.

_____. "Justice Good As Ever." *Entertainment Weekly*, December 5, 1997, pp. 61–62.

BOOKS

Bartlett, John. *Bartlett's Familiar Quotations*. New York: Little, Brown, 1980.

Denby, David. *Great Books*. New York: S & S/Touchstone, 1996, p. 93.

Haun, Harry. *The Movie Quote Book*. New York: Bonanza Books, 1986.

Moriarty, Michael. *The Gift of Stern Angels.* Toronto: Exile Editions, 1997, pp. 14–15, 44, 46–47, 51, 55, 78–79, 133, 263.

Partington, Angela. *The Concise Oxford Dictionary of Quotations.* New York: Oxford University Press, 1996.

Stanislavski, Konstantin. *An Actor Prepares.* New York: Routledge/Theatre Arts Books, 1989, pp. 281–313.

TELEVISION INTERVIEWS

Michael Moriarty on *Pamela Wallin Live,* CBC Newsworld (Canada), November 20, 1997. (Courtesy of Phyllis Greenberg)

Michael Moriarty on "Too Much *Law & Order,*" *W5,* CTV network (Canada), January 1997.

Michael Moriarty and Paul Sorvino on *McLaughlin,* CNBC Talk Weekend, June 19, 1991. (Courtesy of Joe Stern)

PANEL DISCUSSIONS

Museum of Television & Radio, *Law & Order* Seminar, Los Angeles, CA, October 29, 1992. Participants: Richard Brooks, Dann Florek, Carolyn McCormick, Michael Moriarty, Robert Nathan, Paul Sorvino, Joe Stern, Dick Wolf. (Courtesy of Joe Stern)

INDEX

ABOUT THE AUTHORS

 SUSAN GREEN is a journalist and film critic who has contributed to magazines such as *Premiere, Box Office,* and *Travel & Leisure.* She also writes for the *Burlington Free Press* and *Vox,* two Vermont newspapers, and has won several first-place awards from the New England Press Association.

A resident of Vermont, she worked on two projects about bread and puppet theater: a 1985 book for Green Valley Press, and a 1986 documentary funded in part by the National Film Board of Canada. Ms. Green wrote a chapter for *Backstory 3: Interviews with Screenwriters of the 1960s,* (1997). Her essay "Madness Along the Milky Way" is included in a 1998 anthology about breastfeeding.

 KEVIN COURRIER was a writer/broadcaster, producer, and film critic at the Canadian Broadcasting Corporation for five years, working on such shows as *Prime Time, Later the Same Day, The Inside Track,* and *Two New Hours.* Before that, he spent eight years on-air as co-host of an interview program called *On the Arts* for CJRT, a Toronto FM radio station. He also produced items for two BBC Radio shows, *On Screen* and *Outlook.*

He has written about popular culture and film for *Box Office,* (Toronto) *Globe and Mail,* the *Toronto Star, Tribute* magazine, *Venue* magazine, *The Financial Post,* and *India Today.* He is the author of a forthcoming interview anthology, *Talking Out of Turn: Confronting the '80s.*